UNIVERSITY
∽ OF ∽
BERKSHIRE
HATHAWAY

UNIVERSITY

~ OF ~

BERKSHIRE HATHAWAY

30+ YEARS OF LESSONS LEARNED

from

WARREN BUFFETT
& CHARLIE MUNGER

at the

ANNUAL SHAREHOLDERS MEETING

DANIEL PECAUT

WITH

COREY WRENN

First Printing: 2017

ISBN: 978-0-9984062-6-8

Design by Mauna Eichner and Lee Fukui
Cover Illustration by Allison Baer

Pecaut and Company
401 Douglas Street, Suite 415
Sioux City, IA 51101

www.PecautandCompany.com

This book is dedicated to my hero, Russell B. Pecaut (1902–2000, Dow Jones Industrial Average: 67–11,551). Papa, as we grandkids called him, was a good-natured, honest, and unfailingly upbeat gentleman. He encouraged me greatly in my career. He taught me that optimism is a choice and that your word is your bond. This world could use a few more like Russell Pecaut. Papa, this one's for you.

—DANIEL PECAUT

CONTENTS

THE ELECTRONIC RECORD
ix

INTRODUCTION
xi

THE
ELECTRONIC RECORD

Asked why he is on TV so much, Buffett responded that he likes having the electronic record, so there is no chance of him being misquoted or misunderstood. If he's on Charlie Rose, he knows the record will be permanent and will be exactly what he said.
—Excerpt from our notes at
the 2010 Shareholders Meeting

What follows in this book is not an electronic record. This is the result of feverish note-taking during 32 years of Berkshire Hathaway's annual shareholders meetings. While we, the authors, believe these notes capture the essential meaning and intention conveyed, we apologize in advance for any misrepresentations.

INTRODUCTION

My dad was also my hero, just like the case with you. Dick clearly was a terrific guy and a sound thinker. You were lucky to have him as a father, teacher, and inspiration.
—WARREN E. BUFFETT
(written on the back of a Pecaut & Company newsletter)

After my dad, Dick Pecaut, passed away in 2009, I wrote a loving tribute to him in my investment firm's monthly newsletter. Days later, I received one of the newsletters back. Handwritten, on the back of that newsletter, was a note from *the Oracle of Omaha*, Warren Buffett. The man whose mindset, strategies, and investing insights my business partner, Corey, and I have studied for three decades. The man whose wisdom we are honored to share with you in the coming pages.

Buffett's short note served as a heartwarming footnote to my father's life work as an investment advisor. It also served as validation of both the newsletters that make up this book and our work as investment advisors.

We have been longtime Berkshire Hathaway commentators. Our analyses of its chairman, Warren Buffett, and vice chairman, Charlie Munger, have been featured in the *New York Times, Money Magazine, Schiff's Insurance Observer,* and a host of other leading investment publications. One of our newsletters was referenced in James O'Loughlin's book, *The Real Warren Buffett: Managing Capital, Leading People.**

For years, we sent our newsletter, unsolicited, to Berkshire Hathaway's headquarters. But until this thoughtful reply, we never knew if anyone actually opened the envelopes.†

---

* A Berkshire-approved reading list pick which was for sale at the 2015 meeting.
† When Corey and I were in Mexico in early 2016, he met a broker from Omaha who had traded with Berkshire in the early 1980s. Corey told him he worked for an investment firm, Pecaut & Company, in Sioux City, Iowa, which is 90 minutes away from Omaha. The broker said, "Pecaut? Oh yeah, I read your newsletter." Corey said, "I don't think we send it to you, do we?" He responded, "No. I get it from someone else."

Corey and I were electrified. Buffett read *our* newsletter! It was an acknowledgment that our writings and insights on value investing are of interest to the master himself. On a personal level, mourning my father, it was one of the warmest and most affirming notes I have ever received. For that, I am eternally grateful.

But it wasn't always like this. We didn't always receive personal notes from the world's greatest investor.

How Did We Get Here?

I graduated from Harvard in 1979 with a philosophy degree. While there, I took only one economics course. I found it too theoretical, not anything like the investing I saw happening in my family's business.

My grandfather, father, and uncle had founded Pecaut & Company, a stockbrokerage firm, in 1960. My grandfather, Russell, often marveled that they made money from day one and never looked back.

My involvement in the family business began in the late 1970s, when I was working summers in the back office. I did the grunt work, including updating the S&P 500 tear sheets.

Back then, the S&P sent its clients color-coded binders that were alphabetized like a set of encyclopedias. Every month, a packet would arrive in the mail with colored sheets that matched the binders. Green sheets were large-company stocks. Yellow sheets were small-company stocks. Blue sheets were for bonds. Someone needed to manually update the binders by replacing old sheets with the new. That was my job. I learned a lot by reading those sheets.

After graduating, I entered the firm as a full-time employee. I felt inadequate and clueless. Our small, family-run operation had no formal training program or structure. My dad rarely sat me down to discuss how things were going. I tortured myself with my own self-judgment about how poorly I thought I was doing. I learned by trial and error.

One error was option trading. It was quick and exciting. You could theoretically triple your money in a short time. Do that a few times, and you'd have a good year. I spent a year trying to develop a successful option trading strategy. And at the end of the year? I had made about a hundred bucks. Calculating that into the amount of time spent, I had made about 10 cents an hour.

Clearly, that wasn't worth it. Trading in the short-term may work for some people, but it wasn't for me. I needed a better approach.

Then, in 1982, I read the book *The Money Masters* by John Train, in which he profiles nine brilliant investors, including John Templeton and Warren Buffett. A light bulb came on when I finished the book. I said, "I'm going back to school. These investors are my professors. My curriculum is everything they say and write." I was excited. I would study the most brilliant investors in the world like they were my professors at Harvard. I was on fire to learn everything I could about them and to figure out how to invest like them.

From that point forward, I saw my role in the firm primarily as a learning organism. My thought was that the more I learned, the better my decision-making would be, and the better I would serve our clients.

Over time, my favorite professors would include Sir John Templeton (of the Templeton Growth Fund),* George Michaelis of Source Capital (a top-performing closed-end fund), Jean-Marie Eveillard (who ran what is now the First Eagle Global Fund), Bob Rodriguez (of First Pacific Advisors), and Marty Whitman (of Third Avenue Value Investors). These experts would all offer tremendous insight and direction.

But of all the brilliant "professors," none of them has been more instructive than Warren Buffett and Charlie Munger of Berkshire Hathaway.

After realizing that Buffett was one of *the* guys to learn from, I devoured all his annual letters to shareholders from Berkshire. When I met a friend who had Buffett's letters from his partnership prior to taking over Berkshire, I devoured those, too. I loved reading them.

From where I lived, it was only a 90-minute drive to Omaha and Berkshire's annual meetings. But to attend, you had to be a shareholder.

Undaunted, I bought a single share of Berkshire Hathaway for $2,570 that year. That share paved the way for over 30 years of first-class tuition from two of the greatest professors you could ever hope to learn from.

The "University of Berkshire Hathaway"

I distinctly remember that first meeting in 1985. It was an electric yet cozy affair at Omaha's Joslyn Art Museum.

---

* In 1987, a group of investors and I traveled to John Templeton's headquarters in the Bahamas to meet with him. In his mahogany-paneled office, he was as gracious and dignified as I'd imagined. That fabulous meeting remains one of the highlights of my career.

A local CPA I knew, Corey Wrenn, was taking tickets at the door.* He was a relatively new employee, hired by Berkshire's audit department in 1983.

After graduating college and working two years in public accounting in Sioux City, Iowa, Corey decided that wasn't what he wanted to do his whole life. While looking for another job, he received a call from a headhunter in Omaha who told him that Berkshire Hathaway was looking for an internal auditor. Corey asked, "Berkshire what?" The headhunter said, "It's run by Warren Buffett." And Corey responded, "Warren who?" He had no idea who or what they were. Nonetheless, he took the job and began working alongside the six or seven other employees in the audit department, auditing Berkshire's subsidiary companies and preparing schedules used for quarterly financial statements and for Buffett's use.

I had felt a pang of jealousy when I found out he had been hired there. I envied how he would be learning firsthand from Buffett.†

But I wasn't focused on Corey at the time. My eyes were on the stage.

Warren Buffett and Charlie Munger sat on the auditorium's stage in front of an audience of 300 shareholders (which at the time I felt was large).

I realized that if I were going to learn, I would have to get up and ask what I was wondering about. I wrote pages and pages of detailed questions with the goal of getting to the microphone.

I nervously asked my one question. Their clarity of mind and high intellect was clear from their answer. I thought, *Wow. That was a fantastic answer. They took my dumb question and turned it into a masterpiece.*

I kept thinking, *What took me so long to get here? Why haven't I been here before?*

At that meeting, I learned that Berkshire owned 80% of Wesco Financial, where Charlie Munger served as the chairman. So I flew out to Pasadena to attend the Wesco meeting. It was a much smaller affair.

---

* Corey was just an observer at the 1984 meeting. With fewer than 50 people in attendance, he wasn't required to do anything. But the next year, the crowd had grown significantly larger, so all hands were on deck. Corey was put in charge of taking shareholders' tickets as they flooded into the venue. But Corey was quickly overrun by the waves of people. Irv Blumkin, one of the executives at Nebraska Furniture Mart, saw Corey's plight and started helping him take tickets.

As Corey was looking down frantically taking tickets, one guy tried to go through without a ticket. Corey called out, "Excuse me! You need a ticket." The man stopped, and Corey looked up at him. It was Warren Buffett. Corey apologized and Buffett continued on. Later on, a woman with an entourage of six or seven people passed through without a ticket. Corey once again called out, "Excuse me, but you need a ticket!" She looked at him and said, "I'm Susie Buffett." So in one meeting, Corey had stopped both Warren and his wife from getting into their own meeting. Corey was quite embarrassed.

† Little did I know that eight years later, Corey would leave Berkshire to become my business partner.

The first Wesco meeting I attended had only 15 people, and half worked for the company. Once again, I had prepared questions. After asking three questions, it was clear I would be asking a lot more.

I felt nervous. Munger has an imposing presence behind his thick Coke-bottle lenses. He seemed like an old professor who doesn't tolerate fools. I got up and stammered, "I'm sorry, I've got a lot of questions. It looks like I'm asking all the questions. I didn't mean to take over the meeting."

He was gracious, saying, "That's what we're here for. I'll answer your questions as long as you've got them. If people want to leave, they can leave. But I'll be here."*

I thought, *Wow. All right, then. Here we go.* I don't know how long it went, but I was in heaven. There's no doubt that having that level of expertise delivered directly to me accelerated my learning.

The "University of Berkshire Hathaway" is what I nicknamed the accumulated wisdom dispensed by Warren Buffett and Charlie Munger.

Each year's curriculum consists of Berkshire Hathaway's annual reports and the lectures at its annual meetings. That course of study, now accessible in these pages, has taught Corey and me far more about investing than any other source.

Pouring over Berkshire's reports, reading Buffett's annual letter, and listening to Buffett and Munger at the annual meeting have all been central to our growth as value investors. It is the core curriculum of our business education—one that easily rivals most MBA programs.†
It is the cornerstone of our continuing education.

It is, without a shadow of doubt, the best investment either of us has ever made.

Once a year, you have arguably the greatest investment team of all time on hand to answer your questions. It is a fantastic annual tutorial on the world of business. Buffett admitted in the beginning that he was

---

* Although I asked many questions to Munger over the years, Corey only ever asked one. His question, alongside Munger's response, was reprinted in another Berkshire-approved reading list pick: *Poor Charlie's Almanack: The Wit and Wisdom of Charles T. Munger.*
  Knowing that Munger had a lake and a cabin where his family went every summer, Corey wrote down and submitted a smart-ass fishing question: "I'll be hitting the Walleye Opener next Friday night at Eagle Lake, Minnesota. Any recommendations concerning lures or bait?" Munger got a chuckle out of it and responded, "I stopped fishing for walleye; I've become a bass fisherman in my old age. But in my lake, they do better with walleye at night."
  † Author Timothy Ferriss said, "As several veterans put it to me before the pilgrimage, 'It's like an MBA in a weekend.' I thought this was hyperbole and hero worship, but I would now take it further: I think it's one weekend that delivers more than most MBAs. Real-world strategies culled from experience? Check. Networking? Big-time check. The only thing the mecca of Buffett seemed to lack was the $100K+ price tag."

terrified of public speaking. (He used to get physically ill at just the thought of it.)

Thankfully, over the years, Buffett and Munger have grown ever-more comfortable as educators. Today, they are excellent teachers. Their wisdom and willingness to share make each annual meeting an invaluable installment in a sublime lecture series.

The Unstoppable Rise of Berkshire Hathaway

Few on Wall Street would dispute the claim that Warren Buffett and Charlie Munger are the greatest investors of our time. Their genius in identifying and evaluating intangibles sets them apart.

As a value investor, your ideal situation is to find a company increasing its intrinsic value. Ideally, the company would be one with a declining stock price, thus creating an even better bargain as time unfolds. No one has employed these principles more effectively than Buffett and Munger. Over the last 50 years, they have consistently sought to own either all or part of good businesses, bought at bargain prices. In addition, to succeed using this approach, one must control one's emotions. Buffett and Munger are set apart by their mastery at business valuation and relentless rationality in implementing this approach.

The results of this have been awe-inspiring.

Under Buffett and Munger's leadership, Berkshire Hathaway has become one of the greatest business stories of the 20th and 21st centuries.

A Short History

Buffett was educated at the University of Nebraska. Afterward, he enrolled at Columbia Business School. He went there to learn from the father of value investing, Benjamin Graham. Buffett became Graham's star student. Afterward, Graham took him on at his investment partnership, Graham Newman.

Buffett used what he learned from that experience to start his own partnership back in Omaha. He did phenomenally well from the very beginning. A $10,000 investment in his partnership in 1956 grew to $200,000 by 1969. That's a 25.9% compounded annualized return. Incredibly, the partnership never had a down year, even though the market had six down years during that period.

In 1959, Buffett met Charlie Munger, who was also from Omaha, at a dinner party. Each man instantly recognized the intelligence of the other. Munger had worked in law, but Buffett convinced him that he should be in the investment business if he wanted to make real money.* Munger started his own investment partnership, Wheeler, Munger & Co., in 1962. From then on, he and Buffett worked on a number of investment ideas together, both formally and informally.

Berkshire Hathaway was originally a New England textile company. It was a deeply discounted stock, with a book value of $19. Its net working capital was over $11 a share. Buffett bought shares at around $7–$8 per share. Buffett was buying shares at a discount to net cash and near-cash items.

The decline of the textile industry was underway. Berkshire Hathaway was consolidating and selling assets. Then, with the cash, it was buying in its stock—which was intelligent because the stock was so cheap. In 1963, Berkshire did a massive buy-in of almost a third of its shares. The owners of Berkshire Hathaway saw Buffett's position and didn't want him in their little fiefdom. They called Buffett, offering to pay him $11.50 a share. He agreed. He'd make about a 40% profit in a short period.

When the letter came for the offer, however, it was less than the agreed-on amount—but only by pennies. Nevertheless, their dishonesty upset Buffett. They were trying to chisel him out of 12.5 cents per share. So Buffett went the other way and started buying increasingly more shares of Berkshire until he took control. He then booted out the guy who had tried to chisel him out. In 1964, Warren Buffett took control of that small New England textile firm, and it became his new base for making investments.

At the time, the move made no sense. Buffett had bought a business in decline that he didn't know how to run. He later joked that he should have taken the money. That would have been the smarter thing to do.

As it turned out, this textile company was an ideal vehicle for making investments. With Berkshire Hathaway's stock, Buffett had a publicly traded corporation with captive capital. The benefits of this corporate structure for managing money are significant.

In his previous partnership, if shareholders redeemed their shares, the money would come right out of the till. Now, when shareholders sell their shares in Berkshire Hathaway, that doesn't affect its available capital.

---

* Munger did want to get rich, "Not because I wanted Ferraris—I wanted the independence. I desperately wanted it. I thought it was undignified to have to send invoices to other people. I don't know where I got that notion from, but I had it."

Capital doesn't leave the corporate shell unless Buffett pays a dividend. He could use this captive permanent capital to invest long-term by buying businesses, in part or in whole. Berkshire's structure also allows for making opportunistic investments in special situations.

Over time, Buffett phased out the textile portion of the business. He sold off assets to create more cash. With the cash, he began to build his wealth-compounding machine.

In 1967, Buffett bought an insurance company, National Indemnity. Insurance has been a core operation at Berkshire Hathaway ever since. He loves the insurance business. With its float characteristics, it creates a powerful platform for compounding wealth.

Insurance companies collect premiums, of which a significant portion goes into reserves to pay future claims. This reserve (the "float") earns money for Berkshire, leveraging the company's return on capital. If you can operate in a way where that float is generated at a low cost and you can grow it over time, you have built a wealth-compounding machine. As Munger once put it, "Basically, we're a hedgehog that knows one big thing. If you generate float at 3% per annum and buy businesses that earn 13% per annum with the proceeds of that float, we have figured out that's a pretty good position to be in." Few investors understand that float is one of the secrets to Berkshire's success.

For every $1 of equity at Berkshire, over time there has been roughly another 50 cents or so in float. By investing $1.50 for every $1 of capital over the years, Berkshire has leveraged its returns. A significant portion of Berkshire's long-term outperformance can be attributed to Buffett and Munger's ability to execute on this brilliant insight. That's not something you or I can go out and do.

In 1972, Berkshire bought See's Candy. While Buffett paid more than he normally might have, he discovered how powerful a cash generator a great brand could be. It taught him about the power of brands and the virtues of companies that don't require a lot of capital to grow. Selling chocolate doesn't require a lot of innovation. It won't become obsolete. If you have a good brand, customers will keep coming back every Valentine's Day for more.

Those two pieces—the insurance company as a platform and high-quality brands as cash generators—built the base for the wealth-compounding machine that is Berkshire Hathaway.

Another significant company Buffett bought was GEICO, a company he had a long history with. His mentor, Ben Graham, owned shares of GEICO at Graham Newman. At the University of Nebraska, Buffett wrote his thesis about GEICO. Looking at it now, he understood that with a terrific basic business model, it just had to be run the right way to be successful.

In the mid-1970s, GEICO got into some trouble, and its stock price collapsed. A new CEO, Jack Byrne, was brought in, and Buffett was confident that Byrne was the man to fix it. Buffett bought a ton of GEICO stock.*

Munger liquidated his partnership in 1976. The Wheeler–Munger partnership had earned 24.3% compounded from 1962 to 1975, versus 6.4% compounded for the Dow Jones Industrial Average. In 1978, Munger became Berkshire Hathaway's vice chairman.

In addition to being Berkshire's vice chairman, Munger served as CEO and chairman from 1984 to 2011 for Wesco Financial, the holding company for Mutual Savings, a savings and loan in Pasadena. Wesco was 80.1% owned by Blue Chip Stamps, which, in turn, was wholly owned by Berkshire Hathaway.† Over the years, Wesco was seen as a sort of "mini-Berkshire" as Munger reallocated the company's assets into reinsurance, CORT business equipment, Kansas Bankers Surety, and shares of some of Charlie's favorite stocks.

Over the years, Berkshire Hathaway has accumulated ownership of many other wonderful businesses: utilities (Berkshire Hathaway Energy), consumer products (shares of Coca-Cola), and even media properties (the *Buffalo News* and shares of the *Washington Post*).

The public has long viewed Berkshire as a sort of mutual fund with large stock holdings. This view underestimates or ignores 1) Berkshire's insurance companies' impressive generation of low-cost float, 2) Berkshire's impressive and growing stable of cash-generating operating businesses, and 3) Berkshire's ability to orchestrate value-enhancing deals.

With billions in cash and fixed income securities, Berkshire is now a financial Fort Knox. During the first decade of the 21st century (a.k.a. "the lost decade"), Buffett was criticized for holding enormous amounts of cash and bonds. During the subprime mortgage crisis, Buffett and Munger went on an investing spree.

Berkshire was in the position of seeing every decent deal in America as the nation's "buyer of last resort." While retail investors were selling, Buffett and Munger bought and bought—and bought some more. Their investments included the acquisitions of a railroad, Burlington Northern Santa Fe (BNSF) and a chemical company, Lubrizol. They

---

* Over time, GEICO steadily bought in more shares, so Berkshire became a larger and larger percentage shareholder over time. Then, in 1996, Berkshire bought 100% control of GEICO, allowing Berkshire to invest aggressively in GEICO's growth. That progression has added a lot of wealth to Berkshire.
† In June 2011, Berkshire Hathaway acquired the 19.9% of Wesco that it did not already own.

did high-yield lending with warrants attached. They made capital investments at BNSF and MidAmerican Energy. All told, Berkshire may have put $100 billion to work at double-digit rates of return during the subprime crisis.

Over the last 32 years, Berkshire has created a collection of fantastic, independently great businesses that generate a lot of cash to grow the enterprise. If Berkshire were strictly in the investment portfolio business, you would need investing geniuses like Buffett and Munger to oversee it and determine when to buy and sell.

But by owning great businesses, it is less essential to have Buffett and Munger there. GEICO will keep selling auto insurance. Burlington Northern will keep shipping stuff by rail. These companies will all keep going without them. In doing this, they have intentionally created Berkshire to extend their success past their own lifespans.

Today, Berkshire Hathaway is one of the world's most powerful conglomerates. In 2017, *Fortune* ranked Berkshire as the nation's second largest companies (trailing only Wal-Mart)—boasting revenues of $223 billion, profits of $24 billion, and assets of $620 billion. With $283 billion of equity and $91 billion of float, Berkshire has substantial capital to fund its operations.

In terms of market value, Berkshire now trails only Apple, Google/Alphabet, Exxon Mobil, and Microsoft for the title of America's most valuable company. Berkshire continues to represent solid value, lower-than-average risk, and unparalleled quality. It is a superb company with better relative value than almost anything else in the U.S. stock market.

Berkshire vs. S&P 500 (or 884,319% vs. 12,717%)

Since Buffett took over Berkshire 52 years ago, its per-share book value has grown from $19 to $172,108. That's a rate of 19.0% compounded annually. Let's compare that to the S&P 500. Since the S&P is a cross-section of American businesses (as opposed to having all your eggs in one basket), it's largely considered a safe choice. To justify the risk of owning Berkshire, it needs to outperform the general market.

Mission accomplished: 19.0% is nearly double the S&P 500's 9.7% gain for the same 52-year period.

Berkshire has consistently outperformed the S&P 500 during negative years. The S&P had 11 down years in the 52-year period. The cumulative loss for those 11 years amounted to 251.4%. Comparatively, Berkshire Hathaway had only two losing years during the same period and had a cumulative gain of 117.8% for those 11 years. That's an incredible 369.2% advantage over the S&P.

More than two-thirds of Berkshire's outperformance over the S&P was earned during down years. This is the fruit of Buffett and Munger's "Don't lose" philosophy. It's the losing ideas avoided, as much as the money made in bull markets that has built Berkshire's superior wealth over the long run.

Utilizing compounding, a small advantage in the annual rate of gain creates a huge advantage in total dollars over time. In terms of the overall percentage gain from 1965–2016, a dollar invested in Berkshire in 1965 experienced an amazing gain of 884,319%, versus a gain of 12,717% for the S&P 500.

Though Corey and I have been aware of the results for a number of years, we still marvel at Buffett's and Munger's incredible achievement. They have presided over one of the greatest records of wealth-building in history. For five decades, money under Buffett's control has grown at a phenomenal rate.

"Woodstock for Capitalists"

As Buffett's and Munger's fame and wealth have grown, so has the frenzy around Berkshire's once humble annual meetings.

As noted, my first meeting in 1985 was a cozy, 300-attendee affair. Since then, the meeting has changed many times. First it was an event, then a spectacle, and now it is a full-fledged, three-day party. But in 1985, 300 attendees was considered large, since only 13 people attended just six years before. Fast-forward to 2015, when 45,000 people were in attendance.*

In a short period, Berkshire's annual meetings morphed from a small private lecture series into a chamber of commerce's dream event. It may be a sign of the times that so many people now flock to Omaha to hear Buffett and Munger speak. It's often called "Woodstock for capitalists." This testifies to the world's rising interest in the realm of investment.

Buffett and Munger are happy to accommodate the hordes of fans, friends, students, and shoppers who flock to Omaha each year. In fact, they have managed to stretch out the whole affair for an action-packed, three-day weekend.

---

* Appendix II chronicles Berkshire's amazing growth over these 32 years.

It's a weekend vacation package where shareholder discounts abound. Stores such as Borsheim's (jewelry) and Nebraska Furniture Mart have exclusive openings and parties for shareholders. Around town, Omaha routinely features events, such as an Omaha Storm Chasers baseball game, where Buffett has signed autographs and thrown out the first pitch.

Over the weekend, shareholders are encouraged to patronize everything in which Berkshire has an economic interest—which brings us to "The Berkshire Mall," a target-marketing retail bonanza for Berkshire subsidiaries.

The ground floor of the CenturyLink Center turns into a mini-mall for Berkshire's shareholders. Dozens of subsidiaries form a midway of booths hawking their wares.*

And then there's the meeting itself, which kicks off with an original short film. Over the years, these films feature skits that have featured every kind of celebrity, including soap opera legend Susan Lucci, boxer Floyd Mayweather, and actor Bryan Cranston (appearing in his role as Walter White from *Breaking Bad*).

The Meeting Itself

With all the furor around the Q&A, you might be forgiven for thinking it was of lesser importance. But you couldn't be farther from the truth. These two men are always the main attraction.

People care deeply about what they have to say and will wait for hours just to ask a single question. In 1985, the Q&A session went on for 2.5 hours. Now, it's considered short if it wraps up in under six hours. Such is the value attendees place on the combined wisdom of these two modern-day sages.

Admittedly, adjusting to the larger numbers of attendees has been, well, an adjustment. With so many people vying to get a question in, the quality of the questions appeared—to Corey and me—to drop off. But perhaps we are being unfair. Having been longtime attendees,† we miss the quieter, more intimate meetings of the past. Fortunately, in 2013, the quality of questions significantly improved by adding a panel of three journalists and three analysts, who now ask a majority of the questions.

Regardless of size, though, the meetings are always informative and full of Buffett and Munger's wit and insight.

---

* To get a full picture of the spending orgy that happens in the lobby, see Appendix III.
† Remember, we saw Warren Buffett and Charlie Munger before they were popular and cool—like seeing the Beatles playing at a bar in Hamburg before they became famous.

A Conversation Across Time

Corey and/or I have taken copious notes during every single Berkshire meeting since that first one in 1984. In 1985, I decided I shouldn't keep them to myself and started sending them out as a newsletter to clients and friends.

While working for Berkshire, Corey was still on my newsletter's mailing list. He remembers reading and enjoying my newsletters while there. He found them to be informative and down-to-earth and thought they captured the essence of the meetings. We talked on the phone from time to time, and I would ask him questions. He said I understood Berkshire's business, from the outside looking in, as well as anyone.

While at Berkshire, Corey had often thought about chronicling what he learned there in a diary, but part of him thought that would be disloyal to the corporation, so he opted against it.

While he didn't formally sit down to take notes, Corey still picked up gems of wisdom as he talked to his coworkers and the executives of the subsidiaries and watched how these exceptional people thought. As a necessity of his job, Corey was always focused on learning. The subsidiaries he worked with varied greatly in their business models. Nebraska Furniture Mart's business, after all, is a lot different from National Indemnity, See's Candies, and Buffalo News.

While working there, Corey also went to graduate school for his MBA and studied organizational theory as part of that. So during his workdays, he observed how effectively Berkshire's decentralized organization functioned through the lens of what he was studying.

Corey became my business partner in 1992. While not disclosing any of the proprietary information he had been privy to, Corey and I discussed Berkshire all the time. He brought a deep understanding of the culture, the values, and of the players involved.

At that time, he personally knew a lot of the people involved and intimately understood the businesses that Berkshire owned. He had spent a lot of time traveling to meet with the subsidiaries.* Ajit Jain, who is often talked about as being Buffett's replacement now, invited Corey for dinner after he spent the day working at his office in New York.

---

* The extensive traveling was the main reason Corey decided to leave Berkshire. His first child was born in 1987. After once returning home from a routine two-week trip, Corey noticed that in that time his daughter had grown and "just looked different." That really bothered him. So he was ready for a change when I approached Corey about becoming my partner.

Corey even had brief interactions with Buffett, talking to him briefly two or three times.*

Corey had seen firsthand Berkshire's high ethical standards. Corey saw how Buffett, from the top, set the tone that Berkshire employees would monitor and respect all laws and rules. When Corey started in internal audit, computers could be purchased online without paying sales tax. But, at Berkshire, if anything like that was purchased, it had to be reported to corporate, so they could file the use tax returns. Buffett wanted to make sure that Nebraska got their sales tax. He was adamant about making sure that Berkshire paid—not more taxes than it had to, but the taxes that it was responsible for.

Taking everything he understood from that experience, Corey has contributed to the notes every year since he came to work at Pecaut & Company in 1992. In the years he attended alone, I based the newsletter on his notes and insights. While I wrote each newsletter, Corey rigorously edited each one.†

Writing feverishly at each meeting, Corey and I jot down what we feel are the most significant of Buffett and Munger's comments and insights. Our rigorous note-taking enables us to highlight, reflect on, and pass along the golden nuggets of what we learned.

Once home, we do a condensed but detailed write-up of each meeting's notes for our clients. Those write-ups are what make up this book.

In addition to their words, we often address what was unsaid, inferred, or implied. Our own expertise as value investors adds a depth of insight that goes beyond a dry, static, verbatim reporting of events.

Much of the mainstream news reporting on Buffett is done without deep insight into the working world of investing.‡ In these pages, you will benefit from our own critical assessment of the meetings.

We have taken hundreds of hours of lectures and distilled them to their most concentrated form. You've been saved the painstaking task of digging through the archives to bring the gold to the surface.

You'll quickly be swept up by the highlight reel of what has been a fascinating, informative, and often hilarious ride through 32 years of the Warren and Charlie show.

---

* Since Munger was off on his own running Wesco Financial in California, Corey never saw him except for when he attended the annual meetings.
† This is why I am the "I" voice in our newsletters.
‡ The 2015 meeting kicked off with Buffett proactively clearing up an issue. A major reporter, who didn't understand accounting, reported that the gross profit of one of Berkshire's businesses was its *net profit*. The difference between the two was huge. The incident highlighted the importance of having a firsthand understanding of scale, terminology, and accounting.

This isn't a book about dusty old "investment theory." This is a curated collection of the best advice and insights Buffett and Munger have shared over the last three decades. Shocking revelations. Funny moments. Devilishly insightful strategies.

These newsletters form a conversation with Warren Buffett and Charlie Munger spanning three decades. We have no doubt that any serious investor will be fascinated and informed, in equal measure, by these letters. (And we challenge you not to laugh out loud at Munger and Buffett's sibling-like haranguing.)

We believe these notes (excluding the annual reports) are the best substitute for attending Berkshire's annual meetings in person over the last 32 years. Of course, if you were at the meetings, then this book is the perfect refresher. The pages to follow will add color and definition to your own memories of events.

The layout of the book is simple. It's designed to put you in the room with Buffett and Munger, every year for the past 32 years (1986–2017).* You will see how Buffett and Munger responded to their own mistakes and faced challenges as the world changed around them. The book unfolds as a journey.

If you decide to jump on board, you will see the remarkable rise of Berkshire Hathaway as it happens. You'll come to understand the genius behind it. You have in your hands fly-on-the-wall analyses of 32 years of annual meetings.

Admittedly, for most companies, that would be like watching paint dry. But Berkshire Hathaway is a different kind of beast.† The company's unique success, and the strategies that made it possible, are legendary.

How To Use These Letters

This book isn't for the first-time investor. It's for the informed investor who sees the value of being able to get deep into the mindsets of Warren Buffett and Charlie Munger. If you want to walk around in their shoes for the past three decades, absorb what works, and then apply it to your own investments, then this book is for you.

Also, one significant personal benefit of value investing is peace of mind. Many investors tough it out in the markets for years, living a life

---

* As you'll note, as the meetings significantly increased in length, so did our newsletters. Since there were more questions asked and answered, we had more data to draw from.
† What other annual meetings do you know of that take over an entire town for a weekend and kick-off with a movie? Or, for that matter, that can boast their own shopping mall? Of course, it wasn't always that way.

filled with anxiety and stress. They constantly fear that their investments will disappear overnight. On the other hand, great value investors, like Buffett and Munger, sleep like a baby—provided they follow simple timeless principles.

We hope that by the time you've finished this book, these principles will be engrained in your consciousness. We hope that your investment decisions will take on a quality and depth that give you a serious competitive edge.

This is not a "how-to" book. This book wrestles with the question, "Why do two of the world's greatest investors do what they do?" The answer is contained in these pages. If you understand it, you will become a better investor. If you can think and behave like they do, particularly under pressure, you will become a great and wealthy investor.

This book will provide you with a deeper insight into how two of the world's greatest investors deal with investment problems as they arise. You'll witness, in real time, their reactions to events like the sovereign debt crisis, the subprime crisis, and nuclear terrorism. Through it all, you get an honest and frank account of mistakes made and obstacles overcome. You'll see firsthand Buffett's rock-solid reasoning for investing in Coke and See's Candy.

You'll also take a long look into the morbidly funny yet jaw-droppingly astute mind of Munger on a range of issues. From the futility of growing corn for fuel to the annual whipping of the modern portfolio theory, Munger never misses a beat.

Had this been just a collection of anecdotes drawn from the last 5–10 years, it would have been too short of a time period to be meaningful. Instead, this is a three-decade, year-by-year analysis of history unfolding. You will be able to view Buffett and Munger's decision-making process from a unique vantage point. You have a collection of insights about what went on beneath the surface of those decisions over time. You see how the same timeless principles are applied to vastly changing landscapes and circumstances (i.e., the internet, the demise of newspapers, booms and busts, and so on).

While reading, you may wonder, *If Berkshire got out of the market, shouldn't I do the same?* or *If Berkshire bought it, should I buy it too?* Buffett and Munger are clear in their advice—people should learn from them and model their advice rather than copy their behavior. The main reason is this: Unless you find yourself in the enviable position that Berkshire operates in, you would do well *not* to copy its moves.

Berkshire Hathaway now represents half a trillion dollars of assets. It makes direct purchases and deals of its own design. Berkshire sometimes buys whole companies. Buffett and Munger play the game at a scale that most investors cannot match. So instead of copying, understand why they made the decisions they did. Then apply those insights to your own decisions and your own position.

In more than one annual meeting, Buffett suggests that the best investment you can make is in yourself. After a lifetime of following his teachings and seeing the success in our own business, we wholeheartedly agree with him.

These letters are a valuable resource of learning and analysis that you can model for your own investing decisions.

But before you dive in, understand that you are about to reap the rewards of the best investment we ever made, as a student at the University of Berkshire Hathaway.

So we invite you to turn the page and step into the fascinating world of *the world's greatest investment team* . . .

All the best,
DANIEL S. PECAUT
Pecaut & Company
April 2018

1986

Venue: Joslyn Art Museum

Attendance: 500 or so

Details About This Year:

- The business of the day was concluded in a matter of minutes, at which time the meeting was opened to 2.5 hours of Q&A.

Stock Price: $2,475

One dollar invested in 1964 would now be worth **$200**.

Berkshire's per-share book value has grown from $19.46 to **$2,073.06** (a rate of **23.3%** compounded annually).

The S&P 500 compounded at **8.8%** annually for the same period.

HIGHLIGHTS FROM 1986's NOTES

Before I reflect on the meeting, let's review Buffett's philosophical framework.

Value Investing

Warren Buffett is the greatest investor of our time and is the most prominent of a group of highly successful value investors who share a common intellectual father, Ben Graham. Graham's books—*Security Analysis* (1934) and *The Intelligent Investor* (1949)—have become the bibles of value investing.

Basically, Graham breaks the art of investing down into two simple variables—price and value. Value is what a business is worth. Price is what you have to pay to get it. Given the stock market's manic-depressive behavior, numerous occasions arise where a business' market price is distinctly out of line with its true business value. In such instances, an investor may be able to purchase a dollar of value for just 50 cents. Note that there is no mention here of interest rates, economic forecasts, technical charts, market cycles, etc. The only issues are price and value.

I should also note that Graham emphasizes a large *margin of safety*. The strategy is not to buy a dollar of value for 97 cents. Rather, the gap should be dramatic so as to absorb the effects of miscalculation and worse-than-average luck. As Buffett puts it, "When you build a bridge, you insist it can carry 30,000 pounds, but you only drive 10,000-pound trucks across it." Over time, diversified portfolios of such stocks have provided superior returns with below-average risk.

Buffett's Track Record

No one has employed these principles more effectively than Warren Buffett. Over the last three decades, Buffett has consistently sought to own either all or part of good businesses for a fair to bargain price. The results have been awe-inspiring.

A $10,000 investment in Buffett's partnership in 1956 grew to $200,000 by 1969, a 25.9% compounded annualized return. Incredibly, the partnership never had a down year even though there were *six* down years in the market during that period. Superior returns with below-average risk, indeed.

In 1969, the partnership dissolved, and Berkshire Hathaway—originally a small New England textile firm—became his base for making investments. Berkshire's stock was $40 a share then. Today it sells around $2,850, a compounded annualized growth rate of 28.5%. Thus, for three decades, money under Buffett's control has grown at a phenomenal rate.

Though I have been aware of the results for a number of years, I still marvel at the achievement.

The Berkshire Hathaway Annual Meeting

So it was with much eagerness I attended my first Berkshire Hathaway annual meeting.

The business of the day was concluded in a matter of minutes, at which time the meeting was opened to 2.5 hours of Q&A. Of Buffett's and Munger's comments, here are the ones I felt to be the most significant.

On Intrinsic Business Value

This concept is the centerpiece of Buffett's approach. Buffett defines it as "what a company would bring if sold to a knowledgeable buyer." This definition departs from Ben Graham's numbers-oriented valuation as it gives value to such intangible items as management talent and franchise value.

It is Buffett's genius in identifying and evaluating these intangibles that sets him apart from the crowd.

On Inflation

Buffett says it's a political phenomena, not an economic one. As long as politicians lack self-restraint, they will print a lot of money at some point. Though it is probably two years or more down the road, Buffett sees "substantial inflation" and "rates we've never seen before."

These are powerful words for Buffett, a man much given to understatement and self-depreciation, so do not take them lightly. If Buffett is correct, long–term bonds and other investments vulnerable to inflation should be avoided.

On Economic Forecasting

True to Graham's principles, Buffett said he pays no attention to economic outlooks. His decisions are based simply on intrinsic business values.

Interestingly, despite his feelings on inflation, Buffett has no plans to alter his strategy (one that has worked for him for three decades). At best, he will try to find businesses that can keep pace with inflation.

On Capital Cities/ABC

"The management of Cap Cities is the best of any public-owned company in the country." Thus, Buffett explained last year's biggest acquisition.

Berkshire helped finance the merger of these two media giants, investing $517 million in three million shares ($172.50 per share) of the new company.

CCB stock currently trades at $240/share.

On the Stock Market

When the lemmings are running, Buffett notes that more money can be made in the market than in buying whole companies. However, such times are rare. Right now, "we see nothing in marketable securities that interests us in the least."

Buffett and Munger have been getting out of the market. Their favorite businesses—media, consumer goods, insurance—have been marked up dramatically in price during this bull market.

You may well ask, "If Buffett's getting out of the market, shouldn't we do likewise?" This is a very difficult question. It is critical to learn from Buffett—not to mimic him.

By selling, Buffett is not predicting a decline, though that will surely come someday. He is simply acting on his observation that the intrinsic business values of his holdings are fully reflected in current market prices.

Berkshire Hathaway now represents $3.1 billion of assets. The number of companies large enough to be meaningful for Buffett is small. Bargains among blue chips are virtually nonexistent. However, we are not so restricted. There are thousands of wonderful small companies we can consider.

Venue: Joslyn Art Museum

Attendance: Over 500

Details About This Year:

- The meeting featured a three-hour Q&A session with shareholders.

Stock Price: $2,827

One dollar invested in 1964 would now be worth **$229**.

Berkshire's per-share book value has grown from $19.46 to **$2,477.47** (a rate of **23.1%** compounded annually).

The S&P 500 compounded at **9.2%** annually for the same period.

HIGHLIGHTS FROM 1987's NOTES

Going on Tour

In the last two months, I have had the great privilege of seeing several of the country's wisest investors:

- George Michaelis of Source Capital, the top-performing closed-end fund over the last decade, April 28, Santa Monica, CA.

- Charles Munger, Chairman of Wesco Financial, April 28, Pasadena, CA, and Vice Chairman of Berkshire Hathaway.

- Warren Buffett, Chairman of Berkshire Hathaway, May 19, Omaha, NE.

- As you may recall, I also had the good fortune to meet with John Templeton in February.

Basically, my associate, Mark Staal, and I have adopted a world-as-our-classroom approach. As such, we will continue to seek outstanding individuals as our "professors." We hope it will make us better investors. At the very least, we will certainly have fewer excuses for our mistakes.

Here is a sampling of their collective wisdom.

On the Market

Like most value investors, they see few bargains. Michaelis holds about a 40% cash level at Source Capital. Buffett and Munger are even more extreme. They have sold *all* their non-permanent stock positions and invested $1 billion in 8- to 12-year tax-free bonds.

As Buffett points out in the Berkshire Hathaway annual report:

> " . . . occasional outbreaks of those two super-contagious diseases, fear and greed, will forever occur in the investment community. The timing of these epidemics will be unpredictable. And the market aberrations produced by them will be equally unpredictable, both as to duration and degree. Therefore, we never try to anticipate the arrival or departure of either disease. Our goal is more modest: we simply attempt to be fearful when others are greedy and to be greedy only when others are fearful.

As this is written, little fear is visible in Wall Street. Instead, euphoria prevails—and why not? What could be more exhilarating than to participate in a bull market in which the rewards to owners of businesses become gloriously uncoupled from the plodding performances of the businesses themselves. Unfortunately, however, stocks can't outperform businesses indefinitely."

Noting that the Japanese stock market has gone to wild extremes, Buffett wryly quoted Herb Stein: "Anything that can't go on forever will end."

Buffett added, "That's about as sophisticated as we get."

On Inflation

Like John Templeton, Buffett believes significant inflation is inevitable due to our government's quick-fix attitude. "The availability of a printing press as a short-term band aid is very tempting . . . Inflation is a narcotic." At the meeting, Buffett went as far as to say we will see a lot more inflation, even more than we saw five years ago.

This has serious implications for fixed income investors.

Note that, to minimize market risk, Buffett's bonds will all mature within 12 years. You should consider doing likewise.

Know Your Limitations/Be Humble

This seems to be the major theme for all of these great investors. Templeton spoke of being humble as the gateway to understanding.

Munger noted that Tom Murphy, CEO of Capital Cities/ABC and considered by Buffett to be the best business manager in the country, prays every day to be humble. And we found George Michaelis to be modest and self-deprecating.

Munger denied being humble (of course) but noted that the key to his and Buffett's success has been that "we've had a very low opinion of our abilities." He said that he'd rather be with a guy with an IQ of 130 who thinks it is 128 than a guy with an IQ of 190 who thinks it is 240. The latter will get you into a lot of trouble.

False Precision

Buffett claimed that it is a terrible mistake to think that things out of a computer are precise. If you have to carry it out to three decimal places, it is too complicated.

As a result, in his 35 years of investing, Buffett says he has seen no improvement in the breed of investment managers. They are no smarter, no more stable psychologically, and they make things more difficult than they are.

Munger added that the worst mistakes are made from the nicest graphs and what is really needed is "enlightened common sense."

Again, knowing your limitations and the limitations of your information seems to be the key. Or as Keynes said, "I would rather be vaguely right than precisely wrong."

On Insider Trading

While applauding the SEC's effort to date, Munger observed, "When incredible rewards go to the casino operators, it is extremely unlikely that civilization has reached nirvana."

On the Insurance Industry

Buffett says the party is over, and the hangover will last longer than the party.

Berkshire Hathaway's insurance companies are seeing a sharp drop off in premium volume. Earnings will look good for a year or two ("the bar closes, but you get to finish your drink"), but business is becoming intrinsically less profitable in a very discernible trend.

Interestingly enough, one of George Michaelis' favorite stocks is the top insurance brokerage company, Marsh & McLennan.

Wall Street has already concluded that the party is over and has knocked the insurance stocks down to depressed levels.

In our portfolio, Hanover and RLI both sell at about six times earnings.

On the Ideal Business

Buffett: "Something that costs a penny, sells for a dollar and is habit forming."

1988

Venue: Joslyn Art Museum

Attendance: 580

Details About This Year:

- The meeting's formal business was concluded in a matter of minutes. The floor was then opened to a three-hour Q&A session with shareholders.

Stock Price: $2,957

One dollar invested in 1964 would now be worth **$239**.

Berkshire's per-share book value has grown from $19.46 to **$2,974.52** (a rate of **23%** compounded annually).

The S&P 500 compounded at **9.1%** annually for the same period.

HIGHLIGHTS FROM 1988's NOTES

On Inflation

As Buffett has been saying for several years, we will have significant inflation eventually. Though the timing and degree of it are unknown, inflation appears inevitable. The reason is "printing money is too easy. I'd do it myself if I could." And it is not unique to the U.S. There is a worldwide bias toward inflation.

On Inflation Hedges

Given that we are going to have major inflation, several people asked whether real estate, foreign currencies, leverage or hard assets should then be considered. Buffett and Munger basically shot them all down:

Real Estate
Munger: "Everyone talks about the big money made in real estate, but they forget to talk about the big money lost in real estate."

Foreign Currencies
Munger: "It's hard enough to understand the culture you've been raised in, much less someone else's."

Leverage
Buffett: "You can leverage up to your eyeballs, but you may not make it across the river."

Hard Assets
Munger: "Someone figured out the Van Gogh painting that sold for $40 million last year yielded a 13% compounded annualized return. Berkshire shareholders have done much better."

The Ultimate Inflation Hedge

What can we do then to mitigate the effects of inflation? The same thing that Buffett and Munger would do if there were no inflation. We'd buy great businesses with excellent management at a fair to bargain price and leave them alone.

While inflation is still undesirable, well-run businesses that employ relatively little capital, that throw off lots of cash and that have pricing flexibility will cope well with inflation.

On Program Trading

Buffett noted that anytime two commodities come together, there will be arbitrage, and that is actually a good and necessary function in capital markets.

The question is whether derivative instruments such as index options should exist at all. Munger's unhedged opinion, "It's a totally asinine idea."

To illustrate the point, Buffett suggested that we imagine that the annual meeting was being held on a tour boat that was blown off course and wrecked on a deserted island. We might elect Buffett to be chairman of the island with a mandate to maximize life on the island. He would probably set half of the shareholders to work raising food, some to building shelter and an inventive few to creating tools and new technologies for the future. Now imagine that an IQ test was given so that Buffett could take 30 or 40 of the best and brightest, give them each a Quotron terminal and have them trade futures on the output of the food producers. It's absurd, of course.

On Predicting Business Cycles

Buffett: "If I live X number of years, I'll go through X number of recessions. But if I spent all my time guessing cycles, Berkshire Hathaway would be $15/share. You can't dance in and out of businesses based on forecasts."*

On Salomon Brothers

Unlike other Berkshire businesses, such as Nebraska Furniture Mart or the World Book, Buffett said he has no idea what the world of investment banking will look like in 10 years. However, there will be lots of capital raised, and Salomon should fill an important function.

---

* Currently, Berkshire is $3,800/share.

Buffett also reaffirmed that they like John Gutfreund, Chairman of Salomon Brothers, very much.

Munger (whose favorite expression seemed to be, "It's one tough business.") made one of his only enthusiastic comments of the day: "Salomon is deep in talent—the ultimate meritocracy—and with that talent may do very well over time."

It appears to me that Salomon Brothers, which is selling below book value, may be an excellent long-term core holding.

On Successor Businesses

In response to a query about the impact of compact laser disks on World Book's business, Buffett characterized himself as an "old windmill enthusiast" and suggested that encyclopedias will be little changed 20 years from now.

In a fascinating digression, Buffett noted that "the fact that you are being obsoleted does not mean you should go into the successor business."

As an example, he explained that if you were a person of vision in the passenger train business in 1930, you might have seen the coming of the airplane. But the answer was not to get into the airline business, which is a terrible business. The answer was to get out of the passenger business altogether.

On the Resilience of the U.S. Economy

Buffett and Munger steadfastly refused to get into a long discussion of macroeconomics.

Buffett noted that the U.S. economic system is strong and can take a lot of abuse. He said that the difference between great economic policy and poor economic policy could be a difference of just 1% annually in the GNP. That is, the GNP might grow at (X-1%) instead of X% due to misguided policies.

John Templeton has shared similar thoughts.

In other words, rather than worry about economic projections, these brilliant investors focus on finding good businesses at bargain prices within our resilient economy.

On the Trade Deficit

Buffett sees the trade deficit as a far more serious problem than the federal budget deficit.

To clarify the point, he noted that Peter Minuit traded trinkets for Manhattan. Now we're trading Manhattan for trinkets! ABC sold its New York office building for $750 million. In return, we buy VCRs.

In other words, he explained, we are trading away the farm. We are sending IOUs out that are slowly being redeemed for pieces of the farm. That is the consequence of a significant trade deficit.

Biographies: Improve Your Friends

My favorite comments are those that give an inside glimpse of what Munger and Buffett are really like.

To a question about what books to read, Munger replied that he is a biography nut and heartily recommended biographies as a way to "make friends among the eminent dead." Buffett quipped, "And they don't talk back."

Munger went on to say that biographies give you marvelous experience, extend your range and may even improve the quality of your friends. He noted that *Golden Arches* and *The Big Store* offer great lessons on business.

Venue: Joslyn Art Museum

Attendance: 1,000+

Details About This Year:

- This year's meeting was delayed 15 minutes as over 1,000 people squeezed into Witherspoon Concert Hall auditorium. Buffett noted, "A lot more people turn out to talk about their money than to look at old paintings."

Fortune 500 Ranking: 205th

Stock Price: $4,711

One dollar invested in 1964 would now be worth **$381**.

Berkshire's per-share book value has grown from $19.46 to **$4,296.01** (a rate of **23.8%** compounded annually).

The S&P 500 compounded at **9.4%** annually for the same period.

HIGHLIGHTS FROM 1989's NOTES

The Trade Deficit:
Our Most Important Economic Problem

Buffett explained that the trade deficit represents the passing out of claim checks that can only be redeemed for assets or consumable items. We are passing out $130 billion of claim checks annually, so we can consume 103% of what we produce. While it may feel pleasant now, such a lifestyle will eventually lead to major trouble.

He likened the problem to eating an extra piece of toast each day. One hundred extra calories per day doesn't seem like much, and it provides immediate pleasure. However, after a month, you've consumed an extra 3,000 calories and gained one pound. Keep it up and eventually you will have a significant problem.

In sum, the trade deficit amounts to the gradual giving away of the farm. As these claim checks are cashed, America gives up more and more of its productive assets. Peter Minuit traded trinkets for Manhattan. Now we are trading Manhattan for trinkets.

Junk Bonds: Who Will Be the Patsy?

Buffett noted that Ben Graham said people got into much more trouble with a sound premise than an unsound premise.

As an illustration, if I recommended Alaska beachfront property to you, you could dismiss it out of hand as nonsense. If I recommended Florida beachfront property, you might have an interest since the premise is sound. Yet many people have lost their shirts buying Florida land.

So it is with the leverage buyout game. The enormous success of a few sensible LBOs has led to wild excess. Buffett and Munger did not mince words about the "creative financing" spawned by the leverage buyout mania.

Zero-coupon bonds (actual payments made only at maturity) and payment-in-kind (PIK) bonds (payments made in more of the same paper) only defer the moment of truth. (Munger noted that if Argentina had PIKs, it would still be current.)

They said that there are large quantities of these bonds that will be impossible to pay under most circumstances. Energies are primarily devoted to laying it off on someone else, to deciding who will be the patsy.

In sum, the LBO junk bond game will go to an extreme and will stop only when it cannot be done anymore. At that time, "there will be blood in the streets."*

Intrinsic Business Value (IBV): The Annual Question

This is the essence of Buffett's value approach.

Buffett said to determine the IBV of an asset, simply take the present value of the net cash flows from here to eternity, based on current bond rates.

The hard part, of course, is predicting the future cash flows. Some businesses are easier to predict than others. Even then, you don't cut it close.

Buffett noted that if he and Munger get a value of X to 3X for an asset, then they attempt to buy it at $1/2$X.†

Insurance Industry Outlook: It Will Get Worse Before It Gets Better

Buffett and Munger had two basic observations: One was that regulation of the insurance industry will only get more onerous. California's Proposition 103 reflects the antagonism that the public feels for the insurance industry. The other was that the industry's underwriting losses will continue to grow for at least two more years.

The Little Bitty Jet: Ridiculous Extravagance

The meetings are always laced with homespun wit and humor.

While Buffett prides himself on never adding the unneeded, Berkshire did purchase a corporate jet a few years ago. When asked about the "little bitty jet," Munger replied, "I am unfamiliar with this ridiculous extravagance." Munger flies coach.

---

* George Michaelis gives a superb summary of the LBO problem in his Source Capital first quarter report. According to Michaelis, to avoid being the patsy, one must do the following:
   A. Avoid financing overpriced takeovers via the high yield bond market.
   B. Avoid the equity of financial companies providing such financing.
   C. Avoid unrealistic valuations in your common stock portfolio based on takeover speculation.
† Buffett paid 23¼ for ServiceMaster in early 1987. We might infer, then, that he calculated ServiceMaster's IBV at that time to be approximately 46 to 140. Today, ServiceMaster is 22⅞.

The Value of Brand Names:
It's Great When You Have One

See's Candy, a Berkshire Hathaway subsidiary, is attempting to market a new chocolate syrup and expects to lose money for some time on the venture. Hershey's is tough competition. It is extremely difficult to break into the food business, and that is precisely why an established brand name product is so valuable.

Similarly, Buffett said that he drank five Pepsis per day until he switched to Cherry Coke. Now he drinks five Cherry Cokes per day. After 50 years of research, he joked that he finally noticed that there are only two companies in the field. Coca-Cola and Pepsi have over 70% of the soft drink market, and their market share grows each year. He finally made a decision and bought one of them.*

Past Is Not Necessarily Prologue

The history of Wall Street has forever been one of boom and bust.

One of the reasons Buffett gave for human excess is an unthinking reliance on the recent past. For example, junk bond advocates point to the last 30 years of attractive "high yield" bond performance and claim, therefore, that they will continue to do well. Buffett noted that such an analysis is akin to thinking the sun rose because the cock crowed. Meanwhile, junk bonds get junkier, and a bad end seems more and more likely.

As Buffett summed up, "If investors only had to study the past, the richest people would be librarians."

---

* Berkshire owns 6.3% of Coca-Cola.

Venue: Orpheum Theater

Attendance: 1300

Details About This Year:

- To handle the fast-growing attendance, the venue was changed to the larger Orpheum Theater.

Fortune 500 Ranking: 179th

Stock Price: $8,696

One dollar invested in 1964 would now be worth **$703**.

Berkshire's per-share book value has grown from $19.46 to **$4,612.06** (a rate of **23.2%** compounded annually).

The S&P 500 compounded at **10.2%** annually for the same period.

HIGHLIGHTS FROM 1990's NOTES

Rites of Spring

Since adopting a world-as-our-classroom approach six years ago, we have attended the Berkshire meeting regularly and selected others as well. This year, we attended the following "classes" with some of our favorite "professors":

- April 30th, Omaha, *Berkshire Hathaway*, Warren Buffett and Charles Munger

- May 7th, Los Angeles, *Source Capital*, George Michaelis

- May 8th, Pasadena, *Wesco Financial*, Charles Munger

They shared a great many insights I would like, in turn, to share with you. However, there was such a striking emphasis on one concept by these gentlemen. I thought it might be most beneficial at this time to review that theme.

Buy Wonderful Businesses

"It is far better to buy a wonderful company at a fair price than a fair company at a wonderful price."
—WARREN BUFFETT

According to each of the above meetings and the Berkshire Hathaway annual report, the key to investment success is to buy wonderful businesses.

Like many great truths, this may seem obvious, but it is not. In fact, it is a complete departure from the value approach recommended by the philosophical father of value investing, Benjamin Graham.

At the Source Capital annual meeting, Michaelis explained that there have been two basic themes in value investing: 1) buy assets and 2) buy earnings power.

The first approach focuses on buying a company well below its liquidating value.

Ben Graham was an asset bargain hunter, which was probably the appropriate approach coming out of the depression as he did.

The problem with buying assets cheap, as Michaelis sees it, is that the only way to increase the value is through some sort of event.

20

Buffett expressed much the same thoughts in his annual report, calling the asset style of investing the "cigar butt approach." Unless you are a liquidator, you may end up waiting a long time for that "puff" of profit.

Michaelis prefers the earnings power approach. If a company earns very high returns year after year, he explained, then, ultimately, those will be the shareholders' returns as well.

At the Wesco Financial annual meeting, Munger put it this way: what he wants are "idiot-proof" businesses. He pointed to Coca-Cola and the *Washington Post* as examples and described them as "first liens against the passage of time."*

Institutional Blindness

What is fascinating is that each of these gentlemen came to the idea of buying good businesses on his own.

Michaelis told me that the subject was never discussed at the Harvard Business School.

At the Wesco Financial meeting, Munger noted that when Ben Graham, one of the most brilliant teachers, taught Warren Buffett, Graham's most brilliant student, the subject *never came up*.

Munger lamented that business schools would produce better managers if they would study what makes a good business good and what makes a bad business bad. But they don't.

When asked why they don't, Munger replied that for business schools to do so would mean calling into question the flawed morals and performance of America's largest corporations, the same corporations that hire many of the business schools' students.

Munger explained that the business schools are merely heeding Ben Franklin's advice: "Keep your eyes wide open before marriage and half shut thereafter."

"Business schools are good at keeping their eyes half shut," Munger concluded.

---

* Buffett has, in the past, credited Munger with steering him toward buying wonderful businesses versus buying asset bargains.

1991

Venue: Orpheum Theater

Attendance: 1,700

Details About This Year:

- Fans were greeted in the lobby by a floor-to-ceiling Coca-Cola display. Coca-Cola President Don Keough and his "minimum wage helper," Warren Buffett, were adorned in red Coca-Cola aprons and serving beverages.

- The 1,700 people who flocked into the old Orpheum Theater marked a six-fold increase over the attendance in 1984. The mere size of the crowd made for a festive atmosphere (and, we believe, less penetrating questions at the meeting). That aside, the meeting was informative as always, full of Buffett's and Munger's wit and insight.

Fortune 500 Ranking: 170th

Stock Price: $6,687

One dollar invested in 1964 would now be worth **$541**.

Berkshire's per-share book value has grown from $19.46 to **$6,437** (a rate of **23.7%** compounded annually).

The S&P 500 compounded at **9.6%** annually for the same period.

HIGHLIGHTS FROM 1991's NOTES

Coke Is It

To explain Berkshire's purchase of 7% of Coca-Cola, Buffett deferred to Coca-Cola President Don Keough, who noted that his company has been selling "simple pleasure" for 105 years and is now available in 170 countries. Big growth should come from overseas. While Coke sells 300 drinks per person per year in the U.S., it sells just 59 drinks per person outside the U.S.

Buffett has frequently mentioned the value of consumer franchises over the years. His appraisal of Coca-Cola is unequivocal: "the most valuable franchise in the world."

Permanent Holdings

Buffett has classified Berkshire's holdings in Capital Cities/ABC, Coca-Cola, GEICO and the *Washington Post* as "permanent" and listed three characteristics for such holdings:

1. Good economic characteristics

2. Able and trustworthy management

3. We like what the company does

He allowed that economics are not the only issue for him ("What's the sense of getting rich if you discard associations you enjoy?"). But even if they were, some permanent holding would be likely. He noted that there aren't that many wonderful, large enduring businesses—even fewer than he thought 15 years ago.*

Buying Stocks: Like Buying Food

Buffett made his annual statement that he will not comment on any investments that Berkshire might be accumulating except as required by securities law. Good ideas are rare, and competition in accumulation may push the stock price up.

Buffett noted that many investors illogically become euphoric when stock prices rise and are downcast when they fall. This makes no more

---

* Berkshire Hathaway certainly fits the "permanent holding" criteria: the economics are powerful, and management could not be more able or of greater integrity.

sense than if you bought some hamburger one day, returned the next day to buy more but at a higher price, and then felt euphoric because you had bought some cheaper the day before. If you are going to be a lifelong buyer of food, you welcome falling prices and deplore price increases. So should it be with investments.

The Financial World

Buffett and Munger have had a great deal to say about the failings of our financial system in recent years. They foresaw problems in the junk bond market, the savings and loan industry and the banking industry.*

Buffett explained that financial disasters come about because stupid decisions in financial companies are not accompanied by immediate pain. Instead, people give you *more* money. Seeing this, competitors indulge in mindless imitation. Thus, when failure comes, it is huge.

Buffett and Munger have pointed to a number of LBO debacles and have taken exception to a "kill-'em-at-birth" mentality on the part of some promoters.

In the case of Interco's bankruptcy, Munger found it hard to imagine more irresponsible conduct. Leveraged to the gills, Interco was virtually assured of failure from the start.

Buffett also cited a need for a better insurance solvency system. As with S&Ls and banking, the present system doesn't catch companies until much damage is done.

Munger commented that despite the "stupid megalomania" at First Executive Life, it received an "A" rating from the rating agencies right up to its collapse. Financial companies don't have to be bad. To the extent there is tough-minded, independent management—such as Carl Reichardt and Paul Hazen at Wells Fargo—such companies can do well. Unfortunately, such managers are rare.†

Media Business: Considerably Less Marvelous

While there will be some cyclical rebound, Buffett believes the secular trend for media is not good.

---

* Read Munger's 1988, 1989, and 1990 Wesco Financial letters for a brilliant treatise on the rise and fall of this economic anachronism.
† As of December 31, 1990, Berkshire owned just under 10% of Wells Fargo (five million shares at an average cost of $57.88 per share) and recently filed to buy up to 22%.

With more electronic ad conveyance and direct-mail substitutes, certain areas of the media industry are quickly turning from marvelous businesses into mediocre ones.

Buffett still considers Berkshire's media holdings to be fine businesses compared to American industry generally, but considerably less marvelous than he would have thought just a few years ago.

Advice to MBA Graduates

Buffett: "Do what you enjoy the most. Work for people you admire. You can't miss if you do that."

I Help the Captain

When asked how he spends a day, Buffett responded that he tap dances into work (obviously, he's following his own career advice), reads a lot, talks on the phone a bit, and that's about it.

When the same question was directed at Munger, he told the story of the World War II Air Force captain who was bored stiff in Panama. As the general reviewed the officers, he asked the captain what he did. The frustrated captain answered, "I don't do one damn thing." The general asked the same of his lieutenant. The lieutenant replied, "Well, sir, I help the captain."

Looking for Seven-Footers

In looking for investments and for business managers, Buffett recommends a cream-skimming approach. He suggests adopting the mindset of a basketball coach who, in a crowd of people, will immediately begin talking to the seven-footers. You only need one good player to make a difference.

Munger also claimed that much can be discerned from "the paper record." The documented record of how people have behaved over many years has far more predictive power than a personal interview. Buffett added that this is why they don't hire fresh MBA graduates. There is no record of on-the-job performance.

The Inefficient Theory: Where's an Orangutan When You Need One?

Buffett and Munger have made a hobby out of tweaking the nose of academia and its pet investment theory, the efficient market theory.

The theory holds that since markets are totally efficient, it does no good to think about businesses.*

Three professors won the Nobel Prize last year for additions to the theory.

Munger calls it a grand structure built on a false premise and bluntly concludes, "A well-educated orangutan could see the success of our approach, and yet no one is doing it."

The Insurance Industry

While Buffett is not upbeat short term, he is upbeat long term about Berkshire's prospects in insurance.

Munger pointed out that a period of major distress is approaching and that declining equity plus asset problems equals opportunity for Berkshire.

Of all their businesses, Buffett believes the insurance business has the greatest potential.

---

* If that's true, Berkshire must be a mirage.

Venue: Orpheum Theater

Attendance: 2,000

Details About This Year:

- The 2,000 people who flocked into the old Orpheum Theater marked an eight-fold increase over the attendance in 1984.

- Former Berkshire Hathaway employee Corey Wrenn becomes a partner at Pecaut & Company.

Fortune 500 Ranking: 158th

Stock Price: $9,068

One dollar invested in 1964 would now be worth **$733**.

Berkshire's per-share book value has grown from $19.46 to **$7,745** (a rate of **23.6%** compounded annually).

The S&P 500 compounded at **10.4%** annually for the same period.

HIGHLIGHTS FROM 1992's NOTES

Guinness: Another International Company

Commenting on Berkshire's investment of $265 million in shares of Guinness PLC, the world's largest purveyor of assorted liquors, Buffett noted that, like Coca-Cola and Gillette, Guinness receives the vast majority of its profits from overseas.

Munger pointed out that liquor can be a status symbol and that Guinness' products enjoy the rare and remarkable quality that the higher the price, the higher the perceived value. Buffett added that some people equate price with value in investment banking services and business schools. So it is with scotch. *

More on The Real Thing

Buffett mentioned that roughly 20% of Berkshire's look-through earnings now comes from international sales, the largest percentage of which comes from Coca-Cola.

Each day, the average person drinks 64 ounces of something. In 1991, 25% of those 64 ounces were soft drinks, surpassing water as America's number one beverage! That means about 730 soft drinks per capita per year are consumed, of which approximately 42% are Coca-Cola products. Worldwide consumption shows remarkably similar patterns, and the number of soft drinks consumed is rising continuously.

Buffett noted that this illustrates why he pays so little attention to macroeconomic factors. Owning the right business is the key.

Coca-Cola went public in 1919 at $40 per share. In 1920, the stock plunged to 19½ as sugar prices changed. After seven decades of wars, depression, etc. that initial $40 share would now be worth $1.8 million (About 16% compounded annually).

It is far more fruitful to decide whether a product can sustain itself than make economic predictions.†

---

* Berkshire's cost translates to about $42.40 per Guinness ADR (American depositary receipt), which currently trade at $55. Given Buffett attempts to buy companies for 50 cents on the dollar, we might infer that he believes Guinness' intrinsic value would be in the neighborhood of $80 or more per ADR.

† The fact that Buffett volunteered the percentage of look-through earnings coming from overseas suggests that he has been intentional in repositioning Berkshire to benefit from growth abroad. We have discussed the boom in free enterprise around the globe numerous times in this newsletter. Buffett may have seen it coming years ago.

Executive Compensation

With many executives making tens of millions in compensation in 1991, this has been a hot topic in the press. Buffett's response:

1. There should be no cap (you simply cannot overpay for truly great performance).

2. Longevity is irrelevant.

3. Relate compensation directly to the performance of the business. (Yardsticks will vary depending on the business and the amount of capital employed).

What he finds objectionable is the large sums being paid for mediocre performance.

The Case for a Non-Executive Chairman

Comments on compensation related to a larger discussion of the role of corporate boards.

Buffett noted that every corporate employee has to answer to someone else, except for the president. Too often the CEO also serves as chairman of the board. Given that the chairman calls the board meetings and sets the agenda, it is difficult for the board to evaluate the CEO properly.

The central question is how do you set up a cooperative institution with an oversight board that will flash a yellow light when necessary but not so often that it disrupts operations. Buffett's idea—one that he has publicly suggested at Salomon Brothers—is a non-executive chairman. Such a person could see to it that the CEO is properly evaluated and monitored.

Speaking of Salomon Brothers

Buffett was asked about his heroic efforts in saving Salomon Brothers from the treasury scandal.

Buffett responded by telling the story of the shark pool at Sea World—which, the tour guide explained, no one had ever dared to swim across despite a $1,000,000 prize for doing so. Suddenly, there was a splash. A man paddled furiously and emerged on the other side, sharks nipping at his heels. The tour guide gushed, "What bravery! You are the first man ever to swim across the shark pool. What will you do with your million dollar prize?" The man responded, "Hire a detective to find the S.O.B. who pushed me in."

Light Hand on the Rudder

When asked about capital allocation decisions at Berkshire's investee corporations, Buffett claimed that he and Charlie were far less influential than we might think.

Munger said they had nothing like control and quoted Clarence Darrow: "Captain of my fate? Hell, I don't even pull an oar!"

Modern Portfolio Theory:
The Annual Rebuttal

Buffett noted with fascination that what is taught about investing has gone backward over the last 40 years.

Munger claimed that it is because professors are so enamored by modern portfolio theory. For the man with a hammer, every problem looks like a nail.

Buffett continued the thought, noting that because computers can generate huge amounts of data, modern portfolio theorists end up looking for answers in chicken tracks. They ignore the simple fact that when you buy a business, you *own a business.*

In conclusion, Buffett mused that he and Charlie, as buyers of good businesses, should support the study of modern portfolio theory: "If you're in the sailing business, you want to set up flat-earth scholarships."

On Market Timing

I found this story remarkable:

When Buffett graduated from Columbia University in the 1950s, both his teacher, Benjamin Graham, and his father told him that it was not a good time to get into the securities business. The Dow had just surpassed the 200 mark. Buffett had $10,000 at the time. If he had waited, he claims he would still have $10,000.

Munger put it this way: "We're predicting how people will swim against the current. We're not predicting the current itself."

I find Buffett's story stunning because the two people who most certainly knew Buffett was one great swimmer (investor) discouraged him from entering the water because they were concerned about the current (market). Even Ben Graham succumbed to the seduction of making a market call, which illustrates just how difficult it is to focus on identifying great swimmers instead of predicting the current.

All Investing Is Value Investing

Buffett commented that the distinction between the growth and value styles of investing is nonsense.

Value is the *only* concern for any economic commitment. To calculate your expected return, compute the discounted present value of the flow of all cash from the business between now and judgment day. To do so, you must A) determine the amounts and certainty of cash flows in and out and B) select a discount rate.

Buffett noted that growth can enhance or *detract* from the calculated value. For example, electric utilities were forced to grow and to invest capital in the 1970s, which lowered their returns.

More dramatically, Buffett noted that the assured growth of the airline industry has been a death sentence to American investors. Since Kitty Hawk, the industry has lost money every year! Yet the industry asks for more money from investors every year. The idea is to find investments that *give* you money, not take it.

Munger observed that studying airlines teaches you about competition in a high fixed-cost business with a fungible commodity.

Buffett also noted that book value is seldom meaningful in analyzing the value of a business. Book value simply records what was put *into* the business. The key to calculating value is determining what will come *out of* the business.

Buffett explained that buying a business is much like buying a bond with no maturity and with a blank coupon. You must write in the coupon, and the accuracy of that coupon is the essence of intelligent investing. If you cannot guess the coupon with any accuracy, then do not invest in the business.

Corporate Returns on Equity: The "Equity" Coupon

A corporation's return on equity approximates its equity coupon.

My question, then, was whether the 13% return on equity that American industry has averaged over the last few decades was likely to change materially in the next few decades.

Buffett cited his 1977 *Fortune* article (in which he discussed his stocks-as-bonds analysis) noting that the average return on equity was 12% then. He saw little to change that. Maybe 13% was okay.

Then he and Munger started to chip away at the 13% noting the following:

- Post-retirement medical benefits amount to a huge liability for corporate America that has been accruing for 20 years but is only now beginning to be reported on balance sheets. Deduct ¼ to ⅜ of a point.

- Stock options and other executive compensation that goes unreported by GAAP accounting. There is another ¼ to ⅜.

- Overfunded pensions that have led to faithfully recorded prepaid pension costs, which are not what they would call earnings.

When they got done, they decided a 12% average return on equity was more likely to be the correct number.

Buffett said there is a bias toward inflating the numbers in U.S. accounting. As Munger so delicately phrased it, "The difference between 12% and 13% is the corruption in U.S. accounting . . . the moral and intellectual failing of the U.S. accounting system."

The General Market: Not Cheap

After restating that the level of the market has no impact on their purchase decisions, Buffett allowed that the market is not cheap.

Munger described the last 12 years as hog heaven and stated that future returns will not be as high—the investment money of the world can only grow so fast.

Buffett was even more emphatic: "There's no way investment returns can match what has been achieved."

Venue: Orpheum Theater

Attendance: 2,000

Details About This Year:

- Bus service was introduced to take shareholders from the venue to and from Nebraska Furniture Mart, Borsheims, various hotels and the airport.

Fortune 500 Ranking: 158th

Stock Price: $11,770

One dollar invested in 1964 would now be worth **$951**.

Berkshire's per-share book value has grown from $19.46 to **$8,854** (a rate of **23.3%** compounded annually).

The S&P 500 compounded at **10.2%** annually for the same period.

HIGHLIGHTS FROM 1993's NOTES

World Markets

Buffett continues to like world markets, noting that a large percentage of the earnings of Coca-Cola (80%), Guinness (80%) and Gillette (67%) comes from abroad.

With over 20% of Berkshire's look-through earnings coming from overseas, Buffett has intentionally positioned Berkshire over the last five years for the globalization of the world economy.

An interesting point—Berkshire's position in U.K.-based Guinness is unhedged. Buffett claimed that currency hedging would be not only expensive and time-consuming but unnecessary as well since Guinness itself already earns money in many different currencies. In the long run, the currency factors should wash out.*

Munger took advantage of the topic to take a shot at the "diseconomies of scale" of bureaucracy. Where a large corporation might go bonkers and develop an entire floor of currency traders—probably hedging the company on currencies for which it had no exposure—Berkshire seeks to keep things simple, "so the chairman can sit and read annual reports all day."

Value Investing: A Mispriced Gamble

As in years past, Buffett pointed out that the rational value of any economic asset equals the discounted present value of all future cash flows (*in* as well as out).

He believed the long-term government bond rate (plus a point or two if interest rates are low) is the appropriate discount rate for most assets. While predicting cash flows for companies is much tougher than for bonds, it can be much more rewarding.

Munger noted that many analysts look at huge bodies of past data looking for clues, which results in enormous misspent effort (generally proportional to the IQs of those doing it). True investing is really more like betting against a parimutuel system, trying to find a 2-to-1 shot that pays 3 to 1. Value investing is looking for a "mispriced gamble."

Buffett chimed in, saying that they would have no edge if they tried to evaluate every horse. They have an edge only if they pick their spots.

---

* Mark Holowesko, director of research at the Templeton Group, says much the same thing.

The danger of relying on historical statistics or formulas is that you end up betting on a 14-year-old horse with a great record but is now ready for the glue factory.

Rate of Change "Normal"

I have often stated to clients that the rate of change in the world is accelerating.

While I still stand by that notion, Buffett disagrees, saying that the amount of change in the business world today is normal. The simple fact is that businesses come and go, and there are always a certain number of 14-year-old horses on their way to the glue factory. (He recommended Carol Loomis' *Fortune* article "The Dinosaurs" as a case in point.)

Generics vs. Brands

Buffett noted that generics are a threat in any industry where the leaders earn high returns on equity. In many industries, that risk is increasing.

Generics have been doing well, but not all brands are alike. Where the pricing umbrella has been raised too high (cigarettes, cornflakes, diapers) and where much marketing muscle has been lost to retailers, brands are quite vulnerable to generics.

In the case of Philip Morris, the price of Marlboro was steadily raised to $2.00 per pack, enabling $1.00 per-pack generics (a $500 per-year differential for a 10-pack-per-week smoker) to grab significant market share. Philip Morris recently responded by dramatically cutting the price of Marlboro.

In contrast, Gillette has a much larger moat around its business castle. The annual difference in the cost of Sensor blades versus the cheapos might be only $10 per year. Plus, there is a substantial quality differential built on lots of technology. (For example, putting those tiny springs in the Sensor required the development of a laser that can make 15 spot welds in a tenth of a second).

Likewise with Coca-Cola, which has kept its pricing low. Coke sold for 0.8 cents per ounce many decades ago, and today sells for 2 cents per ounce. Few food items have gone up less in price. Put another way, with 700 million 8-ounce servings worldwide every day, Coke sold 250 billion servings last year and made $2.5 billion, or 1 cent per serving. That leaves Sam's Cola with very little room to maneuver. In addition, Coke has a worldwide infrastructure that is very impressive.

See's Candy vs. generic chocolate? Buffett said he just hopes that few men, come Valentine's Day, will say "Here, honey, I took the low bid."

Danger in Derivatives for Salomon

Regarding the alarmingly rapid growth of derivatives, Buffett said there is no question in his mind that there exists the possibility of an explosive chain reaction with huge financial outcomes.

Munger added that the derivatives market is bigger than the futures markets now and that to have money cascading in on people who sit in front of computer screens all day is a reliable source of craziness. The pyramiding of intertwining contracts and abilities to pay is very dangerous.

While Salomon Brothers is alert to the danger, Buffett noted that Salomon cannot hedge away the systemic risk of a collapse in derivatives.

Berkshire Stock Split?

Every year Buffett explains that he wants Berkshire to have great long-term shareholders and that splitting the stock would only work against that. Instead, it would attract people like the man who ordered a pizza and, when the vendor asked if he wanted it cut into eight pieces or four, the man replied, "Make it four, I could never eat eight."

Munger added that $13,000 is a perfectly reasonable amount to pay for a partnership interest in a fine business.

Reinsurance Opportunities

Buffett noted that with risks growing faster than the cost of living, the world is groping for a new reinsurance concept. Many companies need reinsurance on a very large scale.

A contributing factor is the collapse of Lloyd's of London, which Munger doubts can be fixed (and whose collapse he believes should be studied worldwide as a case study in stupidity).* †

---

* Our sense is that Buffett and Munger see huge opportunity here and would look for the amount of reinsurance underwritten to expand.
† Wesco Financial, 80% owned by Berkshire, recently announced the sale of its Mutual Savings subsidiary, freeing up over $300 million of capital. Berkshire can now cede significant amounts of reinsurance to Wesco's Wes-FIC insurance arm. Wesco Financial's stock has rocketed from 90 to 110 in recent weeks.

Inflation Will Return

While amazed at how low inflation has stayed, Buffett said that, at some point, inflation will return. "It's just in remission."

Munger agreed, noting in his characteristically upbeat way that "the failure rate of all great civilizations is 100%."

Though no business benefits by inflation, Buffett believes Berkshire is better positioned for it than most.

Key to Successful Investing

When asked for great investment books to read, Buffett cited *The Intelligent Investor* (as always) but then downplayed the idea that investment secrets are hidden in books.

Investing is not that complicated, he explained. Other than learning accounting, which is the language of business, the real key to investment success is to have the *right mindset* with a temperament compatible with those principles. As long as you stay within your circle of competence (and know where the perimeter is), you will do fine.

Munger put it even more succinctly, noting that few humans have an edge if they try to follow 40 companies or more (such as yours truly). Eight or 10 in a lifetime, or even one, will get you your return.

1994

Venue: Orpheum Theater

Attendance: 3,000

Details About This Year:

- After nine years of working the meetings as an employee of Berkshire, our own Corey Wrenn was finally able to sit and enjoy the meeting.

- Buffett mused that the only place large enough to hold next year's meeting might be AK-SAR-BEN—the local race track. Years ago, the meetings were held at the Joslyn Art Museum. Buffett observed that in moving from a temple of culture to an old vaudeville theater and, prospectively, to a den of gambling, Berkshire was sliding down the cultural scale.

Fortune 500 Ranking: 158th

Stock Price: $16,348

One dollar invested in 1964 would now be worth **$1,322**.

Berkshire's per-share book value has grown from $19.46 to **$10,083** (a rate of **23%** compounded annually).

The S&P 500 compounded at **10.2%** annually for the same period.

HIGHLIGHTS FROM 1994's NOTES

Derivatives

At last year's meeting, Buffett noted that the use of derivatives has exploded and that he would not be surprised if a failure in derivatives triggered a financial catastrophe sometime in the decade ahead. Since then, the rest of the world has taken heed.

Asked for a follow-up, Buffett emphasized that derivatives actually serve a useful purpose. However, when ignorance is combined with borrowed money, you get interesting outcomes.

Alluding to Proctor and Gamble's embarrassing loss in derivatives, Buffett noted that anytime you go from selling soap to putt writing on bonds, you have made a big jump.

When asked if he had anything to add, Munger, in his usual gregarious fashion, said, "No." Buffett quipped, "I may have to shut him off."

Super Catastrophes

Catastrophe coverage in the insurance industry is in disarray.

Buffett noted that the industry still has its head in the sand regarding worst-case scenarios. Too many insurers make the mistake of underwriting based on experience rather than exposure.

Buffett claimed that the insurance industry has vastly underestimated the full potential of what a super catastrophe could do.

For example, the LA earthquake was a pretty big one (but not the Big One). Loss estimates of $4.5 billion seemed low to Buffett.* But a catastrophe would need to exceed $8 billion to trigger any of Berkshire's supercat policies. Yet these losses have already exceeded many companies' estimates of "probable maximum loss." If it had been the Big One, a number of companies would have been wiped out.

Likewise, Buffett estimates that a hurricane hitting Long Island or Miami could easily be a $15–$20 billion event, an event for which the insurance industry is insufficiently prepared.

Swimming Naked in the Reinsurance Pool

With $5 billion of new money entering the reinsurance field last year, Buffett acknowledged that there is more competition in the catastrophe reinsurance business.

---

* They have since been revised to $6 billion.

In the short run, this has led to some price deterioration. In the long term, Buffett remains optimistic, noting that new competitors may feel pressure from their investors to "do something" (i.e., writing business whether or not the price is right), while Berkshire can pick its spots.

In addition, Buffett noted that Berkshire's premier strength and reputation constitute a significant competitive advantage.

He observed that the nature of reinsurance seems to lead to stupid things done en masse. All of a sudden, the money is gone. "You don't find out who's been swimming naked until the tide goes out."

The Indefensible

Buffett accused Munger of planting a question about Berkshire's corporate jet, The Indefensible. The parsimonious Munger reputedly flies coach.

Buffett admitted that Charlie has pointed out to him that the back of the plane invariably arrives at the same time as the front and acknowledged, "Charlie's even more of an expert on buses."

Evaluating Management

Buffett gave two criteria for evaluating the performance of management: 1) How well do they run the business? and 2) How well do they treat the owners?

Business performance should be compared to that of the competition, include review of capital allocation decisions and take into account the hand management was dealt.

While good managers might think about the owners, Buffett said that he has found poor managers seldom do. Finding good managers is a difficult, but essential task.

Munger shared the story of the headmaster who told the graduating class, "5% of you will become criminals. I know exactly who you are, but I'm not going to tell you because it would deprive you of an air of excitement."

Job Description

Buffett explained that one of his jobs is to identify and keep good managers. The trick is, since most such managers are financially independent, they need another reason to work.

Buffett tries to keep it fun and interesting, to compensate them fairly based on performance and to leave them alone to do what they do best.

Munger observed that the concept of treating the other fellow as if the roles were reversed was a sound one.

Buffett's other job is to allocate capital. "Aside from that, we play bridge."

Greenspan

Buffett said he felt the actions of Federal Reserve Chairman Alan Greenspan were quite sound given that part of his job is "to take away the punch bowl at the party."

Buffett noted that it is not an easy job. As you lean against the wind, if the wind changes, you will fall flat on your face.

When Buffett asked Munger for his assessment of Greenspan's performance, the monosyllabic Munger replied, "Fine." Buffett exclaimed, "Greenspan is safe!"

What vs. When

Berkshire, Buffett explained, is in the business of acquiring businesses and, in the manner of people buying groceries or cars, welcomes lower prices.

Buffett said that they know how to evaluate businesses. They do not know how to predict market swings. "It is crazy to give up something you know for something you do not."

Munger added that they are agnostic on macroeconomic factors. Instead, they spend all their time on individual businesses. "To think about *what* will happen versus *when* is a far more efficient way to behave."

Acquiring 100% of Businesses

When acquiring businesses, Buffett's preference is to buy the entire company. Unfortunately, sellers of 100% of a business tend to demand a fair price. At the same time, competing buyers operating with OPM (other people's money) tend to pay more optimistic prices. Most corporate managers believe they are better off if they are managing something larger, especially if the purchase is made with OPM. They get the upside with no downside. "Animal spirits compete in 100% purchases."

As a result, a greater percentage of Berkshire's corporate holdings consist of partial ownership positions purchased in the stock market, where more foolish prices can prevail.

Wesco Financial Valuation

Part of the game with Berkshire is to try to calculate its intrinsic business value. While Buffett and Munger give plenty of clues, the shareholders are challenged to come up with their own appraisal of intrinsic business value.

Buffett says he has been pleased with the way Berkshire's share price has generally reflected its value over the years.

In a surprising break from tradition, Munger actually calculates the value of Wesco Financial (80% owned by Berkshire) in the Wesco annual report, coming up with $100/share.

Munger explained that he thought the buyers of the stock were a little crazy (Wesco Financial peaked at 149, and the current price is about 117), and he did not like attracting people in at high prices. He called it "a one-time quirk."*

Modern Portfolio Theory Described

Buffett and Munger took their annual shot at debunking modern portfolio theory.

Buffett defined risk as "the possibility of harm or injury."

In modern portfolio theory, beta is used as a measure of the volatility and, thus, the risk of an investment. However, Buffett sees the use of beta as nonsense, emphatically stating, "Volatility is no measure of risk to us."

For example, super catastrophe insurance *will lose* money in a given year, but over a decade, Buffett expects to make money—more money than writing something predictable.

He said it is Wall Street nonsense to say that something that earns a lumpy 20% to 80% is "riskier" than something that earns a predictable 5% year after year.

Buffett said that while he is risk averse, we would be surprised at how much he might put on a seven-to-five flip. "We go where the probabilities are good."

Munger summed up, "We act as if we never heard of modern finance theory, which can only be described as disgusting."

---

* When is the last time you heard a chairman talk his own stock *down?*

What's the Tax Rate in Bangladesh Anyway?

Buffett said he believes in progressive taxes, though he would prefer a steeply progressive tax on consumption rather than on income.

Munger noted that there is a point where income tax becomes counterproductive, but we are not there yet.

Buffett pointed out that the rich are very well-treated in America. For those who feel unfairly burdened, Buffett suggested transporting them to Bangladesh, so the rich could find out how much of their wealth is them and how much is society.

Information Hypeway

Asked about the boom in information technology, Buffett replied that his primary information source is the same as it was 40 years ago: annual reports.

He emphasized that it is *judgment* that has utility in measuring price and value. What is needed is not quick information, but good information.

Buffett concluded that if the mail and quotes were delayed three weeks, he would do just fine.*

Think for Yourself

The need for independent thinking has long been a theme at Berkshire meetings.

This year, Buffett cautioned that you cannot let the market think for you—"you cannot get rich with a weathervane."

Buffett said to beware projections ("Don't ask the barber if you need a haircut.") and to keep things simple ("I'd rather multiply by three than by pi.").

Munger noted that it is such an obvious point, yet many believe if they just hire someone, they can do something difficult. He labeled it "one of the most dangerous human ideas" and told the story of a man and his building. The man said he had learned to fear three things: an architect, a contractor and a hill.

Munger concluded that you do not need hierarchical thinking.

---

* In a similar vein, John Templeton told us that his investment results improved when he moved to the Bahamas, where the *Wall Street Journal* arrived three days late.

1995

Venue: Holiday Inn Convention Center

Attendance: 4,300

Details About This Year:

- A number of foreign countries were represented in the audience this year, as well as shareholders from 49 of the 50 states (those ever-practical Vermonters stayed home).

- To handle the record crowd, Berkshire continued its slide down the cultural scale: from the Joslyn Art Museum years ago to the Orpheum Theater to the Holiday Inn Convention Center.

- Prior to the meeting, giant television screens replayed Nebraska's Orange Bowl win over Miami. (The locals apparently found this to be in extremely good taste.)

- The Q&A went on for nearly five hours.

Fortune 500 Ranking: 295th

Stock Price: $20,435

One dollar invested in 1964 would now be worth **$1,652**.

Berkshire's per-share book value has grown from $19.46 to **$14,426** (a rate of **23.6%** compounded annually).

The S&P 500 compounded at **9.9%** annually for the same period.

HIGHLIGHTS FROM 1995's NOTES

Buying Businesses

Normally the business portion of the meeting is railroaded through in a few minutes. This year's took longer as shareholders approved a motion that would allow Berkshire to issue up to one million shares of preferred stock. Buffett called it another form of currency with which to buy businesses.

Buffett noted that Berkshire is equally willing to acquire companies whole or in part. Quoting Woody Allen, "The advantage of being bisexual is you've doubled your chances for a date on Saturday night."

One recent 100% purchase for Berkshire was Helzberg's, a Kansas City-based chain of 150 jewelry stores.

Buffett praised Barnett Helzberg as just the sort of talented, high-integrity operator Berkshire seeks.

Buffett predicted that Helzberg's will become a big factor for Berkshire over time and added that he may have one or two more such purchases to report for next year's meeting.

Asked if he had anything to add, the taciturn Munger shook his head. Buffett quipped, "For a minute there, I thought Charlie was going to have a near-life experience!"

EVA: No Value Added

Each year, Buffett and Munger toss cold water on hot academic theories. This year's variation was an inquiry about "Economic Value Added," or EVA.

Munger noted it is less silly than the capital asset pricing model, but it forces the right answer.

Buffett added that people market these fad theories to justify needing high priests. "If all it takes is the Ten Commandments, it makes it tough on religion. 'Listen to your customers' as a business principle does not require a 300-page book."

On Projections

In another poke at human foibles, Munger claimed projections do more harm than good as they are prepared by people desiring a certain outcome.

He quoted Mark Twain: "A mine is a hole in the ground owned by a liar."

Buffett said the meticulous preparation of most projections tells you it is simply a ritual to justify what an executive wants to do anyway.

Munger concluded that the paper record is key. "Something with a lousy past record and a bright future . . . that's an opportunity we're going to miss."

Salomon Brothers

Despite recent problems, Buffett and Munger expressed confidence that Salomon Brothers will be around for a long time.

Munger observed Salomon had a bad break with having a bad year right on the heels of installing a new compensation system.

Regarding the exodus of executives at Salomon, Buffett noted that some left of their own volition and that some did not. Those that stayed have more of the owner/manager mindset Salomon seeks to build.

Munger added that Wall Street has more jealously effects than elsewhere even though "jealousy is the only sin you can never have any fun at."

On Newspapers and Elevators

While not as attractive as they were 15 years ago, Buffett noted that newspapers still have exceptionally good economics. He went so far as to say that if he could own only one business, it would probably be a newspaper in a one-newspaper town.

Munger scoffed at the paranoia of newspaper proprietors who worry about rising newsprint prices: "People don't care what floor the elevator is on, just which way it's going."

Buffett added that a 15-year graph of newspaper advertising rates versus newsprint prices would show ad rates have done far better.

Intrinsic Business Value

A central concept of Buffett's philosophy is intrinsic business value, the value a knowledgeable buyer would pay for the business.

Buffett said shareholders are presented all the numbers needed in the Berkshire annual report to estimate Berkshire's intrinsic business value.

He dropped a hint saying the discussion of Berkshire's $3 billion of float was the most important page in the report.

He went even further, saying, "Berkshire's price relative to our intrinsic business value offers more value than most any stock we see."

Derivatives

Buffett predicted derivative calamities two years ago. Since then, there have been a number of them, from Barings PLC to Orange County.

Buffett noted, when million-dollar nonphysical transactions swing on just a signature, there is potential for lots of mischief.

He observed that derivatives, instead of transferring or moderating risk, *create* risk on a huge scale (rendering regulation of borrowing limits on securities meaningless).

Munger registered strong disapproval: "If I ran the world, there would be no option exchanges . . . The world has gone bonkers."

Keeping It Simple

Regarding Berkshire, Munger noted that few companies have ever been constructed that require so little intelligence to maintain.

He reminisced that someone once subpoenaed their staffing papers regarding an acquisition. "Not only did we not have any staffing papers, we did not have any staff!"

Stocks

In discussing the $268 million write down of Berkshire's USAir preferred stock from the original investment of $358 million, Buffett noted you do not have to make it back the way you lost it.

Munger said that mistake is made frequently by those who gamble, continuing to gamble when the right thing would be to walk away.

Buffett emphatically summed up his case for reason over emotion: "A stock does not know you own it, the price you paid, who recommended it, the prices someone else paid . . . the stock does not give a damn."

Business Castles

Munger said the ideal business has a wide and long-lasting moat around a terrific castle with an honest lord. The moat represents a barrier to competition and could be low production costs, a trademark, or an advantage of scale or technology.

They regard Coca-Cola as the standard (of which Berkshire owns 100 million shares).

Buffett noted it is important to differentiate between a business where you have to be smart once versus one where you have to stay smart. For example, in retail, you are under assault at all times versus a newspaper, where you just need to be first.

Buffett quoted the Southern newspaper publisher who, when asked of the secrets of his success, replied, "Monopoly and nepotism."

Financial World

With holdings in Freddie Mac, Wells Fargo, Salomon Brothers, PNC Bancorp and American Express, Berkshire has a significant stake in the world of finance.

While finance is not an inherently attractive industry, Buffett believes there will be opportunities for shrewd operators of scale to earn above-average returns as the financial industry consolidates.

Buffett expects significant change over the next 20 years with Microsoft even perhaps finding a way around the present system.

Similarly, Berkshire has built enduring advantage in the highly competitive catastrophe insurance market. Berkshire has $13 billion of equity. Its largest competitors have less than $1 billion.

Accounting

Accounting is the language of business, and Buffett and Munger are critical of those who abuse it.

Regarding a failed FASB proposal for the accounting of stock options, Buffett expressed sharp disappointment with American business leaders who were cynical in the way they persevered in "seeing the value of pi stay at three."

Munger concluded, "Corruption won."

On a general note, Buffett said, when accounting appears confusing, avoid the company. The confusion may well be intentional and reveal the character of the management.

National Debt

Buffett noted that debt is meaningless without looking at the ability to pay.

With a 35% annual profit interest (tax) in America's corporate earnings and a 15%–33% share of personal income, the government is very solvent.

Even with U.S. national debt at 60% of GDP (versus 125% of GDP at the end of World War II), Buffett does not think the national debt is a big worry.

Learning

In a fascinating digression, Munger pointed out that no one has ever found a way to teach, so all are wise.

Munger rued that he has had great difficulty communicating even to his own children. "It's extraordinary how resistant some are to learning."

"Especially when it's in their own interest to do so," Buffett continued.

He concluded, quoting Bertrand Russell, "Most men would rather die than think. Many have."

Venue: Holiday Inn Convention Center

Attendance: Over 5,000

Details About This Year:

- Buffett threw out the first pitch, "a premature sinker," at the Saturday Omaha Royals baseball game.

- A pre-meeting comedy video featured appearances by, among others, Tom Brokaw, Susan Lucci and Bill Gates.

- Attendees lined up hours before the meeting for a good seat. CNBC stationed a camera crew outside the doors for daylong meeting coverage.

Fortune 500 Ranking: 292nd

Stock Price: $32,165

One dollar invested in 1964 would now be worth **$2,600**.

Berkshire's per-share book value has grown from $19.46 to **$19,011** (a rate of **23.8%** compounded annually).

The S&P 500 compounded at **10.7%** annually for the same period.

HIGHLIGHTS FROM 1996's NOTES

The "B" Shares—A Non Event

The first 75 minutes of the meeting involved questions about Berkshire's filing to issue "B" shares, which would have ⅟₃₀th the value and ⅟₂₀₀th the voting rights of the "A" shares.

Buffett explained the purpose of the "B" issuance was to head-off the creation of unit trusts by brokerage firms that would buy Berkshire shares for unit trust holders. People purchasing units of such trusts would incur unnecessary costs and tax consequences and could well have unrealistic expectations about future returns.

Buffett noted the "B" shares would create a flexible supply of shares (as each "A" share would be convertible into 30 "B" shares) and would avoid false inducements to buy. In fact, Buffett stressed that neither he nor Charlie think the stock is undervalued.

Buffett also stressed the supply of "B" shares on the underwriting would be expanded to meet demand.*

Buffett noted that on many initial public offerings (IPOs), Wall Street firms intentionally limit supply, so the stock has a big first-day pop, creating a "hot issue." However, that just means Wall Street's favorite clients, not the company, are getting the enormous benefits of a hot IPO market.

At Berkshire they engaged in a bit of reverse engineering—"How do we keep people from buying our stock?"

Buffett likened the thought process to singing a country song backward . . . "then you get your house back, your wife back."

According to Munger, the "B" offering was a non-event, amounting to only about 1% of Berkshire's shares outstanding.

When Buffett asked if he had anything else to add, Munger said, "No." Buffett quipped, "Charlie does not get paid by the word."

Microsoft

The founder of Microsoft, Bill Gates, and Buffett have become good friends.

---

* The original filing was for 115,000 shares. The actual offering totaled 517,000 shares at $1,110 each.

The pre-meeting video made light of their recent trip to China, reporting that a computer nerd and a carpet salesman from Omaha had endangered U.S.-Sino relations.

Buffett spoke highly of Gates' managerial talent and business focus. But, ever principled, Buffett said technology is just not something they want to bet on.

GEICO: We'll Be Very Happy

In 1976, Berkshire started buying shares of GEICO, whose direct marketing method of selling auto insurance gives it an enormous cost advantage.

GEICO has since grown to become the seventh largest auto insurer in the U.S.

At year-end 1995, Berkshire's $45.7 million investment had grown to $2.4 billion. In 1995, Berkshire agreed to buy the rest of GEICO for $2.3 billion.

Buffett said he believes the move is a huge plus for Berkshire, noting that GEICO is an outstanding company with a low-cost distribution method and has widened its competitive moat by its focus on lowering costs. With 2.5% of the U.S. auto market, GEICO has a huge pool to grow from.

Buffett believes GEICO can flourish a bit more by being wholly owned by Berkshire. "In five years, we will be very happy with GEICO."

Intrinsic Business Value

Each year, Buffett is asked about the intrinsic business value of Berkshire. Each year, he notes that all the information required for such a calculation is in the annual report.

He did point out that to look merely at break-up value is a mistake. Such a process misses the interesting dynamics of Berkshire's collection of businesses. A better method would be to calculate the stream of cash generated by Berkshire and discount it back to the present.

As an example, he noted that a break-up value analysis of the $8.7 million Berkshire paid to Jack Ringwalt to buy National Indemnity 29 years ago would have missed entirely the value of the float-generating characteristics of the business (float which now totals $7 billion!).

Buffett admitted that the value of that acquisition was far greater than he knew at the time.

Add the $7 billion of float to Berkshire's $5 billion of deferred taxes, and you have an extra $12 billion in "assets" that a break-up valuation would miss.

Buybacks: Intensify Ownership

On a related topic, Buffett noted that corporate stock buybacks add to shareholder value only if the purchases are made at prices below intrinsic business value. Pay above intrinsic business value and you hurt shareholder value.

He added, however, for a really wonderful business, he would come up with a much higher intrinsic business value than most.

As an example, he noted that Berkshire's original 7% stake in Coca-Cola is now 8% with about 1% being added via buybacks.

Even more dramatic, Berkshire's 33% stake in GEICO grew to 50% with 20 years of stock repurchases.

Such repurchases proved very wise, even when GEICO was selling at twice book value.

Buffett summarized, "With a scarce and powerful business, cap shrink intensifies our ownership."

Float

Buffett offered a beautiful explanation of float, comparing it to bank deposits.

Bank deposits provide banks funds to invest. They come at an explicit cost, the rate of interest paid to the depositor plus operating costs. Similarly, insurance companies generate funds for investment (i.e., float) as policyholders pay premiums upfront in return for a promise of financial coverage in the event of future calamities.

Unlike bank deposits, however, the costs of float are unknown until the policies expire and the claims are settled.

For Berkshire, the float, on average, has cost *zero*. In addition, it has grown dramatically from $7 million in 1967 to $7 billion today.

Buffett cautioned that ordinary insurance is not a good business and that float, per se, is not a blessing. To make it work, the insurance company must be run right, ideally with competitive advantages and the ability to maximize them. If you can get float cheap and in increasing quantities, float becomes a very important asset—something even more important than Buffett could have guessed in 1967.

Munger concluded that one of Buffett's tricks is that he keeps learning.

Warren Hit By a Truck? Too Damn Bad

Every year, Buffett gets the "What-if-you-get-hit-by-a-truck?" question.

Munger asked rhetorically, "Will Coca-Cola stop selling Cokes because Warren is no longer here? Will Gillette stop selling razor blades because Warren is no longer here?"

He noted that Berkshire's collection of businesses has been lovingly put together so as not to require continuous intellect at headquarters.

Munger finishes, "And if you are upset that Berkshire would lose Warren's capital allocation skills, well, that is just too damn bad."

Buffett joked, "Ever the sympathetic ear."

Annual Reports

Buffett said he prefers annual reports that read like a half partner filling you in on what is going on. Unfortunately, he sees no way to mandate such reports.

Still, he noted that it is amazing what you can do with "outside" information. All kinds of information is available, but you have to read it yourself.

Buffett claimed that in 40 years, he has never gotten an idea from a Wall Street report.

Diversification: Twaddle

Buffett and Munger took their annual poke at modern portfolio theory (MPT) by zeroing in on popular notions about diversification.

Buffett noted that he likes to put a lot of money in things he feels strongly about. Diversification makes no sense for someone who knows what they are doing. "To buy number one on your list equally with number 37 strikes us as madness. Diversification is a protection against ignorance, a confession that you do not know the businesses you own."

Buffett claimed that three wonderful businesses is more than you need in this life and would serve you much better than 100 average businesses.

Munger took off the gloves, "Much of what is taught in corporate finance classes is twaddle."

Buffett continued, saying that MPT has no utility. It is elaborate with lots of little Greek letters to make you feel you are in the big leagues.

The ever understated Munger claimed that as a student of dementia, he would rate MPT as beyond classification.

Buffett concluded that his trust owns only one stock, and he is perfectly content.

Borsheim's

Buffett announced that last year's special Sunday opening for Berkshire Hathaway shareholders set a single-day sales record at Borsheim's. This year's crowd bested that record by 60%.

Munger reported with great relish that a shareholder bought $54,000 of jewelry at Borsheim's and asked Munger to autograph the receipt.

Munger exclaimed, "Now that is the kind of autograph we like to give! Go thou, and do likewise."

Buffett added that the autograph hound was not a member of Charlie's family.*

Disney: Share of Mind

With Disney's takeover of Capital Cities/ABC, Berkshire has become a major owner of Disney.

While there is plenty of competition in the entertainment business, Buffett said he would rather start with Disney's hand and Michael Eisner running the show, by far.

The key according to Buffett is "share of mind." What place will Disney have in the minds of billions of children? He noted that while it is hard to beat the name recognition of Coca-Cola, Disney is up there.

It is also nice to recycle Snow White every seven or eight years. Buffett likened it to having a huge oil field where you pump and sell all the oil, it eventually seeps back into the ground, and you get to sell it all over again.

Wonderful Companies

Munger allowed that Berkshire's portfolio is a product of their "slender abilities."

---

* A related story—when Bill Gates was in the market for a wedding ring, Buffett flew him to Omaha for special treatment at Borsheim's. Buffett noted that when he got married, he spent 6% of his net worth on the ring. He encouraged Gates to do likewise.

Buffett added that they are slim in their ability to predict where change will lead. Thus, they are much better at products where change will not mean as much: soft drinks, candy, shaving, chewing gum. "There's not a whole lot of technology going into the art of the chew."

Buffett said the mindset of owning wonderful companies has worked far better than he would have predicted 20 years ago.

We Love Focus

Buffett was emphatic in saying that they love focused management. Coca-Cola and Gillette both lost their focus along the way. When they regained their focus, it added billions of dollars to shareholder wealth. GEICO lost its focus in the early 1970s and nearly went out of business.

Buffett said he loves the focus Coca-Cola and Gillette have on maximizing their potential for global distribution with 80% and 70% of profits, respectively, coming from abroad now.

Downsizing

While it is no fun being the village blacksmith when the car comes along, Buffett noted that it is in the interests of society to get maximum output per unit of input. Businesses should become more efficient, not less so. Since 1900, efficiencies in farming have freed much of the farm workforce to pursue other activities.

He encouraged people to read a recent *Forbes* article on how jobs have changed over the past 100 years. He claimed that there is no more displacement now than 10 years ago, though it is in the interests of society to care for those who are displaced.

Munger said to think of the problem in reverse. While he could not name one business ruined by downsizing, he could think of many ruined by bloat.

He concluded, "There's no social benefit to idle employment."

Ownership: Cost of Capital

Buffett has long chastised the way stock options are handed out in boardrooms.

He said it is awful the way businesses reward executives with no regard for capital. For example, a 10-year fixed price option is basically an interest-free loan. A more appropriate option plan would set the strike price at not less than fair intrinsic business value and would have a yearly step-up relating to the cost of capital. Executives would still have no downside, but at least there would be a carrying cost of ownership.

Munger said he preferred the old-fashioned way—have executives buy stock in the market.

Buffett concluded that there is a very easy way to think like a shareholder: Become one.

Venue: AK-SAR-BEN

Attendance: 7,700

Details About This Year:

- In past years, we have privately accused the University of Berkshire Hathaway of becoming a party school. This year Buffett admitted as much, calling it the "capitalist's version of Woodstock."

- It may be a sign of the times that so many thousands of people flocked to Omaha to hear Buffett and Munger speak. People came from all 50 states and over a dozen foreign countries.

Fortune 500 Ranking: 132nd

Stock Price: $34,159

One dollar invested in 1964 would now be worth **$2,761**.

Berkshire's per-share book value has grown from $19.46 to **$25,488** (a rate of **24.1%** compounded annually).

The S&P 500 compounded at **11.1%** annually for the same period.

HIGHLIGHTS FROM 1997's NOTES

McDonald's: Not Inevitable

In this year's annual report, Buffett referred to Coca-Cola and Gillette as "The Inevitables" due to their massive market dominance.

Normally, Buffett does not discuss recent purchases but did so with McDonald's (as of year-end, Berkshire owned over 30 million shares of McDonald's at a cost of $1.265 billion).

He explained that with food, you will never get the total certainty of dominance of Coca-Cola or Gillette. People move around with restaurants, seeking variety. Convenience is a huge factor—people stop at the one they see.

In contrast, Buffett claimed there will never be another major soft drink company. Coke's infrastructure is incredible.

Munger noted that many have failed at having a successful chain of restaurants (e.g., Howard Johnson's). The restaurant business is much tougher than the razor business. With food, people will switch with competitive pricing. Meanwhile, Gillette sees few customers changing their shaving habits to save a few dollars. The Gillette Sensor has been a huge success.

Irrational Exuberance

Buffett repeated his warning in the annual report that you can pay too much even for a wonderful business and that the overpayment risk is currently quite high.

Munger was emphatic, guaranteeing that real inflation-adjusted returns will be lower in the long-term future.

Buffett said it would not surprise him in the least if stocks averaged a 4% return over the next 10 years.*

Buffett explained that falling interest rates and a huge earnings improvement over the past decade combined to produce much higher U.S. stock valuations. Those factors are widely recognized now.

Buffett noted that after a while, people can become captivated by rising prices, and the conditions are there for bubble-type excess.

---

* Contrast this to the Louis Harris & Associates survey (commissioned by Liberty Financial) where the majority of mutual fund investors polled expect double-digit returns to continue.

Returns on Equity

On a related topic, Buffett admitted he never thought average returns on corporate equity would go to 22%.

He added that it does not seem sustainable with long-term interest rates of 7% and a substantial savings rate. Competitive forces should come into play to drive returns lower.

Munger cited two contributing factors:

1. It became fashionable for corporations to buy-in shares

2. Anti-trust became more lenient toward acquisitions of competitors.

Munger noted it cannot go on forever. At 15% a year, stock returns are growing far faster than the economy itself. Sooner or later, something has to happen.

Buffett added, if real GDP grows at 3% annually and the capitalized value of American industry grows at 10% annually, eventually it gets absurd. With a $7 trillion GDP and a $7 trillion market cap, we are not there yet, but projecting it out, it goes off the tracks.

Buffett allowed that, if current returns on equity are sustainable and there is no change in interest rates, you can justify 7000 on the Dow. However, if interest rates move up or returns on equity decline, market values would be pulled down.

Flightsafety International

Last year, Berkshire Hathaway acquired Flightsafety International.

Munger joked that due to a counter revelation, they would change the name of the Berkshire corporate jet from "The Indefensible" to "The Indispensable."

Buffett said Flightsafety's simulators are so good that a pilot may spend 100% of a five-week training program on them. A joint venture with Boeing provides global growth opportunities for Flightsafety.

Business Risk

Owning a stock means owning a piece of a business.

Accordingly, Buffett noted there are several key business risks.

The first involves capital structure. A company with a ton of debt could be a candidate for foreclosure.

The second relates to the nature of the business and its capital requirements. With commercial airlines, for example, tons of capital is required upfront, and competition is intense.

A third risk occurs with commodity businesses. Unless you're the low-cost producer, these are poor businesses to own.

Overall, Berkshire seeks low-risk businesses with sustainable competitive advantages and strong capital structures.

Market Risk

If the business is sound, there remains the risk of paying too much. Here, the risk is time versus loss of principal. If you overpay, it will take time for the business value to catch up to the price paid.

The key is to remember that the market exists to serve you, not instruct you. Volatility is a huge plus to real investors.

Intel

Buffett noted one of his rules is understanding the business, to be able to have a pretty good idea where it will be in 10 years. That excludes a very large group of opportunities, from cocoa beans to rubles. As a result, Berkshire has seldom invested in technology, passing on even Intel and Microsoft.

In a fascinating digression, Buffett recounted how he was on the Grinnell College endowment committee in the 1960s when Grinnell bought 10% of the private placement that founded Intel. Despite knowing the chairman of Intel, who explained the business to him at length, Buffett claimed he was a poor student. A few years later, the investment committee sold Grinnell's Intel shares.*

GEICO

Buffett proclaimed GEICO is doing even better than he expected when Berkshire bought it out.

Voluntary auto insurance grew 10% in 1996, GEICO's best year in two decades. The first four months of 1997 have been even better with premium growth approaching 20%.

With the growth in float and high policy-retention rates, Buffett noted GEICO's growth in intrinsic value is larger than its growth in reported earnings.

---

* Don't cry for Grinnell—it's the best endowed private college in Iowa.

Already the seventh largest auto insurer in the U.S. with 2.7% of the market, GEICO should see significant market share gains in the decade ahead.

The Ovarian Lottery

When asked what the ideal rate of taxation on capital gains might be, Munger recalled Aristotle's observation that systems work better when perceived as fair.

Buffett launched into an intriguing thought problem he called "the ovarian lottery." You are to be born in 24 hours. You are also to write all the rules that will govern the society in which you will live. However, you do not know if you will be born bright or retarded, black or white, male or female, rich or poor, able or disabled. How would you write the rules?

Buffett said how one comes out in this lottery is far more important than anything else to one's future. He and Munger were huge winners having been born American ("in Afghanistan, we wouldn't be worth a damn"), male (at a time when many women could only be nurses and teachers), white (when opportunities for minorities were slim) and good at valuing businesses (in a system that pays for that like crazy).

Buffett noted it is important to take care of the non-winners of the ovarian lottery. Therefore, some sort of taxation is in order. Given that few people with money and talent are turned away from free enterprise under the current system, the 28% capital gains tax is probably okay.

Filters

In the Berkshire report, Buffett claims he can give an answer on a prospective acquisition in five minutes.

He can do so, first, because he is already familiar with most of the companies of the size large enough for Berkshire to consider. Second, filters simplify the decision-making process. Munger noted people underrate the importance of a few big ideas. Filters work really well because they are so simple.

Over the course of the meeting, they gave out numerous such filters. Here are a few:

> **Opportunity Cost**—Munger noted that for any corporate stock, a bond is an alternative. You must choose the best opportunity you can understand. He summed up, "Life is a whole series of opportunity costs."

Quality People—Buffett said he looks for a manager who bats .400 and loves it. Munger noted there are many wonderful people and many awful people. Avoid the awful. Stick to those who take their promises seriously.

Good Businesses—Go with those that are understandable with a sustainable edge. The pond you choose is far more important than how well you swim.

Executive Compensation

Buffett and Munger took their annual shot at executive stock options, the use of which has become epidemic.

Buffett argued such options should have a step-up in exercise price. Otherwise, they simply become a royalty on the corporation's buildup of retained earnings.

In addition, Buffett argued such options should reflect the business' intrinsic value, not simply the market price.

Munger remarked that the accounting of options is weak, corrupt and contemptible.

Buffett chimed, "Other than that, we're undecided."

In Munger's view, the payment of options has gone to wretched excess.

Despite the excess, Buffett said the real sin is mediocre management. That is what costs the shareholders money. It is almost impossible to overpay for good management.

For example, Coca-Cola's market value was $4 billion and stagnant when Roberto Goizueta took over in 1981. Today, the market value is $150 billion.

The right manager can have an absolutely huge impact. Find people with brains, energy and integrity, and you can own the world.

Insurance

Berkshire takes on very large exposures (up to $1 billion) with its super-cat writings.

Buffett explained that, while such exposures can be large dollar amounts, Berkshire knows exactly what they are.

Munger noted that a billion-dollar loss would be just 2.5% of liquid assets. The real supercat risks are those borne unwittingly by insurance companies that could be wiped out by an unforeseen event.

Buffett recalled Twentieth Century Industries, which all but went broke after the Northridge Earthquake.

Buffett intoned, "Surprises in insurance are never symmetrical. They are all bad."

With $7 billion of float, momentum at GEICO and unmatched capital for supercats, Buffett concluded, "Insurance will be a very good and very big business for us."

Wesco Financial: Coin Flip

In past years, Buffett and Munger have repeatedly cautioned that Wesco Financial is not a miniature Berkshire. However, this year, Buffett called it a "coin flip" as to which was a better buy.

He allowed that Wesco is the logical place for the small acquisition, unless it's a business Berkshire is already in.*

On Learning

Munger noted that Buffett is the most rational person he has ever known and that Buffett's ability to learn has been essential to the success of Berkshire.

For example, the notion of buying only understandable, predictable businesses came from painful lessons learned after owning third-level department stores and manufacturers of pumps and windmills.

Munger claimed that See's Candy taught them the virtues of a franchise-type business. Seeing how See's played out in the marketplace led directly to their bold purchase of Coca-Cola shares in 1988.

Buffett was emphatic, "Without See's, we would not have bought Coke."

Munger bristled at the notion that he and Buffett are "aging executives," exclaiming "I don't know anybody who's moving in the other direction!"

Rather than age, learning is the name of the game. Munger noted it is essential to learn from both the mistakes of others as well as your own.

He quoted Patton: "It's an honor to die for your country. Make sure the other guys get the honor."

---

* Wesco Financial did buy Kansas Bankers Surety last year, and Buffett's comments imply there may be more to come. This change in tune may account for Wesco's 25% run-up since the annual meeting.

Buffett and Munger each expressed amazement at how little successful businesses are studied, from GEICO to State Farm (which went from nothing in the 1920s to an incredible 25% of the personal auto market today) to Berkshire itself.

Buffett summed up, quoting Yogi Berra, "You can observe a lot just by looking."

Venue: AK-SAR-BEN

Attendance: 10,000

Details About This Year:

- During the event, this year's Berkshire Mall sold:

    - 3,700 pounds of See's Candy

    - 4,000 Dilly Bars

    - 1,635 pairs of Dexter shoes

- The annual report was printed in white and red to celebrate Nebraska's NCAA football championship.

- This year is the exception that proves the rule. 1998 is the only year we didn't publish a newsletter about the meeting. In its absence, we sent out the following two articles, from July and August 1998, about Berkshire Hathaway.

Fortune 500 Ranking: 150th

Stock Price: $46,080

One dollar invested in 1964 would now be worth **$3,725**.

Berkshire's per-share book value has grown from $19.46 to **$37,801** (a rate of **24.7%** compounded annually).

The S&P 500 compounded at **11.7%** annually for the same period.

HIGHLIGHTS FROM 1998's NOTES

Berkshire Hathaway's Mega Merger

"Berkshire Hathaway Inc. and General Re Corporation to Merge

OMAHA, Neb. and STAMFORD, Conn.—(BUSINESS WIRE)—June 19, 1998—Berkshire Hathaway Inc. and General Re Corporation announced today that they have reached a definitive agreement to merge.

Under the agreement, General Re shareholders will have the option at closing of accepting either 0.0035 Class A shares or 0.105 Class B shares of Berkshire. The transaction is expected to be tax-free to General Re shareholders. Based on Thursday's closing prices, the value of the consideration to be received by General Re shareholders is approximately $276.50 per General Re share. The total consideration for the transaction will be approximately $22 billion. The merger will be accounted for by Berkshire as a purchase.

Pro forma for the transaction, Berkshire would have had GAAP net worth of approximately $56 billion, as of March 31, 1998, the highest of any company in the United States, and a market capitalization today of approximately $120 billion."

So begins a most remarkable press release.

Warren Buffett has long poked fun at the "animal spirits" of CEOs and their overwhelming urge to merge.

Seldom has empire (and ego) expansion been more evident than in this age of the mega-merger. Now Buffett has joined the fray with his biggest deal to date.

While our numbers are very rough, we find the merger with General Re especially fascinating in a number of ways:

Lack of Coverage

The most brilliant investor of our time just made the biggest deal of his life, yet we've seen just two stories in the *Wall Street Journal* since the initial press release. The silence is deafening.

Buffett bought $700 million of silver, and the media chattered about it for weeks. Now Buffett makes an investment *30 times* larger, and there is silence.

Scale of Deal

This is not simply Buffett's biggest deal—it is his biggest deal by a factor of *10*. The $22 billion transaction amounts to 60% of Berkshire's shareholder equity of $34.8 billion (as of March 31, 1998). This is a "bet the company" deal.

History

Berkshire purchased National Indemnity in 1967. Insurance has been the core operation at Berkshire Hathaway ever since.

One of the shrewdest minds in the insurance industry, Buffett has now purchased the world's third largest reinsurance company.

This deal suggests far-reaching implications for the insurance industry.

Buffett is Selling (I): All-Stock Deal

Issuance of shares is a sacred issue at Berkshire.

Buffett has long said he would never issue stock unless he received more than fair value in return.

In the 1997 annual report, Buffett even issues a "confession," stating that "when I've issued stock, I've cost you money," and concludes, "you can be sure Charlie and I will be very reluctant to issue shares in the future."

Berkshire/General Re is an all-stock deal. Either Berkshire stock is ridiculously overvalued or this is an exceptional deal—or both.

Buffett Is Selling (II): Changing the Bond-Stock Ratio

With a 36% capital gains tax rate and over $30 billion in unrealized capital gains, Berkshire would pay a heavy price to sell its stocks. To a large degree, Berkshire is trapped into holding on.

Only under very extreme circumstances would Buffett sell. Yet in the 1997 annual, Buffett admits to selling some stocks[*] in an effort aimed at

---

[*] Positions in Disney, Wells Fargo, Freddie Mac, and McDonald's were reduced.

"changing our bond-stock ratio moderately in response to the relative values that we saw in each market, a realignment we have continued in 1998." Clearly, Buffett is a seller of stocks.

The purchase of General Re dramatically changes Berkshire's bond-stock ratio.

	Investment Assets	Stocks	Stock %
Pre-Deal Berkshire (3/31/98)	$50 billion	$40 billion	80%
Added from General RE (12/31/97)	$24 billion	$5 billion	21%
Post-Deal Berkshire	$74 billion	$45 billion	61%

In one fell swoop, Berkshire reduces its stock holdings as a percentage of investment assets from 80% to roughly 61%.

In effect, by doing a stock merger, Berkshire is trading away 18% of its holdings in Coca-Cola, American Express, Gillette, etc., but doing so in a way that Berkshire *pays no taxes.*

As my kids would put it, "Way cool."

Float

In past Berkshire annual reports, Buffett has discussed the attractive float-generating characteristics of his insurance companies.

Since 1967, Berkshire's average float has grown from $17 million to $7 billion.

Buffett has argued that if such float can be generated without an underwriting loss, a dollar of float is worth at least as much as a dollar of equity even though it appears on the balance sheet as a liability (mostly under "net loss reserves and loss adjustment reserves"). If the float is generated with an underwriting *profit*, it is clearly worth more than equity.

Berkshire has had an underwriting profit each of the past five years.

In the case of General Re, the underwriting record is superb with an average result of breakeven (a 100.4 combined ratio) over the past 50 years.

By our calculation, General Re generates over $15 billion of float. Post-deal, Berkshire will have over $22 billion of float, a *tripling* of Berkshire's float. (In addition, Berkshire can probably nudge the float higher yet by establishing higher retention rates on General Re's existing business. This is suggested in the press release: "General Re will be free to reduce its reliance on the retrocessional market over time, and thereby have substantial additional funds available for investment.")

Deferred Taxes

As alluded to earlier, Berkshire has over $30 billion of unrealized capital gains.

As a result, Berkshire carries a liability (labeled on the balance sheet as "Income taxes, principally deferred") of about $11 billion to reflect the tax Berkshire would pay if it realized all of its gains at once.

However, it is unlikely Berkshire would sell all at once. Thus, the actual amount of this liability lies between $11 billion (sell all now) and $0 (never sell).

Given Berkshire's post-deal bond-stock ratio, the *likelihood of never selling is markedly increased.*

Therefore, we would argue, most of the $11 billion deferred tax liability may be added back to equity.

Adjusted Shareholders' Equity

Taking these comments on float and deferred taxes to task, here is our estimate of the "adjusted" shareholders' equity (i.e., stated equity plus float plus deferred taxes) of the new Berkshire (in billions).

	Shareholders Equity	Float	Deferred Taxes	Total
Old Berkshire (3/31/98)	$35	$7	$11	$50
General RE (12/31/97)	$8	$15	NM	$39
Purchase Goodwill	$13			
New Berkshire	$56	$22	$11	$89

Purchase goodwill reflects the premium over book value that Berkshire is paying for General Re.

With 1.5 million shares out post-deal and roughly $89 billion of adjusted shareholders' equity, the new Berkshire will have about $59,300 of "adjusted book value" per share.

Valuation

In terms of assets, with Berkshire A shares selling at around $78,000/share, Berkshire is selling at 1.3 times our estimate of "adjusted shareholders' equity."

On assets, 1.3 times equity is not particularly cheap for a leveraged balanced fund.

In terms of income, adding $995 million of net income from General Re to Berkshire's $1,930 million of look-through earnings and assuming a 10% growth rate, post-deal Berkshire would produce roughly $3.2 billion of prospective look-through earnings (about $2,145 per post-deal share).

The A shares then sell at about 36 times earnings.

On earnings, a PE of 36 is rich, but there are certainly worse things to own than a collection of fabulous businesses overseen by a brilliant allocator of capital.

Especially with Internet stocks trading at 100 times *revenues*! Our favorite comment from this year's Berkshire annual meeting: When asked how he would teach business students, Buffett said, "For the final exam, I would take an Internet company and say 'How much is this worth?' And anybody that gave me an answer, I would flunk."

A small tip—by purchasing General Re at recent prices (around $258/share), investors can create ownership in Berkshire—assuming the deal is going through—at about a 6% discount to Berkshire's current price.

Buffett's Connections

Time and again, Buffett's reputation and relationships have paid dividends for Berkshire shareholders.

It seems reasonable to assume the ability to trust Buffett was essential to the deal. The trust goes both ways as Ron Ferguson, CEO of General Re, will join Berkshire's board.

Buffett Is Selling Stocks

In our recent analysis of Berkshire Hathaway's $22 billion merger with General Re ("Berkshire Hathaway's Mega Merger"), we contend that Warren Buffett is selling stocks in at least two ways.

First, he is issuing $22 billion of Berkshire stock to make the purchase.

Second, we speculate that by merging Berkshire's stock-heavy portfolio with General Re's bond-heavy portfolio, Berkshire will dilute ("sell") pro rata its holding in Coca-Cola, Gillette, American Express, etc.

This marks Berkshire's most significant sale of stock since 1969.

The notion that Buffett is selling elicited only moderate response from our clients. Apparently, we have been cautious for so long, it is the sort of thing you expect to hear from us.

However, we want you to know the idea has sparked interest from the media. The July 31, 1998, edition of *Grant's Interest Rate Observer* featured the sale as its lead article. Mr. Grant was so kind as to refer to our piece as "the clarifying analysis of the landmark transaction."

Grant's, in turn, is read by a fairly sophisticated investment crowd (from which we have received a few calls this week).

Be prepared for the idea "Buffett is selling stocks" to surface elsewhere in the media.

Buffett Is Selling Bonds

Buffett disclosed in Berkshire's 1997 annual report that he had purchased $4.6 billion of long-term zero-coupon bonds as a bet on declining interest rates.

In announcing its second quarter results this week, Berkshire said that it had sold its entire position of zero-coupon bonds for a substantial gain.

Clearly, Buffett does not think interest rates will go much lower from here.

Cash Is King

The most brilliant investor of our time is selling stocks and long-term bonds, raising cash.

This at a time when liquidity levels of public and private pension plans are the *lowest* in 15 and 40 years, respectively. Equity mutual fund cash levels are at a 22-year low of 4.6%.

What does it mean?

At a minimum, it means Buffett believes neither stocks nor long bonds offer an adequate margin of safety and/or an expected return above the risk-free rate of 5% offered by Treasury bills. Better to hold cash and keep the powder dry for better risk/reward opportunities.

More precariously, it could presage a significant sell-off. The predominant fear among today's investors has been missing out on a soaring stock market. High expectations and high equity valuations leave little margin for error. No one should be surprised if we have a major downdraft in the market.

Indeed, according to a recent *Wall Street Journal* article, such a sell-off is already underway.

1999

Venue: Holiday Inn Convention Center

Attendance: 15,000

Details About This Year:

- In addition to selling See's Candy, Dexter shoes and Quikut knives, a Berkshire apparel line was unveiled in The Berkshire Mall.

Fortune 500 Ranking: 112th

Stock Price: $70,134

One dollar invested in 1964 would now be worth **$5,670**.

Berkshire's per-share book value has grown from $19.46 to **$37,987** (a rate of **24%** compounded annually).

The S&P 500 compounded at **12.2%** annually for the same period.

HIGHLIGHTS FROM 1999's NOTES

The Market

As in years past, Buffett was asked what he thought about the stock market. As in years past, he said, "We don't think about it."

His focus has always been to find great businesses. When he finds one with great management and great economics at a reasonable price, he buys it either in whole (an acquisition) or in part (a stock market purchase).

Currently, Buffett sees no bargains among large cap stocks. When he cannot find things to buy, the money piles up. When he does find something, he piles in.

Munger noted that for decades, Berkshire had 100% of its book net worth in marketable securities and owned companies to boot. While they may have trouble investing new money today, it is really no "trouble" to have a pile of money.

He concluded, "There shouldn't be any tears in the house."

Future Returns

As they said last year, the real long-term rate of return for the U.S. stock market has to go down.

Buffett suggested dramatically reduced expectations were called for by investors. With 4%–5% GDP growth and 1% inflation, it is unlikely that corporate profits will grow faster than 5%–6%. Otherwise, profits will eventually be greater than the GDP!

Buffett quipped, "Sort of like New York having more lawyers than people." If profits cannot grow 5% or more, how can equities grow at 15%?

Buffett put it another way: imagine a farm (the Fortune 500) valued at $10.5 trillion that produces $334 billion of profits. Paying $10.5 trillion for that farm would not produce a good return on investment.

The $200 Million Club

As in years past, Buffett allowed that technology and pharmaceuticals are two big areas in which he has not participated.

However, he again highlighted his willingness to trade away big pay-offs for certainty. It is much easier to pick the relative strength of Coca-Cola than it is to pick a winner in software.

Buffett reiterated the importance of staying within one's circle of competence. Jet airplane technology has been pretty static the past 20–30 years, making NetJets quite predictable. The Dilly Bar is more certain than any software company over the next 10 years.

Buffett put it another way. He noted there are some 400 companies in the U.S. that earn more than $200 million in after-tax profit. In five years, the list may grow to 450–475. Maybe 20 of those additions will come from nowhere.

However, dozens and dozens of small companies are priced to do so currently. Many will disappoint shareholders.

Similarly, biotech stocks were all the rage five years ago, yet how many are making $200 million today?

In a capitalist society, everyone is watching you. Competition is fierce. The $3 billion market cap company is rare.

He concluded, "You want to think about the math of it."

General Re

We remain amazed by how little attention has been paid to Berkshire's largest ever acquisition—last year's $22 billion purchase of General Re.

One of the most important elements of the Berkshire Hathaway wealth-compounding machine has been the generation of low-cost float by its insurance operations.

With General Re, Berkshire's float now totals $24 billion (up impressively from a humble $17 million in 1967).

In the short run, Buffett sees little growth in float from General Re due to the current softness in reinsurance markets. GEICO's float generation will have a more significant growth rate.

In addition, with limited investment prospects currently, investment returns on the float will remain unexciting in the short run.

Long term, Buffett and Munger are impressed with the talent and quality of the people at General Re and look forward to the opportunities that being the world's premier reinsurer may offer.

GEICO

Buffett continues to be enthusiastic about prospects for Berkshire's largest subsidiary, GEICO.

He expects the direct writer of auto insurance to have 4.5 million policyholders by year-end (double the number GEICO had in 1995, the year prior to its acquisition by Berkshire).

Closing in on 4% of the U.S. auto insurance market currently, Buffett believes GEICO will be many times bigger 10 years from now.

He sees the Internet as a plus. GEICO's low prices and national reputation have already generated Internet sales.

In time, Buffett believes GEICO's direct model should grow more and more powerful.

Retail and the Internet

Buffett sees that the Internet will have a huge impact on retailing.

In some areas, the Internet threat is so significant that he would avoid them altogether (greeting cards, for example).

However, in other areas, the Internet will have less of an impact. Buffett believes Berkshire's furniture stores, for one, will be little affected by the Internet.

Brand names will be important. Buffett doubts that people will go to brand "X" over the Internet. For example, Buffett believes online jewelry sales will go to a name people trust, such as Tiffany's or Borsheim's (look for Borsheims.com).

Buffett also noted that real estate dedicated to retailing would be affected. For Internet retailers, there is no rental expense. Cyber real estate is free.

Tough to Predict

With a fascinating bit of history, Munger explained that it is tricky attempting to predict what changes in technology will do:

The development of the streetcar led to the rise of the department store. Since streetcar lines were immovable, it was thought that the department store had an unbeatable position. Offering revolving credit and a remarkable breadth of merchandise, the department store was king. Yet in time, while the rails remained, the streetcars disappeared. People moved to the suburbs, which led to the rise of the shopping center and ended the dominance of department stores.

Now the Internet poses a threat to both.

Business Moat

Buffett noted that a dollar of earnings from ".com Inc" and a dollar of earnings from "Horseshoe Corp" are equal.

What really matters is the "moat" around the business. The greater the moat, the greater the certainty and the amount of future cash flows.

The key dangers relate to changes in market share, changes in unit demand and the allocation skills of management.

The bigger the moat, the less great management is needed. As Peter Lynch has said, "Find a business any idiot could run because eventually one will."

Buffett cited Wrigley's and Coca-Cola as businesses with wide moats. With Coke, he noted that its share of mind with the world's six billion people is remarkable. Even the container is identifiable.

Telecommunications

Buffett agreed that there is a lot of money to be made in telecommunications for those who understand it.

While Walter Scott (Berkshire board member and chairman of Level 3) has tried to explain those changes, Buffett feels he has no big insight into them.

However, Buffett added that there is a big difference between identifying a growth industry and minting money.

He noted that AT&T's return on equity over the years has been poor. Change has hurt the company more than it has helped.

Similarly, he cited the airline and auto industries as examples of huge growth industries where very few got rich.

Munger piped up that it reminds him of the World War II aircraft officers: When asked by the commanding officer what they did, Lieutenant Jones replied, "I do nothing, sir." The second replied, "I help Lieutenant Jones."

Munger concluded, "That's been my contribution to our telecommunication investments."

Living Rich

Buffett contended that the average college student has the same standard of living as he does. Same food. No important difference in clothes, cars, TVs. (Though Buffett could not resist yet another plug, admitting that he does travel better thanks to NetJets.)

After you have enough for daily life, all that matters is your health and those you love. Likewise in work, what really matters is that you enjoy it and the people with which you work.

Munger concluded humorously, "What good is health? You can't buy money with it."

Accounting Abuse

Buffett claimed that it has become fashionable to play games with the accounting of revenues and expenses.*

According to Munger, "big bath" accounting and the subsequent release of reserves back into earnings have, together, probably been the biggest abuse.

Buffett believes the auditors should have fixed the problem, but it probably is now up to the SEC and Arthur Levitt (whom Buffett greatly admires).

Munger warned that corruption in accounting systems was a significant factor in Japan's collapse over the past decade—a lesson in how important it is not to let slop into the system.

NetJets

Buffett is enthusiastic about the prospects for Executive Jet Aviation (EJA), which Berkshire purchased for $750 million last year.

Through its NetJet program, EJA sells fractional shares of jets and operates the fleet for its many owners.

As Buffett likes to put it, EJA makes calling up your plane like phoning for a taxi.

He credits Rich Santulli, CEO of EJA, with having the guts and the vision to turn the idea of fractional jet ownership into a major business.

With EJA as part of Berkshire, Buffett believes the dominance and speed of growth of EJA have been enhanced.

He expects EJA to be a very big global company in 10 to 15 years.

Supercat Insurance

While current premium rates are soft, Buffett believes Berkshire's pre-eminent position in the supercatastophe reinsurance market is stronger than ever.

There is only a short list of competitors for the high-level covers that Berkshire can offer. After the next supercat, Berkshire's "Fort Knox" reputation will be extremely valuable, he predicted.

---

* The 1998 Berkshire annual report includes several pages of discussion on the topic.

Berkshire and the S&P 500

Currently, 6%–7% of investment funds in the U.S. are indexed.

Berkshire is not in the S&P Index, though it qualifies in all respects save one: liquidity.

Buffett suggested a 12-month phase-in process, which has been used in Australia.

As indexing continues to grow, liquidity problems will prevail for Berkshire and throughout the market. Eventually, the S&P will need to adjust for that.

Munger concluded that Berkshire will be in the S&P Index, sooner or later.

Always Coca-Cola

Dismissing concerns about Coca-Cola's prospects with the strength of the dollar, Buffett said what really matters is share of market and share of mind.

Coca-Cola's market share is marvelous, and its share of mind is overwhelmingly favorable with a ubiquity of good feeling. The keys to analyzing Coca-Cola's economic progress are 1) unit cases sold (more is better), and 2) number of shares outstanding (the fewer the better).

While it's true case growth slowed over the last four quarters, Buffett believes that is temporary and unimportant to a 10-year projection.

(Munger interjected that 10–15 year projections can tune out a lot of noise.)

Buffett concluded that it's hard to think of a better business in the world. There may be companies that could grow faster, but none as solid.

Venue: Omaha Civic Auditorium

Attendance: 10,000+

Details About This Year:

- Corey and Dan split meeting duties this year. Corey attended the Berkshire meeting in Omaha while Dan attended the Wesco Financial meeting in Pasadena, California.

Fortune 500 Ranking: 64th

Stock Price: $56,177

One dollar invested in 1964 would now be worth **$4,541**.

Berkshire's per-share book value has grown from $19.46 to **$40,442** (a rate of **23.6%** compounded annually).

The S&P 500 compounded at **12.4%** annually for the same period.

HIGHLIGHTS FROM 2000's NOTES

General Re

Despite recent losses at Gen Re, Buffett and Munger remain steadfast in their long-term optimism for their reinsurance operation.

They believe Berkshire has advantages in its ability to pay, willingness to pay and pricing discipline verses the competition.

Buffett claimed that if he had known what Gen Re's losses would be prior to Berkshire's takeover, he still would have done the deal.

Share of Mind

Buffett returned to a concept he has brought up numerous times, relating that "if share of mind exists, the market will follow."

He noted that consumer product organizations understand this. For example, 75% of the people in the world have something in their mind about Coca-Cola, and overwhelmingly, it is favorable.

Similarly, most Californians have something in their mind about See's Candy, and overwhelmingly, it is favorable.

Add a few more California minds over the years, make thoughts a little more favorable and See's future growth will be assured.

Buffett regaled shareholders with the trials and tribulations of American Express, which has maintained a very special position in people's minds about financial integrity and worldwide acceptance.

When banks closed in the 1930s, American Express Travelers Cheques actually replaced bank activity to some degree. Despite some big mistakes over the years, the American Express name has huge value and cachet (which is growing even stronger under current management).

Technology Stocks: Chain Letters

Buffett and Munger were much more strident this year than last in their comments on the market, claiming that stock speculation today is probably the highest ever in the U.S. history.

Munger called it the most extreme event in modern capitalism.

To illustrate the craziness, Buffett said that a company may have a market cap of $10 billion but would be unable to borrow even $100 million at the bank. Yet the owners may be able to borrow many, many times that amount.*

Buffett compared the technology sector's run-up to a "chain letter" in which early participants reap rich rewards at the expense of those that follow.

He referred to the dramatic increase in casino-like day-trading activity as "asinine."

Buffett noted that "in the last year, the ability to monetize shareholders' ignorance has never been greater" and warned that average investors should reduce expectations.

Munger was especially acerbic about Internet speculation: "You are mixing a good concept, such as the Internet, with irrational excess. But if you mix raisins with turds, they are still turds."

Internet Lowers Profit Margins

At the Wesco Financial meeting, Munger claimed that the single biggest outcome of the Internet has been little understood: buyers are the winners. And that means it is quite likely *corporate margins will shrink* with greater bandwidth. And that, in turn, may not be good for stock prices.

Munger noted that high profits on capital often rely on information inefficiencies. A really efficient auction system will remove such inefficiencies as it enables the buyer to find the low price.

He related the story of IBM computer tab cards. With a monopoly on tab cards, IBM made 25% profits. When IBM was forced to open up the tab card market, lots of little companies entered the business. Bids were competitive. Prices collapsed. Tab cards became a pure commodity. This may well be the net effect of the Internet.

At the Berkshire meeting, Buffett noted that a certain streetcar intersection in Omaha had once been prime retail real estate. At the time, people thought, "Who would ever tear up the streetcar lines?"

He concluded, "With the Internet, the streetcar lines get torn up every day."

Big Truth: Know What to Avoid

At the Wesco Financial meeting, Munger took aim at performance chasers, noting that investors need only to have a sensible way to keep wealth

---

* Some banks eager to get IPO fees have reportedly been lending to dot-com owners with dot-com stock as collateral.

growing (especially if they are already rich). If someone else is getting rich, so what? Someone else will *always* be doing better.

He asserted that the notion that an investor or investment manager should be "required" to beat everyone else is nonsense. The real key is to know what you really want to *avoid* and give those things a wide berth (such as a bad marriage, an early death, and so on). Do this and life will go much better, he advised.*

Against the Grain

Buffett and Munger believe shareholders are poorly served by many of today's corporate compensation packages.

Buffett expressed concern about the lottery ticket mentality inherent in the massive issuance of stock options. In particular, he noted that, when the top person gets an outrageous amount, that gets pyramided through the organization.

Munger concluded that a lot of the corporate compensation plans of the modern era work just about the way things would work for a farmer if he put a rat colony in the granary.

Microsoft Trial

Buffett thinks the U.S. Department of Justice attempt to break Microsoft apart is unwise. "We've got something working very well. It doesn't make sense to tinker with it."

He noted that 20 years ago, the U.S. had an inferiority complex over its place in the world. American industry was falling behind that of Japan or Germany.

But with software development now, "We've just swept everyone aside. We're so far ahead that it is difficult to see who is number two." He predicted that the software sector will become ever more important.

Small Expectations

At both the Berkshire and Wesco Financial meetings, a reading and rereading of Buffett's *Fortune* article was recommended.

---

* It was as if Munger was responding to the following quote from Kindleberger's *Manias, Panics, and Crashes*: "Nothing is so disturbing to one's well-being and judgment as to see a friend get rich."

In it, Buffett suggests that expectations of a 6% annual return in stocks over the next 17 years would be rational.

At the Berkshire meeting, Buffett said, "We do not think the general ownership of equities is going to be very exciting over the next 10 to 15 years."

At the Wesco Financial meeting, Munger noted that after the 1930s, America developed a moral aversion to stocks.

As one comedian of the time put it, "They told me to buy stocks for my old age. It worked perfectly. I bought stocks, and within six months, I felt like an old man."

Today stocks are extremely popular, making opportunities few and far between.

Not despairing, Munger quoted Mr. Macawber: "Something will turn up."

As reported in recent letters, Berkshire is increasing its activity in the purchase of wholly owned businesses. Berkshire bought several businesses last year, and Wesco Financial purchased Cort, a furniture rental business.*

Effective Rationality

For several years, Munger, ever the philosopher, has been promoting the idea that we should all employ an interdisciplinary approach to solving human problems.

By learning the primary models in each major discipline (such as compound interest and probability in math and break-points and back-up systems in engineering) and applying all of them, he asserts that people will make better decisions.

In particular, the errors created from overusing any one model ("for the man with the hammer, every problem looks like a nail") can be avoided. As an example, Munger discussed the economic collapse of Japan.

Over the past decade, Japan did all the things Keynesian economics would recommend, including lowering the interest rates and increasing the money supply. The Keynesian "hammer" was surprisingly ineffective. It was Japanese *psychology* that the economists failed to take into account.

---

* According to the 10-K, Wesco Financial even took advantage of the Internet boom, selling roughly $30 million of Homestore.com that Cort owned in February.

Chastened by their losses in the 1990 Japanese stock market crash, Munger concluded that people were afraid to borrow and that banks were afraid to lend no matter what the rates were.

At the Wesco Financial meeting, Munger recommended "effective rationality" as a lifelong pursuit.

Venue: Omaha Civic Auditorium

Attendance: 10,000+

Details About This Year:

- Corey's rigorous note-taking enables us to pass along the following golden nuggets, as Daniel was absent this year.

Fortune 500 Ranking: 40th

Stock Price: $71,120

One dollar invested in 1964 would now be worth **$5,749**.

Berkshire's per-share book value has grown from $19.46 to **$37,920** (a rate of **22.6%** compounded annually).

The S&P 500 compounded at **11.8%** annually for the same period.

HIGHLIGHTS FROM 2001's NOTES

One Big Idea: Float

Few investors understand one of the great secrets to Berkshire Hathaway's wealth-compounding machine: float.

Insurance companies collect premiums, of which a significant portion go into reserves to pay future claims. This reserve ("float") earns money for Berkshire, leveraging the company's return on capital.

Low-cost float has turbo-charged Berkshire's returns. Furthermore, Buffett has grown the float incredibly from $17 million in 1967 to $27 billion at year-end 2000.

Buffett looks for twin virtues of increased growth and reduced cost for Berkshire's float in 2001.

At the same time, he expects that float to grow to $30 billion (roughly 10% of the U.S. total). Buffett expects the cost of float, absent a mega-catastrophe, to drop under 3% on an annualized basis (versus a 6% cost of float last year), with additional improvements in years to come.

The value of float is powerful leverage.

As Munger put it, "Basically, we're a hedgehog that knows one big thing. If you generate float at 3% per annum and buy businesses that earn 13% per annum with the proceeds of that float, we have figured out that's a pretty good position to be in."

Reduced Expectations

In his 1999 *Fortune* article, Buffett talked about the unlikelihood of corporate profits in the U.S. getting much higher than 6% of GDP.

The range has been 4%–6% historically, and we've been up around 6% recently.

Buffett continued that if you're already capitalizing those profits at a very big multiple, then you have to conclude that the value of American business will grow roughly at the rate of GDP growth. That growth, in turn, should probably be around 5% a year with a couple of points a year of inflation as well.

Buffett concluded that stocks are a perfectly decent way to make 6% or 7% a year over the next 15 to 20 years. But anybody that expects to make 15% per year is living in a dream world.

Pension Scandal

Buffett said it was particularly interesting how, back in the 1970s, when the prospects for stocks were better, pension funds were using assumptions in the 6% range. Now, when prospects are way poorer, most pension funds have built-in assumptions of 9% or better.

He said he didn't know how pensions were going to make 9% or better, but if assumptions were reduced, it would significantly reduce the companies' reported income. And no one wants to do that.

Buffett said it will be interesting to watch how quickly assumptions change as pension shortfalls mount in the years to come.

Munger concluded that pension fund accounting is drifting into "scandal" because of these unreasonable assumptions.

He compared the situation to living on an earthquake fault, building-up stress and projecting that the longer it's been without a quake the less likely a quake is going to occur. It's a dumb way to write earthquake insurance and a dumb way to do pension fund planning.

California Utility Crisis

Munger observed that the production of electricity is an enormous and fundamental business. But the California mess exposes a flaw in our education system as all sorts of smart people—utility executives, governors, journalists—have difficulty realizing the most important thing with a power system is to have *surplus capacity*.

Everyone knows you build a bridge that can handle a lot more than the maximum load. That same margin of safety is essential in a power system. Yet according to Munger, very intelligent people are ignoring this single most important and most obvious fact.

Buffett elaborated that the power system probably should have about three elements from a societal standpoint.

One is to be efficient. A second would be to produce a fair but not excessive return on capital to attract capital for future needs. Third, you'd want Munger's margin of safety, an ample supply.

In the old regulated system, operators were paid to stay 15%–20% ahead of the demand curve. However, in the old regulated system, operators were not paid to be efficient, so some sloppiness could result.

However, Buffett noted, the problems of some sloppy management are nothing compared to the problem that results from inadequate generation.

As California deregulated, ownership of utility assets shifted to people who had no interest in excess supply. In fact, they wanted too little supply since a shortage would increase their return on assets.

So Buffett explained that a situation was created where the interests of the operators diverged from those of society. You simply cannot have utility plants built for X sold to entrepreneur operators for 3X and expect electricity prices to fall. Buffett concluded that this was a very, very basic mistake.

That said, Buffett said there will be a need for more power generation. As the electricity industry grows, it will need lots of capital, and there should be ways to participate in that where Berkshire can get reasonable returns on capital.*

The Biggest Mistake: Opportunity Cost

Munger observed that the most extreme mistakes in Berkshire's history show up as *opportunity costs*.

While few managements think about it, Buffett claimed blown opportunities have cost Berkshire's shareholders "billions and billions and billions of dollars."

Munger gave a dramatic example of how, with the power of compounding, blown opportunities can cost an awesome amount of money.

In his younger days, Munger was offered 300 shares of Belrich Oil, which, by his analysis, offered no possibility of losing money and a large possibility of making money. He bought. Three days later, he was offered 1500 shares, which he refused since he'd have to sell something to buy them.

Munger claims that mistake, traced through to today, cost him $200 million.

Buffett qualified the notion of mistakes as those things within their circle of competence. Missing a big move in cocoa futures is not an error since that is something they know little about. An error is when it's something they understand, but then they don't act on it in a big way.

Munger elegantly calls it "thumb-sucking."

Liability Awards: Lottery Tickets

Buffett was quite concerned about mushrooming product liability awards.

* Berkshire's utility subsidiary, MidAmerican Energy, recently announced plans to build two new power plants in Iowa.

The asbestos liability mess is just one example. Unless there is a legislative solution, Buffett sees more and more of GDP going to liability awards.

He noted that an attorney can gamble a modest amount of time and have a payoff of tens or hundreds of millions.

Paraphrasing Lincoln, one of Buffett's attorney friends reportedly said, "I'm just looking for 12 jurors you can fool all of the time."

Munger noted that the increasing power of the bar was especially pernicious. State supreme justices are on for life unless they upset some particular special interest group.

Munger claimed this accounts for far too much tolerance for junk science, junk economic testimony and trashy lawyers. And he sees few signs of improvement.

Buffett concluded that the liability trend will probably accelerate, and therefore, investors should build a margin of safety to account for it.

Sugar

Buffett believes that food companies are probably not at much risk of product liability.

In the case of sugar, Buffett noted the average human body eats something like 550 pounds in dry weight of food in a year, and about 125 pounds (over 20%) of that consists of sugar in one form or another. Yet the average life span of Americans keeps going up.

Buffett concluded that he would not be at all worried about product liability for Coca-Cola, See's Candy or Dairy Queen.

The Internet: A Huge Trap

The idea that you could take almost any business and turn it into wealth on the Internet has been pretty much discredited.

Buffett reported that the Internet threat to Berkshire's furniture and jewelry business has diminished substantially. Very prominent dot-coms in both industries that had valuations of hundreds of millions have vanished in short order.

What the Internet really did, asserted Buffett, is give promoters the chance to monetize the hopes and greed of millions of investors through venture capital markets. A lot of money transferred from the gullible to the promoters. Very little real wealth has been created.

He concluded, "The Internet has been a huge trap."

Munger interjected that he and Buffett were once in the grocery delivery business, a "terrible business." Munger observed that someone got the idea it was a great business and turned it into an idea on the Internet.

Buffett noted that the grocery store in question was the "infamous" Buffett and Son, which barely supported the family for 100 years.

The only way it worked, Buffett joked, was to hire guys like Munger as slave labor.

While they took orders with a pencil instead of a keyboard, once they started hauling them on trucks, they ran into the same costs as Webvan.

Brand vs. Retailers

Buffett explained that there will always be a battle between brands and retailers. The retailer would like his name to be a brand. And to the extent that people trust Costco or Wal-Mart as much as they trust the brands, then the value of the brand moves over to the retailer from the product itself.

Munger observed that brands such as Kellogg's have seen a power shift toward grocery chains like Wal-Mart and Costco.* He went on to say that the muscle power of Sam's Club and Costco has gotten very extreme.

Munger boasted that a woman thanked him for her pantyhose, which she'd purchased at Costco at his recommendation (Costco has co-branded with Hanes).

Buffett quipped, "She must be pretty desperate if she's consulting with you about her pantyhose."

Extrapolating the Past: Massively Stupid

Reprising Buffett's *Fortune* article in the fall of 1999, Munger said the shareholding class in America should reduce its expectations a lot.

In his usual understated way, Munger asserted, "It's stupid the way we extrapolate the past. Not just stupid, massively stupid."

Buffett noted that it's a mistake for any company to predict 15% growth, yet plenty of them do. For one thing, unless the U.S. economy grows at 15% annually, the 15% number catches up to you. Very few large companies can compound at 15%. Yet during the bubble, people were valuing businesses at $500 billion, and there was no mathematical calculations that would possibly lead you to justify those valuations.

---

* Munger is on the board of Costco.

Munger said that to some degree, stocks sell like Rembrandts. Instead of selling on the value people will get from looking at the picture, they sell based on the fact that Rembrandts have gone up in price in the past. If you fill every pension in America with Rembrandts, Rembrandts will keep going up and up.

Buffett asserted that the biggest money made in Wall Street in recent years has not been made by great performance, but by great promotion.

Munger claimed the current scene is "obscene," with too much misleading sales material and television emphasis on speculation.

Starting Early

Buffett advised younger attendees to start saving early.

He acknowledged that he was fortunate that his dad paid for his education. As a result, he was able to save $10,000 by the time he was 21—a huge head start.

He noted that it's much easier to save during your teen years when your parents are taking care of your financial obligations. He surmised that every dollar saved then is worth $20.

He also suggested that getting knowledge about business has a similar compounding effect.

He recommended learning about local businesses—which ones are good and why, which ones went out of business, etc. As you go, you'll build a database in your mind that is going to pay off over time.

Invest in Yourself

Buffett asserted that the very best investment you can make is in yourself.

Buffett shared that, when he talks to students, one of the things he tells them is what a valuable asset they have in themselves.

Buffett would pay any bright student probably $50,000 for 10% of their future earnings for the rest of his life. So each student is a $500,000 asset just standing there. What you do with that $500,000 asset should be developing your mind and talent.

Know the Big Cost

Buffett and Munger have repeated year after year that they seek to buy businesses with enduring competitive advantages. This year, they treated listeners to an extended discussion of one key element of a wonderful business: the cost structure. A superior cost structure is often fundamental to a business' sustainable advantage.

At Flightsafety the key is quality simulators, so Berkshire is investing $200 million annually in flight simulators.

At NetJets, first-class pilots are essential, so for that business, costs are very people-intensive.

In the carpet business, Buffett continued, only 15% of costs relate to employees. The big cost in that industry is the raw materials, fibers.

In the insurance business, the big cost is future claims, which involves lots of estimating since claims might be paid five, 10 or 20 years later.

In retail, the big cost is rent, with labor being a significant secondary cost.

Buffett summarized that the big cost can vary enormously by the type of business you're in.

He said he doesn't really care whether they're buying into raw-material-intensive businesses, people-intensive businesses or capital-intensive businesses. The key is to understand a company's costs and why it's got a sustainable edge against its competitors.

Labor Costs

This line of thought continued with a fascinating review of the airline industry.

Buffett noted that the big problem with airlines is not so much aggregate revenue, but whether your average costs are out of line with your competitors. Since airline travel is pretty much a commodity business, costs are the key factors. The biggest cost is labor.

However, Munger noted that the pilots' union is very tough since the union knows no airline can stand a prolonged shutdown with the chaos it causes to routes. The figure to look for with airlines, then, is cost per available seat mile and the cost per occupied seat mile.

At USAir, for example, when Munger and Buffett were directors for a time, the costs were 12 cents a seat mile—which was fine until Southwest Airlines came in at 8 cents a seat mile.

In airlines, as with many other industries in a capitalistic society, business will eventually gravitate to the low-cost player.

In contrast, Buffett claimed that fractional jet ownership is not a commodity business. NetJets' clients care enormously about service and safety.

He wryly observed that if you were going to buy a parachute, you wouldn't necessarily take the low bid.

If NetJet can maintain and grow its excellent pilot force, it should do well for years and years to come.

Playing Chicken

One of the best stories of the day was how Buffett handled a strike shortly after he bought the *Buffalo News*.

In a fascinating real-life study in game theory, Buffett noted that sometimes the weaker you are, the stronger your bargaining position may be.

(Buffett joked that buying the *Buffalo News* was Munger's idea: Munger was stuck in Buffalo during a blizzard, and he called Buffett to ask what he should do. So Buffett told him to go out and buy a paper.)

In the early 1980s, the *Buffalo News* and the *Courier-Express* were in a kind of death struggle. Thus, dealing with the union became a game of chicken because if the paper closed down, everyone would lose his job.

The union struck on a Monday.

Buffett recalled that some union leaders had tears in their eyes because they knew it would put them out of business.

Buffett took the position with the union that if you come back in a day, we're competitive. If you come back in a year, we're out of business. If you're smart enough to figure out exactly how far you can push us where we still have a business and you still have a job, you're smarter than I am, so you go home and figure it out.

They came back to work on Thursday, and the *Buffalo News* made it.[*]

Buffett observed that it was out of his hands. If the union had decided to strike long enough, his investment and their jobs would have been lost.

The *Buffalo News'* weakness proved to be its bargaining strength.

The Berkshire Advantage

While Buffett lamented Berkshire's size as an anchor to future growth, he also enumerated some of Berkshire's advantages.

For one, its checks clear.

Buffett noted that Berkshire is a preferred purchaser for many companies because they know the deal will not have any financing difficulties.[†]

---

[*] Eventually, the *Courier-Express* folded.
[†] Berkshire currently has $30 billion in cash.

For example, Berkshire bought Johns Manville for cash at $13/share just after a $15/share offer fell through due to the other bidder's financing difficulties.

Sellers also know Berkshire's ownership structure is stable and that they will be able to run their businesses as before.

Buffett anticipated that Berkshire might buy 40 companies, roughly two a year, over the next 20 years.

While the investment arena is extremely competitive, Buffett guaranteed that sometime in the next 20 years, people will do something exceptionally stupid in equity markets. The question for Berkshire is, will it be in a position to take advantage of it when the time comes.

Buffett added that there is no master plan. They will just keep allocating capital as rationally as they can.

Munger asserted that it's a sure thing that in 20 years, Berkshire will have way more strength and value behind each share.

And he added, it's an absolutely sure thing Berkshire's annual percentage rate of progress will go way down from what it has been in the past.

Venue: Omaha Civic Auditorium

Attendance: 14,000

Details About This Year:

- Nebraska Furniture Mart did $14.2 million in sales for the "Berkshire Weekend." This was up from $5.3 million in 1997 when special event pricing was first introduced.

Fortune 500 Ranking: 39th

Stock Price: $75,743

One dollar invested in 1964 would now be worth **$6,123**.

Berkshire's per-share book value has grown from $19.46 to **$41,727** (a rate of **22.2%** compounded annually).

The S&P 500 compounded at **11%** annually for the same period.

HIGHLIGHTS FROM 2002's NOTES

Dampen Expectations

Munger asserted one of the smartest things to do now is to dampen expectations way down.

Buffett noted there is nothing wrong with earning 6% to 7% on your money.

With inflation so low, how much more return is capital entitled to?

Munger described Berkshire's large bond holdings as a "default option" reflecting their lack of enthusiasm for stocks.

Buffett and Munger like the Berkshire model in this environment. With low-cost float, significant earnings power and occasional bargains, Berkshire should do just fine.

Float

From modest beginnings of $12 million in float generated by National Indemnity in 1967, Berkshire has grown float, incredibly, to $37 billion.

Buffett believes that to be roughly 9% of the estimated $400 billion float generated by the U.S. property and casualty insurance industry.

Visuals

UBH went multimedia this year featuring several slides.

Buffett's enthusiasm was evident as he showed a slide of the Berkshire's insurance group's underwriting profit in Q1, a sharp reversal from last year's 13% cost of float. In addition, the slide showed Berkshire's float grew $1.8 billion in the quarter.

If Berkshire can consistently underwrite profitability, this $37 billion of float constitutes an interest-free loan with which to leverage Berkshire's earnings.*

Buffett credited new General Re (Gen Re) CEO Joe Brandon with doing a great job in redirecting Gen Re's culture.

Buffett predicted Gen Re will be Berkshire's No. 1 asset.

---

* Invested simply in 10-year Treasuries, this float will generate $1.9 billion in annual pre-tax income.

Float and Oil Wells

Buffett compared float to oil wells where, every day, some goes out. As you pump the oil, you must seek to replace it.

Buffett noted that Berkshire's float has less natural run-off then any other company because much of it is "long tail" business—like a long-lived oil well.

In addition, Buffett noted that Berkshire seems to attract lots of special transactions.

Munger concluded, "Growing float at low or no cost is almost impossible. We intend to do it anyway."

GEICO

The nation's largest direct writer of auto insurance grew policies in force, modestly rising to 4.8 million.

Buffett noted that each GEICO policyholder was worth at least $1,000 to Berkshire.

While GEICO'S inquiry rate has slowed, a higher close rate per inquiry and rising retention rate bode well for GEICO to increase its free (as long as it underwrites profitability) and growing float.

Greatest Asset: Self

With graduation season upon us, Buffett offered some appropriate worldly wisdom.

Imagine a genie comes to a 17 year old and offers to get him any car he wants. However, there is one catch—whatever car he chooses he must make it last a lifetime. Well, you can imagine that the young man would read the owner's manual 10 times, would change the oil twice as often as suggested, etc. to help that car last 50 years.

In the same way, Buffett continued, we each receive one body and one mind for a lifetime. You cannot repair them at age 60. You must *maintain* them.

One's greatest asset is one's *self.*

Develop your mind and good health habits when you are young, and it will enhance your life. If not, you may have a wreck at age 70.

Asbestos Litigation: Cancer on the Economy

Buffett and Munger offered dire predictions for spiraling liability awards related to asbestos litigation.

Unless Congress steps in to cap awards, Buffett predicted it will get much worse.

Munger opined that asbestos litigation has morphed into fraud, leading to meritless claimants (and their attorneys) receiving huge sums while merited claimants go begging.

Buffett reiterated that this is a huge problem for corporate America, "a cancer on the economy."

Always seeing opportunity in the rubble of disaster, Buffett did suggest that the asbestos mess may offer opportunities for Berkshire to acquire companies freed from asbestos liability—as it did with Johns Manville.

Terrorism: Reality

Buffett noted that humanity will always include a certain percentage of psychotics, megalomaniacs and religious fanatics.

However, where the deranged few could do little more than throw rocks for centuries, modern technology has enormously increased our ability to inflict damage.

He added that, unfortunately, humankind has not progressed similarly in our ability to get along.

Munger noted pragmatically that to the extent we are less weak, foolish or sloppy, 9/11 will be a plus. While we may deeply regret what happened, we should not regret facing reality with more intelligence.

He added the current installation of safety measures should have been done long ago.

Buffett shared that he has long been worried about a terrorist nuclear disaster, and 9/11 leaves his view unchanged.

With millions and millions of people who hate the U.S., Buffett sees the likelihood of such an event someday as a near certainty.

Terrorism and Insurance

While the insurance industry may have long recognized the potential damage by the lunatic fringe, it never wrote it into the contracts.

Buffett noted that this was a huge error, similar to what happened to the insurance industry in England in the 1940s—only after the war did companies think to exclude war coverage from contracts.

Berkshire's new policies exclude NCB (nuclear, chemical, biological), as well as fire from a nuclear event.

Without such exclusions, Buffett asserted that a nuclear act or two could destroy the entire insurance industry.

Insurance companies have long tried to avoid natural aggregation, such as limiting homes insured on a shoreline.*

Now, Buffett asserted, companies need to think about *manmade* aggregation risks.

As an example, while most folks think of the World Trade Center disaster as primarily a property/casualty loss, Buffett noted it will easily go down as the largest *workers' comp* loss in history.

While not being specific, Buffett noted that a biological terrorist event could create workers' comp claims that would boggle the mind.

My Crooks Look Like Crooks

Munger noted that enormously talented people drift into fraud. The culture carries them there.

Munger suggested the best response to fraud is to avoid it and that there are whole fields to avoid.

Buffett asserted, "We won't get defrauded. My crooks look like crooks—normally, they tell you things too good to be true. They have a smell about them."

Munger remarked that sometimes it's annoyingly obvious. Robert Maxwell of England, for example, was nicknamed "The Bouncing Check."

Munger wryly observed that as a satire, it would be too extreme to be funny. Yet Salomon aggressively pursued business with Maxwell.

Buffett added that it's a hobby of theirs to keep track of the Maxwells of the world. He asserted that Wall Street is *no* filter—Wall Street loves their investment banking fees.

He noted First Normandy was IPO'd by Salomon Brothers even though he and Munger were on the board and told them First Normandy's record was complete baloney. The IPO was cancelled a day after the public offering. Salomon's only explanation of this embarrassment was that the underwriting committee approved it.

Munger added that he knew of no subsequent changes on the underwriting committee.

---

* Yet natural aggregation errors occur frequently. Twentieth Century Industries nearly failed in 1994 when it wrote lots of homeowners insurance along the fault line of the Northridge earthquake.

EBIDTA: More Fraud

In a similar vein, Munger noted that the fraud group percentage is high for those who talk "EBIDTA."*

Buffett noted that such enormously successful companies as Wal-Mart, GE and Microsoft never mention EBIDTA. Those who do are probably conning you or conning themselves or both.

As an example, Buffett chided telecom companies that talk about "cash flow" when they are spending every dime they get. It isn't cash flow if it's all flowing *out.*

Professor Buffett continued that the "D" (depreciation) not only reflects a real cost, but the worst kind of cost. Depreciation reflects cash that is spent first, and the deductions only come later.

Berkshire vastly prefers businesses where you get the cash up front (like insurance).

Similarly the "T" (taxes) is a real cost. To pretend otherwise is delusional.

Buffett concluded that it was amazing to him how widespread the usage of EBIDTA has become.

Derivatives: Sewage

Berkshire is shutting down the derivatives operation at Gen Re.

Buffett likened derivatives to hell: "easy to get into and tough to get out of." He noted that the unwinding of Enron's derivatives contracts reveals that they were all money losers.

Munger concluded with a gem that may prove prophetic if derivatives unravel elsewhere: "To say derivative accounting in America is a sewer is an insult to sewage."

Stock Options

Buffett and Munger shared their disgust with the flagrant abuse of stock options in corporate America.

Munger asked rhetorically, if you handed 60-year-old surgeons at the Mayo Clinic a bunch of stock options, would that improve their behavior?

Munger concluded that the fact that U.S. corporations routinely dole out hundreds of millions of dollars to CEOs is "demented and immoral."

---

* Earnings before interest, depreciation, taxes and amortization.

Buffett added that options are not bad in and of themselves.

He asserted that options that included a cost of capital factor and were issued only at or above the company's intrinsic business value would be logical. However, that's not how it's been done.

Buffett also decried the shameless and self-interested way corporate CEOs have been lobbying against treating options as an expense.

Munger summed it up as a "Mad Hatter's Tea Party where the only consistency is that the whole thing is disgusting."

Creative Accounting

Munger noted that one of the great inventions of all time was double-entry bookkeeping by an Italian monk.

Accounting that undoes the monk's work is merely a tool for folly and fraud, and hurts society.

He called Enron one of the most disgusting examples of a business culture gone wrong. Though, he noted, good may come of it to the extent others take notice.

He concluded, "creative accounting is a curse to civilization."

Index Funds and PE's

Buffett suggested that for those who believe U.S. businesses will do well over time, dollar-cost-averaging into a broad-based index is a reasonable approach.

As to whether a PE (price earnings ratio) of 25 is "too high," Buffett stated emphatically that no one ratio really works. *It couldn't be that easy.*

Munger cautioned that it is possible for prices to get so high that index funds won't do well.

In Japan, for example, the Nikkei Index returns over the past 13 years have been negative.

Furthermore, Japan made all the right Keynesian moves, lowering interest rates and providing massive fiscal stimulation, to no effect. The models of the past failed to predict it.

It's crazy for Americans to assume that what happened to Argentina and Japan won't happen to us.[*]

---

[*] Again, Berkshire has voted with its feet. Berkshire is now less invested in U.S. stocks than any time since the early 1970s.

Fruit of the Loom

What goes around comes around.

For a second time, Buffett has participated in the purchase of Fruit of the Loom.

Buffett thanked Mickey Newman, his friend and former employer at Graham-Newman, for helping Berkshire to complete the acquisition of Fruit of the Loom from bankruptcy.

Buffett explained that Fruit of the Loom was victimized by too much debt and poor management.

Berkshire's bankruptcy bid for Fruit of the Loom was contingent on retired CEO John Holland returning to run the company. Holland agreed, and the deal was done. Buffett considers Holland and the brand as Fruit's key assets.

This was not the first time Buffett participated in the acquisition of Fruit of the Loom.

He reminisced that in the 1950s, a Graham-Newman controlled entity, Philadelphia and Reading Coal and Iron (P&R) purchased Union Underwear from Jack Goldfarb for $15 million.

Subsequently, Union bought the license of the Fruit of the Loom name and, along with P&R, was merged into Northwest Industries. Fruit went on to achieve annual pre-tax earnings of $200 million. *

Just Say No

Success in insurance, Buffett intoned, depends on taking understandable risks properly priced without undue aggregation. The ability to say no is crucial.

He noted that Jack Ringwalt, who founded National Indemnity in 1941, was not an insurance guy. But with old-fashioned common sense, he beat the pants off the guys in Hartford.

Buffett said he wanted Berkshire's insurance arm to be exposed to as much business around the world as possible through a disciplined staff.

Munger concluded that in insurance and investing, if you combine a vast exposure with a vast decline rate, you can do very well indeed.

---

* In a similar vein, Buffett wrote his college thesis on GEICO, presaging Berkshire's purchase of a large position in GEICO in the mid-1970s and eventual takeover of GEICO in 1996. With Coca-Cola, there is the story that as a boy, Buffett counted bottle caps in pop machines to see which brands sold best. Fifty years later, he bought 200 million shares of the stock.

Waiting For the Fat Pitch

In a similar vein, Buffett has frequently used his "waiting for the fat pitch" baseball analogy to describe Berkshire's asset allocation approach.

In a fascinating digression, he noted that few other corporations do likewise, and as a result, the aggregate allocation record for American business is poor.

He recalled that GEICO, which has a great business, felt compelled to make three acquisitions over the past 30 years. All were duds.

Gillette, with a 71% worldwide market share in shaving products, felt compelled to issue stock to acquire Duracell, thereby trading stock in a great business for ownership of an inferior one.

Buffett shared that he came across a company that made 10 deals in five years. As of 2001, this company was 0 for 10 on successful deals.

In fact, Buffett estimated the aggregate profits of the 10 purchases were *one-quarter* of the projected amounts.

Munger noted many corporations have large M&A departments spending huge amounts of time to do huge amounts of due diligence. Yet at least two-thirds of acquisitions are duds.

In contrast, Munger noted that Berkshire has done many great deals with no such time spent. They wait for the no-brainer, the fat pitch.

Friends and Partners

Buffett and Munger met in 1959, and they've been friends ever since.

Buffett suggested it is helpful to list the qualities you would want in a friend and then seek to instill those qualities in *yourself.*

He emphasized that it's a matter of choice, not DNA. Anyone can develop good character and quality lifetime habits.

Munger interjected that they know very successful businessmen who do not have one true friend . . . and rightly so. "That's no way to live a life," he concluded.

Keys to Investing

Buffett claimed that successful investing is not complicated. The Rosetta Stone of investing is to remember that a stock is part ownership in a business. That principle provides the foundation for rational investing.

Buffett read Ben Graham's book, *Security Analysis,* in 1949 when he was a student at the University of Nebraska, and he's read nothing since that improves on Graham.

He added that temperament is very important, especially a willingness to go away from the crowd.

He recommended realism in defining one's circle of competence and discipline to stay within the circle. He added that it helps to insulate yourself from popular opinions. You're better off sitting and thinking.[*]

Coping With Reality: Just Ask Why

Munger shared that it helps to have a passionate interest in knowing why things are happening. That cast of mind over a long time, he asserted, will improve its ability to cope with reality. Those that don't ask why are destined for failure, even those with very high IQs.

Buffett noted that lots of folks with very high IQs fail financially.

---

[*] As Sir John Templeton did by moving to the Bahamas and as Buffett has done by staying in Omaha.

2003

Venue: Omaha Civic Auditorium

Attendance: 19,000

Details About This Year:

- In the lobby, two-time U.S. chess champion Patrick Wolff took on all comers—blindfolded. Champion bridge, backgammon and scrabble players were also on hand to compete with shareholders.

Fortune 500 Ranking: 28th

Stock Price: $72,865

One dollar invested in 1964 would now be worth **$5,890**.

Berkshire's per-share book value has grown from $19.46 to **$50,498** (a rate of **22.2%** compounded annually).

The S&P 500 compounded at **10%** annually for the same period.

HIGHLIGHTS FROM 2003's NOTES

Great First Quarter

Buffett's opening remarks featured a review of Berkshire's first quarter results, the best in the company's history.

Berkshire earned $1.7 billion and generated $1.3 billion of float, a total cash generation of $3 billion (or $100 million a day).

While the non-insurance subsidiaries were sluggish, reflecting the economic slowdown, the insurance units are hitting on all cylinders.

Buffett estimated that float grew 13% to $42.5 billion, though he doubted whether it could grow much from here.

With total U.S. property and casualty insurance float of roughly $500 billion, Berkshire now accounts for about 8% of total float. More importantly, Berkshire is posting underwriting profits, which means the float is created at no cost.

Buffett noted that this "free" float has the utility of equity without the dilution of issuing shares.

From modest beginnings of $12 million of float generated by National Indemnity in 1967, this float growth has been spectacular and a major driver of the growth in Berkshire's net worth.

Buffett compared the compounding of wealth at Berkshire to a large snowball going downhill. He noted the Berkshire snowball is good-sized, can attract a lot more snow, and there is probably a lot of mountain and a lot of snow left.

Acquisitions

Berkshire can be seen as a collection of great businesses. Buffett's favorite activity is adding to that collection.

He discussed Berkshire's most recent acquisition activity.

For one, Berkshire has offered $1.7 billion to buy Clayton Homes, the nation's best-run builder of manufactured housing.

Distress in the industry made obtaining financing from fearful lenders difficult.*

By selling to Berkshire, Clayton will have access to capital and Berkshire's AAA credit rating.

---

* The industry distress stemmed most notably from the bankruptcy of Conseco, which was the largest insurer of manufactured housing mortgages, and for which Berkadia—a joint venture of Berkshire and Leucadia National—made an unsuccessful bid.

Buffett spoke highly of the Clayton family's management record and added that Berkshire will retain the mortgages Clayton originates.[*]

Buffett also discussed Berkshire's acquisition for $1.5 billion of Wal-Mart's McLane subsidiary, a food distribution company that serves convenience stores, fast-food restaurants and other retailers.[†]

For those potential customers loathe to do business with Wal-Mart, McLane is now a more palatable distribution source.

NetJets

Resale prices of pre-owned (industry jargon for "used") jets have plunged in this soft economy.

While that means losses for NetJets in the near future, Buffett noted that NetJets has 75% of the market, or triple that of the next three largest competitors combined. Furthermore, those three major competitors are all losing money.

Buffett predicted an industry shakeout but assured the shareholders that NetJets "will not be one of the shook."

Long term, he predicted that fractional jet ownership will be a big global business and that there could eventually be a 10-fold increase in the number of folks flying this way.

Accounting

Asked if he recommended any books on accounting, Buffett advocated getting all the accounting you can if you are in business.

Read lots of annual reports. Learn accounting by reading good business articles, especially those on accounting scandals. Try to know how the numbers are put together.

Then, if you cannot understand it, it is probably because management doesn't want you to understand it. Management always obfuscates the facts for a reason.

Munger complimented Buffett's command of accounting, saying, "You might as well ask him if he has any good books on breathing." Munger concluded that it takes years to integrate an understanding of accounting with life's realities.

---

[*] We see this as a major Berkshire advantage—using its AAA balance sheet and massive capital to reduce financing costs and to retain profitable business that less well-capitalized companies cannot.

[†] McLane has revenue of $22 billion, of which $7 billion comes from Wal-Mart, by our calculations.

Option Accounting

Buffett and Munger have been stern critics of option accounting ever since the rules were changed in 1993.*

Buffett began by noting that any option has value. It's silly to think otherwise.

Options issued as compensation can work if there is 1) a cost of capital associated with them, and 2) the issuance is tied directly to performance.

Unfortunately, almost all option issuance breaks both of these rules. Instead, options have served more as lottery tickets or royalties on the passage of time.

In the 1990s, they served as the conduit for a major wealth transfer from shareholders to employees. Boards awarded options as if they were handing out candy. Consultants promoted option issuances as if it were play money. CEOs looking to juice earnings were pleased to issue options as they were not treated as an expense. Employees enjoyed the free lottery tickets.

No one in the system acted to protect the shareholders. The system lacks what Buffett called a "parity of concern."

More Accounting

As Buffett and Munger warmed to the topic, Buffett railed against all sorts of expenses being hidden in the footnotes: "Why not put everything in the footnotes, then you could have just two lines to report: revenue and income?"

Buffett warned investors that management that refuses to expense options or has fanciful pension assumptions will likely take the low road on other matters as well. He cautioned, "There's seldom one cockroach in the kitchen."

Buffett also decried the use of EBITDA (earnings before interest, taxes, depreciation and amortization) as if depreciation wasn't a real expense.

Not only is it an expense, Buffett asserted, it is the worst kind of expense where all the money is spent upfront.

Munger brought down the house with this teaching tool: "Everywhere you see 'EBITDA' in some analyst's report, simply insert the words 'bullshit earnings.'"

---

* We remember attending the 1993 Berkshire meeting but not understanding why they were so critical of FASB. After options started being issued like candy during the bubble, we finally understood.

Inflation

Buffett noted that inflation is the enemy of the investor.

He suggested that if we had 3% real GDP growth plus 2% inflation, that would equal 5% nominal GDP growth.

With 1% to 2% in dividends (less frictional costs), returns of 6% to 7% for equity investors seem a reasonable expectation and not bad in a low-inflation world.

With a nation of 100 million workers and a $10 trillion GDP, having shareholders receive a 6% to 7% return is a perfectly acceptable outcome.

Quality GDP

Buffett made an interesting observation that we had not heard before.

He noted that GDP is often presented as a gross number. However, he emphasized that *per capita* GDP is far more meaningful.

He added that "quality of GDP" would be an added factor worth knowing. GDP that leads to improved standards of living is one thing. Increased GDP from hiring more security guards is another—a lower quality GDP than the former.

Inequality Helps

Munger is fond of saying the fail rate of all great civilizations is 100%.

However, he noted that one of the keys to a successful society is the perception of fairness. Fostering this perception in America are the changes at the top of America's most wealthy families. If the same families have the greatest wealth for decades, it can breed resentment. But that seldom happens here—the DuPont heirs, for example, have given way to the hard-charging managers at the Pampered Chef.*

And thus, the people see the system as fair.

Taxes

Likewise with taxes—Buffett spoke against the Bush plan to eliminate double taxation of dividends.

If approved, Buffett could dividend out hundreds of millions of dollars to himself, effectively lowering his tax rate to less than 1%, while his secretary continued to pay taxes at a 30% rate. Such a differential could only breed resentment.†

---

* Pampered Chef founder Doris Christopher, a home economics teacher starting out of her basement in 1980, took annual sales from $50,000 to more than $700 million in just 22 years.
† Buffett recently penned an op-ed piece in the *Washington Post*, making a case against the Bush tax plan.

Insurance Risks

Buffett and Munger noted that in insurance, you get handed a lot of money for pieces of paper, and that can tempt you into doing very silly things. A few large mistakes can completely undo years of wealth accumulation.

As an example, they recounted how Mutual of Omaha got into reinsuring property and casualty insurers and, in short order, wiped out half of Mutual's net worth, a net worth that took decades to build.

Another incredible example, GEICO wrote a paltry $72,000 of net premium in commercial umbrella and product liability insurance from 1981 to 1983. This small "bite of the apple" was enough to create a breathtaking loss of $94 million, or about *130,000%* of the net premium it received. Most of the loss was due to uncollectable receivables from deadbeat reinsurers.

Part of what makes the industry dangerous, according to Buffett, is that if you are willing to do dumb things in insurance, they will find you.

He painted an elaborate picture: If you were in a rowboat in the middle of the Atlantic Ocean and just whispered a really dumb insurance price, insurance brokers would be swimming to you from shore . . . with their fins showing.

Correlation

Buffett continued that when things go bad, all kinds of things correlate that you wouldn't think of. Buffett said this is deadly. If you are not aware of these correlations, you have an unrecognized concentration of risk.

When telecom debt collapsed, for example, people found that all of it was correlated.[*]

Munger warned that derivatives have the same sort of danger and that the accounting for them exacerbates the problem.[†]

Lifetime Learning

Munger noted that one of the most remarkable qualities of his friend, Warren, is that he continues to get better with age and continues to keep learning.

Munger recalled how, in negotiating for the purchase of See's Candy, he and Warren would have walked if the sellers had asked for $100,000

---

[*] According to Jim Crowe, CEO of Level 3, there have been 180 bankruptcies so far in the bubble burst of the telecom sector.
[†] At last year's meeting, Munger said he would compare derivative accounting to a sewer, but that would be an insult to sewage.

more. Ira Marshall told them they would be crazy to do that. They should be willing to pay up for quality.

Marshall was right—since paying $23 million for See's in 1971, the candy company has generated over $1 billion of pre-tax profits for Berkshire. That would have been a lot to give up for a paltry $100,000 difference.

Munger asserted that their ability to take constructive criticism has been a key factor in Berkshire's success, that "Berkshire has been built on criticism."

Buffett added that Ben Graham's quantitative approach was easy to teach.

In contrast, Munger emphasized the qualitative. They have learned by experience that they have made more money with a wonderful business at a fair price than a fair business at a wonderful price. While the qualitative insight was much harder to come by, it has proved much more valuable.

Regarding investment learning, Buffett recommended building your database so that you accumulate knowledge over a lifetime.

They mentioned the *Wall Street Journal* and *Fortune* as favorite sources and included the usual corporate filings.

One thing Buffett said he never reads are analysts' reports. "If I read one, it was because the funny papers weren't available," he quipped.

Opportunity Cost

Buffett and Munger agreed that their biggest mistakes have been errors of omission rather than commission.

Despite the lesson learned at See's Candy, Buffett confessed to a tendency to stop buying shares of wonderful companies if the price moves up. Buffett said that he stopped buying shares of Wal-Mart at one time, and his recalcitrance cost shareholders $8 billion.*

Munger claimed that he and Warren have been slow learners. The opportunity cost of the amount of money blown by headquarters at Berkshire has been "awesome."

Warren agreed.

Having already taken a swing at consultants, accountants, politicians and analysts, Munger then took a shot at CEOs and their M&A departments.

---

* In past years, Buffett mentioned a similar mistake with Fannie Mae. This is the first time we have heard him mention Wal-Mart in this regard.

Munger asserted that all intelligent people base decisions on opportunity costs. The alternative returns available should weigh on whether you make a particular investment. It is freshman economics.

Meanwhile, Munger continued, the rest of the world has gone on a crazy kick to use wild and elaborate models for gauging the cost of capital and other formulas for decision-making, resulting in "perfectly amazing mental malfunctions."

Buffett quipped, "Is there anybody we have forgotten to offend?"

The Fat Pitch

Buffett advised attendees that the "market is there to serve you, not to instruct you."

Munger advocated developing a temperament of owning securities without fretting. If you focus on the price, you are really saying that you believe the market knows more than you do. If you think of the value of the business instead of the price, you will sleep better. If the market were to shut down for five years, Acme Brick would still be turning out bricks, and Dairy Queen would still be selling Dilly Bars.

They suggested that investing is more like parimutuel betting, where you need only be right a few times as long as you don't take a big loss.

Munger noted that most financial institutions do exactly the opposite, fielding large research departments to track all 500 companies in the S&P 500.

In contrast, Buffett said he only needs one or two good ideas a year. In this way, Buffett seeks to emulate batting-great Ted Williams, who knew his success resided in waiting for the fat pitch.

Big Opportunity in Energy

Buffett suggested to shareholders that MidAmerican Energy was already a big business for Berkshire but could become much bigger, especially if outdated laws are changed.

The energy field represents billions of dollars of opportunity: "We're not dealing with lemonade stands here."

In addition, Buffett believes that they have fabulous managers with David Sokol and Greg Abel.

Buffett noted that Berkshire brings something to the utility field, and in fact, in 2002 it brought it, buying pipelines from companies that would have otherwise gone into bankruptcy.

Derivatives Warning

Buffett and Munger have warned of the dangers of derivatives for several years.

Concerned that the warning has not been acted upon, Buffett allowed *Fortune* magazine to reprint his thoughts on derivatives shared in the annual shareholder letter, where he referred to them as "financial weapons of mass destruction."

In the energy field, nearly every utility in the country was brought to ruin with participation in the sort of derivatives trading championed by Enron.

In 1998, Long-Term Capital Management nearly paralyzed the entire financial system with troubles magnified by the use of derivatives.

Munger grumbled that with engineering, safety is an enormous concern, but with derivatives, it's as if no one gave a damn about safety.

Furthermore, both parties of the typical derivative trade book an immediate profit on the trade—this false accounting has sparked a ballooning of the business.

Buffett added that, while participants claim derivatives help spread risk, he believes that they have actually *intensified* risk since a few large players do much of the business.*

Buffett cautioned that the counter-party risk in the system has been little examined despite the warnings of past mishaps.

Munger stated that he would be amazed if he lives another five years and doesn't see a significant blow up.

The Best Story

The stories from the early days are always a treat.

This year, Buffett told the story of how Berkshire purchased National Indemnity in 1967 from Jack Ringwalt.

Buffett said he had noticed that Ringwalt got into a fit of pique each year for about 15 minutes, in which he would threaten to sell the company.

Buffett said he put a mutual friend, Charlie Heider, on alert to call him the next time Ringwalt had an episode, so he could buy the company.

Sure enough, Heider soon called: "Jack's ready."

Buffett made the deal in the 15-minute zone, though he could tell Ringwalt regretted it. Ringwalt tried to back out, asking, "I suppose you'll want to see audited financials?"

---

* This same thought has been put forward in past newsletters by Jean-Marie Eveillard, manager of the First Eagle Global Fund.

Sensing that Ringwalt was looking for an excuse to nix the deal, Buffett replied, "I wouldn't dream of asking to see audited financials."

For $7 million, National Indemnity belonged to Berkshire.

Buffett also noted that Ringwalt was 10 minutes late for the meeting because he was looking for a parking meter with a few minutes left on it.

Buffett joked, "That's when I knew he was my kind of guy."

Identical Twins

Buffett suggested the following thought problem.

Suppose you are in a womb with an identical twin. You are alike in all ways. A genie appears with a proposition: "You will be born in the next 24 hours. One of you will be born in Omaha, the other in Bangladesh. You two decide. You start the bidding with how much of your estate goes back to society."

Buffett said he would not hesitate to bid 100% of his estate, noting that he probably would have died years ago of malnutrition had he been born in Bangladesh.

The odds were 50 to 1 of his being born in the United States. He said he was very lucky to be born here.

Successful Living

Buffett claimed that you are successful if the people you hope love you, do love you.

He and Munger agreed that making money is no replacement for friendship and happiness.

Buffett said they knew people with buildings named after them but had no one who loved them. That's no way to live.

Munger concluded with this joke: A minister presiding over a sparsely attended funeral asked the crowd for a few kind words about the deceased. After an awkward silence, he pleaded, "Isn't there anyone who can say a kind word for the deceased?" A voice from the back croaked, "Well, his brother was worse."

Venue: Qwest Center

Attendance: Nearly 20,000

Details About This Year:

- The Qwest Center offers 194,000 square feet of exhibition space for Berkshire subsidiaries. The expanded Berkshire Mall now includes a 16,000 square foot Clayton Home.

Fortune 500 Ranking: 80th

Stock Price: $84,378

One dollar invested in 1964 would now be worth **$6,821**.

Berkshire's per-share book value has grown from $19.46 to **$55,824** (a rate of **21.9%** compounded annually).

The S&P 500 compounded at **10.4%** annually for the same period.

HIGHLIGHTS FROM 2004's NOTES

Inflation Protection

With perhaps the most significant statement of the meeting, Buffett asserted that inflation is heating up in the U.S.

This explains Berkshire's shift from bonds to cash.

For inflation strategies, Buffett suggested, as a first line of defense, that one increase his/her earning power. For example, if you are the best surgeon or the best plumber in town, your wages will likely be more than indexed to inflation.

As a second strategy, Buffett recommended owning businesses that can price through inflation and have low capital expenditures to maintain the business.

He cited See's Candy as an example, noting that See's has been a business that can maintain its value regardless of current changes.

The worst sorts of businesses to own in an inflationary environment are ones that require lots of capital to stay in the game and provide no real return.*

Inflation is not the investor's friend. Munger noted that it is virtually ironclad that most people will get only a small return after inflation and taxes.

As another line of defense, Munger suggested avoiding having "a lot of silly needs in life."

Buffett exclaimed, "Charlie, we're selling consumer goods in the other room! It's OK to talk that way at home, but not here."

To which Munger replied, "I do talk that way at home, but it doesn't do any good."†

Independent Directions

In the furor over the lax behavior of directors, even Buffett has received heat.

Recently, Calpers challenged his independence as a board director of Coca-Cola.

In rebuttal, Buffett said that there is no substitute for thinking. There is no magic checklist that is going to tell you in all cases whether a director is independent.

---

* This describes most technology companies.
† As my grandmother used to say, "Be rich in the fewness of your wants."

Buffett argued that you could grab a man off the welfare line, pay him a $100,000 annual director's fee and he would meet the proposed qualification of "independent." Yet the man's entire income would ride on his fee!

Meanwhile, Berkshire owns roughly $10 billion worth of Coca-Cola stock, but Buffett is not considered "independent" by the proposed checklist. Yet who could care more about seeing that good decisions are made but the largest shareholder?

Buffett concluded, quoting Bertrand Russell, "Most men would rather die than think. Many do."

Good Compensation

Buffett allowed that managers can make a lot of money at Berkshire, but the bonuses are always related to *performance*.

For a good compensation agreement, he advised, you must understand the keys to the business and keep it simple.

In a rather remarkable digression, Buffett shared how he knew that the managers at MidAmerican Energy (David Sokol and Greg Abel) were extraordinary, but what compensation arrangement would be appropriate? He took three minutes to sketch out a proposal, showed it to Walter Scott, talked to Sokol and Abel about it, made some slight adjustments, and it was done.

He noted that the simple agreement they made with Chuck Huggins, manager of See's, in 1972 is still in place. Likewise, Berkshire's agreement with John Holland to run Fruit of the Loom runs a couple of paragraphs. At GEICO, bonuses are based on the two variables that count.*

Bad Compensation

In contrast, executive compensation in America exploded beyond all reason over the past decade.

Buffett noted that executive compensation spun out of control due to an "unequal intensity of interests." While the board might see it as play money, the CEO sees it as his livelihood. Thus, the CEO is most motivated to seek pliant board members.

Buffett quipped, "They don't look for Dobermans. They look for Chihuahuas that have been sedated."

---

* From past annuals, we believe those variables would be growth in policy holders (units) and the combined ratio (profitability).

Likewise, compensation consultants are brought in to make the CEO's case.

Munger concluded with characteristic understatement, "I would rather throw a viper down my shirt than hire a compensation consultant."

Guys Behaving Badly

Buffett and Munger went on to take their familiar shots at lawyers and the need for tort reform, at accountants and how they sold out America with spurious accounting and crooked tax shelters, at the mutual fund scandal and how hundreds knew but no one told, and more.

Rather than reprise all the discussion of the morally marginal here, we will summarize with Munger's quote about the old robber barons: "When they were talking, they were lying, and when they were silent, they were stealing."

Hair Trigger Markets

Munger noted that Berkshire had $31 billion of cash at year-end because they had no compelling alternatives.

Buffett remained hopeful for opportunity because "prices sometimes do amazing things in securities markets."

He noted that junk bonds in the fall of 2002 collapsed to where they had yields to maturity of 35%–40%. Some of these same bonds now yield just 6%—an incredible turnaround in just 18 months.

The St. Petersburg Paradox

Buffett asserted that the tendency to project out very high rates of growth has caused investors to lose tons of money.

The "new economy" bubble was characterized by many such projections.*

Buffett recommended an article by Durand written 30 years ago on the St. Petersburg Paradox for additional illumination.

As Buffett has often taught, the intrinsic value of an asset is the cash it will earn from here to eternity, discounted back to the present. However, if your estimated growth rate is greater than your discount rate, you get a value of infinity.

Clearly, Munger noted, you need to then back off to more realistic numbers.

---

* Bob Rodriguez of FPA has said the same thing, referencing parabolic curves.

While many analysts and companies persist in making 15% plus growth projections, Buffett observed that this year's Fortune 500 includes a 50-year retrospective that shows only a very few companies were able to grow at even 10% or better over that period.

Derivatives: A Mad Hatter's Tea Party

Buffett warned last year that derivatives could prove to be financial weapons of mass destruction. They have only gotten larger since.

While the original idea of derivatives was to disperse risk, he explained, the system now has intensified risk on a few institutions. "There is much more risk in the system because of derivatives," he concluded.

In the case of Freddie Mac, Buffett noted that the financials were scrutinized by hundreds of analysts, a congressional oversight committee, capable directors, auditors . . . and yet earnings were misstated by $6 billion—much of which was related to derivatives. It could just as easily have been off by $12 billion.

Buffett warned that the scale of derivatives gets ever-larger, yet most executives do not have their minds around them.

He confessed that he did not have his mind around the derivatives at Gen Re, and Berkshire is still unwinding that mess.*

Buffett noted another brush with derivatives for him occurred with the Salomon Brothers government bond trading scandal. Salomon very nearly filed bankruptcy with $1.2 trillion in derivatives. With Salomon having contracts in Japan and the U.K., as well as in the U.S., the bankruptcy judge would have had an enormous mess on his hands.

Munger noted the common error is not thinking through the consequences of the consequences.†

Buffett reflected that lots of things correlate that people don't expect to correlate.

Munger surmised that the whole thing is a Mad Hatter's Tea Party and that the accountants sold out.

Investment Temperament

Another fascinating discussion involved the role of temperament in investing.

While intelligence is helpful, Buffett and Munger asserted that having the proper temperament was far more critical.

---

* Six years after the acquisition.
† Garrett Hardin's 'ecolate' filter in his book *Filters Against Folly* asked, "And then what?"

Buffett mentioned the need to spend lots of time looking at companies and building your database and business understanding.

Munger agreed that one must read a lot to be wise, but curiously noted that he has found few among those who read a lot that have the proper temperament. Most get confused by the mass of information.

Buffett claimed that successful investing requires not extraordinary intellect but extraordinary discipline. Few have it. In fact, he mused, "What we learn from history is that people do not learn from history."

As a final proof, Buffett observed that Sir Isaac Newton, one of the most brilliant men in history, wasted a good portion of his days trying to turn lead into gold and lost an enormous sum in the South Sea Bubble.

Math

Munger boldly stated, "It is as if God made the world so only math can understand it."

He noted that if you are innumerate in business, you'll be a klutz. However, business does not require high math, and it may even be a disadvantage to know high math.

Buffett concluded with a smile, "When my mother sang me songs about compound interest, there was no need to go further."

Errors of Omission

Buffett noted that not maximizing the rare good idea has cost shareholders more than his sins of omission.

Though sins of omission do not hit the financial reports, Munger said that they still rub their noses in it.

Buffett said his failure to buy Wal-Mart has cost Berkshire shareholders $10 billion to date.

He said that he initially ran the idea by Charlie who said, "It isn't the worst idea you've ever had," which, coming from Charlie, Buffett took as "ungodly praise."

But he got anchored on a price of $23. When the price moved up, he stopped buying.

Our Own Worst Enemy

Munger observed that throughout history, people have gone crazy trying to know the future.

Ancient kings would have the royal fortuneteller look at sheep guts to make decisions. Today, people are still just as crazy as that king, looking for people who pretend to know the future, giving Wall Street economic incentive to sell its nostrum.

Combining the under-performance of the average mutual fund with the public's habit of frequently shuffling funds, the general public has gotten poor performance from contacting the "experts."

Buffett asserted that his underlying premise is that business will do well in America. While negative factors may move fearful investors to sell, it is important to remember that at any given point in history, there have always been negative factors. Yet despite wars, depressions, epidemics, etc., the Dow went from 66 to 10,000 during the 20th century.

He concluded, "It won't be America that does in investors. It will be the investors themselves."

Thinking About the Unexpected

Buffett noted that he spends a lot of time thinking about what could go wrong in big unexpected ways.

With low probability events, he asserted that people underestimate them if they haven't occurred for a while and overestimate them if they occurred recently.

He jokes, "Noah ran into that."

If there is, for example, a 10% chance of major nuclear disaster in a given year, then in 50 years, there is but a 0.5% chance there will not be such an event. To raise the odds to 1.0% would be meaningful improvement.

Last Man Standing

Financial calamities occur more often than natural ones, Buffett observed. So he advised, over the next 50 years, conduct yourself so that if there is a financial crunch, you'll get through.

That's why they don't believe in a lot of leverage at Berkshire. Throughout history, it is leverage that wipes people out.

Buffett marveled at the all the high-IQ people with huge desire to make money that got killed in the junk bond collapse in 2002. Wall Street is awash in money and talent, yet there are these huge swings in securities prices. This doesn't happen with apartments in Omaha or McDonald's franchises.

Munger noted that derivatives contracts can work just like margin accounts (a form of leverage). If a counterparty has a ratings downgrade, it has to put up more collateral, which, in turn, could cause a domino effect of selling to raise collateral.

Buffett cautioned that there only has to be one day you cannot meet a margin call.

He noted that absent the ability to raise capital, Gen Re could have run into terrible financial trouble after 9/11. Equities fell. Capital shrank. It could have triggered calls on that capital for derivatives positions.*

Buffett summed up with regard to financial calamities: (1) don't let it wipe you out, and (2) be prepared to take advantage. Berkshire is so positioned.

Buffett stated emphatically, "In a cataclysm, Berkshire would definitely be the last man standing."

National Indemnity: Getting the Incentives Right

Our favorite discussion of the day ensued after David Winters of Mutual Series asked about Berkshire's insurance underwriting disciplines.

As if he had been waiting for that question all day, Buffett whipped out slides showing National Indemnity's operating history.

Professor Buffett's first slide showed huge swings in premium volume over the past two decades at National Indemnity (NI) as the company executed its unique philosophy of writing for profit, not volume.†

At the same time, Berkshire kept the employees. Buffett was willing to suffer "high overhead" in low-volume times to teach employees that they would never be laid off for lack of volume.

This was reflected in an expense ratio that ranged widely from as low as 26% to as high as 41%.

Remarkably, staff count in 1980 was 372 and, in 2003, was 358.

With that focus on quality and discipline, NI has been profitable nearly every year, a record that Buffett claimed has left others in the dust.

The key has been having incentives in place to get the right employee behavior. And for that, you must think the business through.

Munger concluded, "Nobody else does it. It's the obvious way to go. Much of Berkshire is like that."

---

* Fully reconfigured, Gen Re is now AAA-rated again.
† Writing feverishly, I jotted down trough-to-peak premiums of 1980/$80 million, 1986/$366 million, 1998/$55 million and 2003/$600 million.

Habits for Life

When asked by a youngster for keys to living a good life, Buffett and Munger were full of advice.

Buffett noted that most people underestimate how important good habits are.

Munger added that it is critical to "avoid dumb stuff" like going to the race track, risking AIDS, experimenting with cocaine or getting into debt. He suggested developing good character and good mental habits and to learn as you go.

On a sobering note, Buffett said he receives letters every day from people in financial trouble, and he tells many of them to take bankruptcy since they'll never be able to catch up.

He warned that it is very tempting to spend more than you make. Buffett also recommended hanging around people better than you.

Munger added, "If that causes problems with your peers, the hell with them."

Buffett concluded with the story of the woman who turned 103 and was asked, "What do you like about being 103?" She responded, "No peer pressure."

Venue: Qwest Center

Attendance: Some 19,000

Details About This Year:

- A new book has been introduced to our curriculum, *Poor Charlie's Almanack* (a nod to Munger's hero, Ben Franklin). The book offers an excellent recounting of Charlie Munger's wit and insights over the years. Corey was especially excited to see that his question from last year's Wesco Financial meeting made it into the book.

Fortune 500 Ranking: 12th

Stock Price: $88,006

One dollar invested in 1964 would now be worth **$7,114**.

Berkshire's per-share book value has grown from $19.46 to **$59,734** (a rate of **21.5%** compounded annually).

The S&P 500 compounded at **10.4%** annually for the same period.

HIGHLIGHTS FROM 2005's NOTES

Don't Ask

Buffett opened his remarks by announcing he would not discuss three topics:

1. Last year's Nebraska football season*

2. What Berkshire is currently buying

3. Details of his testimony to regulators regarding the AIG probe as investigators prefer witnesses not talk publicly about their testimonies.

Pricing Power

Buffett noted that corporate profits as a percentage of GDP were very high and that corporate taxes as a percentage of total taxes were very low. Some reversion to the mean for corporate earnings is to be expected.†

Munger noted it is hard but essential to know who can pass through cost inflation.

Buffett added that "it is not a great business when you have a prayer session before raising prices a penny."

Buffett noted that he loves companies with untapped pricing power. See's Candy was an example where, in 1972, it sold 16 million pounds annually for $1.95 a pound (and a $25 million profit!). It could easily raise prices 10 cents a pound. Today, even newspapers and beer companies have found it much tougher to raise prices.

Buffett concluded that you can learn a lot about the durability of the economics of a business by observing price behavior.

Hair Trigger

Buffett claimed that there has never before been such a high percentage of money at a hair trigger with hedge funds, currency markets, the carry trade, etc.

There are billions of dollars riding on the press of a key.

This "electronic herd" could very well stampede due to some exogenous event a la Long-Term Capital Management in 1998.

---

* Please don't ask Corey, either.
† Bob Rodriguez of FPA and Michael Sandler of Clipper Fund also predict shrinking corporate margins with a likely dampening effect on the stock market.

While determining the timing is very difficult, predicting what will happen is easier.

Unlike a crowded theater where you can just leave your seat and run for the exit, in finance, you must find someone to take your seat. Someone must be on the other side of the transaction.

Munger summed up that it will end badly.*

Hard Landing?

Buffett asserted that current U.S. trade policy will have very significant consequences if unchanged.

He noted neither candidate addressed the issue in the last election.

Buffett disagreed with many observers who see a soft landing. With a $618 billion trade deficit, how do such numbers correct "softly"? And if they don't correct, the net international investment position will grow and compound.

To support his position, Buffett cited an op-ed piece in the *Washington Post*, in which former Fed Chairman Paul Volker shared his apprehension about these huge and possibly intractable imbalances.

Munger added that he is repelled by the lack of virtue in the use of consumer credit and the way public finance is run. Fortunately, Munger noted, a great civilization can bear a lot of abuse.

He went on to predict that we are at the apex of this great civilization.

Dollar Decline

Buffett noted that he could not see how we will have a rising dollar.

Buffett gave the analogy of a rich family with an estate so large they could not see the outer reaches of their domain. They simply waited at the porch for the produce to come in. They were unaware that they were consuming 6% more than what was being produced. And thus, they were trading away a portion of their estate in the process.

In a similar way, the U.S. is trading away $2 billion per day of her assets as we consume roughly 6% more than we produce. In time, our children will be paying "tribute" to foreign investors for our current over-consumption.

However, Munger challenged Buffett's sense of alarm, suggesting that if foreign holders eventually owned, say, 10% of the U.S. but our GDP grew 30% in the process, would that really be such a bad thing?

---

* With $66 billion in cash and bonds at the end of the first quarter, Berkshire stands ready to be the buyer of last resort.

Munger added that it is a queer occurrence to prefer currencies of socialized Europe to that of the U.S.

Buffett concluded that Berkshire has $21 billion in foreign exchange contracts. If it was up to him, they would have more. If it was up to Charlie, they would have none.

Asia Could Do Well

Buffett observed that global competition is heating up as everyone adopts our "best practices," and that is a good thing for all. More trade is better. With six billion people in the world, we should hope that a high percentage can live well in 20 years.

Munger concluded that America will get richer over time but may lose position in the world.

He suggested that Asia could do amazingly well.

Gold

While gold may be a refuge from a declining currency, Buffett observed that is true for *any* physical asset.

For example, if Berkshire sold See's Candy's and people dealt in seashells, Berkshire would get the appropriate number of seashells. Likewise for Coca-Cola, oil, an acre of land. Meanwhile, gold has little real utility. Some 3,000 to 4,000 tons of gold go from South Africa to Fort Knox annually and do not do much along the way.

Ever subtle, Munger noted that with the opportunities of Berkshire averaged out, gold is a dumb investment.

Buffett quantified: In 1940, gold was $35 per ounce. Sixty-five years later, it is $400 per ounce (not including carrying costs).*

Buffett concluded, "This is not something that causes me to salivate."

Real Estate Bubbles

Numerous questions were asked about real estate.†

Buffett reminisced about the bubble in farmland in Nebraska and Iowa 25 years ago. Cash was trash as inflation was out of control. This perception fueled the flight to farmland.

Buffett noted that north of Omaha, farmland got to $2,000 an acre—land that he bought after the bust from the FDIC for $600 an acre.

---

* A 3.8% compounded annual return.
† Which Corey and I take as a sure sign of a bubble.

Currently, Munger sees California and Washington D.C. as real bubbles with a 4 to 1 price ratio versus Omaha.

Buffett said he sold his Laguna Beach home for $3.5 million. He figured the house was worth $500,000, so the one-twentieth of an acre lot went for $3 million. He surmised that $60 million an acre is a pretty fancy price for any kind of land.

Munger recounted that a friend of his sold a modest home with an ocean view for $27 million.

Buffett quipped, "For $27 million, I'd rather stare at my bathtub."

Correlation of Risk

Buffett warned that when there is trouble, everything correlates. Thus, in managing catastrophic losses, one must think through the ripple effects.

California, for example, has had 25 6.0 earthquakes in the last 100 years. Such a quake in a populated area would have enormous consequences. At Berkshire, not only would it hit the insurance operations, but it would correlate with the businesses of See's Candy, GEICO, Wells Fargo and other Berkshire subsidiaries.

Buffett noted that the most powerful quake in America occurred in Madrid, Missouri, which has had three quakes of greater than eight on the Richter Scale.

Buffett observed that if you take a centuries-long view, you will see that extraordinary things have happened.

Munger noted that they have even contemplated a 60-foot tidal wave hitting California (which is not known to have ever happened).

He doubted that any other insurance company considers risk more rigorously than Berkshire.

Buffett added, "It's Armageddon around here every day."

Buffett concluded that with the way Berkshire conducts its affairs, he won't lose sleep no matter what.

Job 1: Nuclear Terrorism

Buffett shared that his number one concern was nuclear terrorism. He recommended a book.*

He also mentioned a website, LastBestChance.org, where they offer a free film sponsored by the Nuclear Threat Initiative.

---

* I believe it was *Nuclear Terrorism* by Graham Allison.

He noted that this issue was also little discussed in the last election.

Insurance-wise, Buffett said their entire book of business has been rewritten now to account for NCBs (nuclear, chemical and biological hazards).

Job 2: Education Reform

After the NCB problem, Buffett sees education as the nation's largest problem.

He believes that a good school system is like virginity: it can be preserved but not restored.

As a country with $40,000 of per capita income, we have the resources. Challenges include the complexity of the system, unions and the opting out of the rich. To the extent the rich go to private schools and the poor go to "armed camps," we create a two-tier system of unequal opportunity.

And Buffett reminded us, equal opportunity has been a big factor in America's success.

Easy Money

Buffett observed that mortgage terms have gotten easier and easier as housing prices have gotten higher and higher.

He noted this is absolutely counter to how the prudent think about lending.

Munger added that easy lending causes more building and higher prices. Eventually, when you have enough new anything, prices will decline.

Munger concluded that such Ponzi effects in society are very important and yet are studied very little.*

Incentives

One of the greatest insights we have learned from UBH is how hugely incentives influence what happens in the world.

Munger asserted that the history of what he doesn't like in modern corporations comes from the directive by headquarters to have earnings go up continually and smoothly, a practice he refers to as "the blood brother of evil."

---

* See *Poor Charlie's Almanack* for more.

Buffett noted that the world just does not work that way, and it leads to a lot of bad things. CEOs with big egos making precise predictions are kidding investors, themselves or both. This, in turn, sets up a system that exerts psychological and financial pressure to do things that people don't want to do.

Buffett said he would be an idiot to jump in a NetJet and say to the pilot, "I'm in a big hurry to get to New York." To rush the pilot through his safety procedures would be dumb. *Yet companies have done this sort of thing time after time with compensation systems that incentivize the wrong things.*

For example, many corporate managers are told to submit budgets and quarterly estimates. This leads to a short-term focus and undue worry about the quarter. A manager who does not want to let the boss down may fudge the numbers. At Berkshire, managers do not submit budgets.

He noted that in long tail insurance, the numbers can be pretty much whatever you want them to be. Berkshire's $45 billion in loss reserves could just as easily be $44.75 billion—especially if he wanted to report $250 million more in earnings.

Buffett opined that the worldwide tendency is for management to understate reserves.

General Motors

Continuing the theme of accounting and accountability, Buffett commented that Richard Wagoner at General Motors (GM) inherited cost structures brought about by contracts made long ago that now make the company uncompetitive.

These benefit obligations are said to run as much as $2,000 per car. With that cost disadvantage, GM has gone from a 50% share of the U.S. auto market to 25% today.

In a very real sense, General Motors could be said to be owned by its retirees, with $90 billion in retirement benefit obligations compared to just $14 billion of equity for shareholders.

The real problems date back to the 1960s. Contracts negotiated at that time bore no accounting consequences. Companies did not have to account for pension obligations on an accrual basis then. And it was not until the late 1980s that companies had to accrue for healthcare benefits.

As a result, earlier management agreed to generous annuity and health benefits for retired workers that have compounded into this enormous liability for the world's largest auto manufacturer.

Munger noted that when you fall from the 42nd floor to the 20th floor and you're doing fine, it does not mean that you don't have a serious problem.

Munger said if he were the owner of GM, he would solve the problem immediately.

Fannie and Freddie and Derivatives

Misbegotten incentives also lie behind the troubles at Fannie Mae and Freddie Mac.

Buffett acknowledged that things have changed a lot since he bought his house in 1958 and his parents sent him to see Mr. Brown at Occidental Savings and Loan. Today, mortgage issuers are geographically distant.

For 25 basis points to guarantee the mortgage, issuers need not worry about the individual property.

Buffett observed that Fannie Mae (FNM) and Freddie Mac (FRE) mushroomed into huge carry trade operations built on the spread between government borrowing costs and lending rates. Yet there is no way one should lend for 30 years to someone who can pay it off (i.e., refinance) in 30 seconds.

In addition, Buffett asserted that the accounting shenanigans have been mind boggling, with errors in the billions of dollars.

The crime of it, for Buffett, is that the government is on the hook for the implied guarantee of $1.5 trillion of mortgages, basically because FNM/FRE *wanted earnings to go up.*

In sum, the government created the two biggest hedge funds in history by issuing a blank check to entities trying to produce 15% per year earnings gains—and did it by accounting means when they could not do it by operations.

Buffett figured the system could absorb the problem if FNM/FRE went into a run-off mode for a time.

Munger added that a lot of the troubles came from the derivatives book. He asserted that stupid and dishonorable accountants allowed the genie of inappropriate accounting to come out of the bottle into the derivatives world.

Munger warned that there is much wrong with derivative accounting, and the full penalty has not been paid yet.

Buffett concluded, "We're a long way from Jimmy Stewart in *It's a Wonderful Life.*"

Great Managers: It's the Wiring

Buffett noted the best way to find great managers is to look at the record.

It's tough to go to the practice tee and predict the best golfers just from their golf swings.

Mixing sports metaphors, he noted that the best batters are the ones with the best batting averages.

Buffett referenced an old study that found the top correlation of great managers to be the age at which managers started their first businesses.

Buffett believes it has far more to do with the wiring than he would have thought 30 years ago.

Munger added that it is also part intelligence and part temperament. Munger found he liked business very early and loved trying to win at games of chance.

Buffett concluded humorously, "Since my dad would not let me be a bookie, I went into investing."*

Be Out of Step

Buffett suggested that the best investment you can make is to invest in yourself. As for where they put their money at Berkshire, they seek to be opportunistic.

Munger noted that Berkshire does no asset allocation. They merely go where the opportunities are regardless of categories, and that is *totally* out of step with modern investment theory.

Buffett noted that they got $7 billion into junk bonds in 2002 but would have invested $30 billion if the bonds had stayed cheap.

Regarding modern asset allocation, Munger concluded, "If a thing is not worth doing at all, it's not worth doing well."

Social Security

Buffett emphasized that Social Security is not insurance but a transfer payment.

He stated his belief that a rich country should take care of the young and the old, so Social Security should not be taken below its current level.

---

* Clearly, Munger and Buffett have the wiring.

Buffett also considered as crazy all this fear of a deficit 25 years from now when we have a $500 billion deficit now. Currently, 4% of GDP goes to Social Security. To think it might go to 5% or 6% of GDP many years from now is not a terrible thing.

Buffett recommend three remedies: means test, lift the $90,000 tax limit way up and raise the retirement age.

Munger allowed that he is a right-wing Republican but still thinks the Republicans are "out of their cotton-pickin' minds" to take on this issue.

He figured a logical way to handle future spending needs would be a consumption tax.

Munger declared that Social Security is one of the best things government has ever done. There is nearly no fraud as it is hard to fake being dead. It is a reward for work, which befits a capitalistic society.

Munger thought it sad that our leaders are wasting goodwill over this "twaddle" when they may need it if we need to face down North Korea or Iran.

10-Year Returns

Buffett noted that Berkshire has a smaller percentage of its net worth in stocks than any time since 1969.

Though there is not as much silliness in the market as there was five years ago, Buffett sees the market in a zone of valuation where he is neither a buyer nor a seller.

From this level, Buffett thought to earn 6% to 7% in stocks over the long run would be a reasonable expectation.

Tax-wise, investors are better treated than at any time in his lifetime. People expecting 10% or more from these levels, however, are unrealistic.

Buffett noted that, while there have been a few times of extreme valuations—1969, 1974 and 1999—most of the time we are in that in-between zone.

Buffett remained hopeful that Berkshire would get the chance to do something "screamingly intelligent" in the next few years.

Long Term, America Richer

When you are buying groceries, you welcome lower prices. Buffett said Berkshire is the same way. They will be glad to see temporarily low prices, so they can put their cash to work.

While concerned about hair triggers and imbalances in the short run, Buffett stated that he is an enormous bull on the U.S. economy long term.

In 1790, there were four million people in America, 290 million in China and 100 million in Europe. Yet 215 years later, America has 30% of the world's GDP.

It is an incredible success story.

Venue: Qwest Center

Attendance: 24,000 or so

Details About This Year:

- This year's meeting lasted the now-expected five to six hours.
- According to Corey's notes, there were 13 people at the meeting in 1980. So this year's turnout suggests a compounded annual growth rate in attendance of nearly 34% over the last 26 years. Berkshire's attendance numbers have surpassed the local university (the University of Nebraska Omaha has 15,000 students).

Fortune 500 Ranking: 13th

Stock Price: $88,710

One dollar invested in 1964 would now be worth **$7,171**.

Berkshire's per-share book value has grown from $19.46 to **$70,281** (a rate of **21.4%** compounded annually).

The S&P 500 compounded at **10.3%** annually for the same period.

HIGHLIGHTS FROM 2006's NOTES

ISCAR Acquisition

Buffett and Munger opened the meeting with the announcement of Berkshire's $4 billion purchase of 80% of ISCAR, an Israeli-based manufacturer of machine tools.

The usually even-tempered Buffett and Munger were very enthusiastic about the deal.

Key points include that it is the first business Berkshire has purchased outside the U.S., that the purchase increases the amount Berkshire will earn in foreign currencies and that the management is terrific.

Buffett was especially taken by ISCAR CEO Eiton Wertheimer and his family-style culture, which was reflected in the fact that ISCAR was not put up for auction.*

Buffett concluded, "I think we'll look back on this in five or 10 years and see this as a very significant event in Berkshire's history."

Cash Going Down

Buffett has been very patient sitting on the Berkshire cash horde through a period of very low short-term interest rates.

At last year's meeting, he mentioned the "D" word ("dividend"). This year, he changed his tune, indicating he thought it likely that over the next three years they will have less cash on hand.

He also said Berkshire needs to keep a minimum of $10 billion around in reserves for mega-cat insurance policies written.

So with around $40 billion on hand currently, Berkshire would need to invest $30 billion over the next three years. Well, not quite. Berkshire will also throw off more than $10 billion in cash annually, so that's another $30 billion over three years for Buffett to invest.†

---

* We wonder if a side benefit of the deal may be that Berkshire can allocate additional capital to Wertheimer's talented management team in the future.

† So Buffett is implying that he thinks it likely that Berkshire can invest $30 billion to $60 billion over the next three years! How? We see at least three large possibilities: more international acquisitions, utility industry acquisitions, and Buffett's stock in trade, bargain shopping in the midst of calamity.

Envy

During the Salomon Brothers government bond scandal, Buffett sat on Salomon's compensation committee and witnessed the "frenzy of envy in investment banking." If one guy received a bonus of $2 million and the next guy got $2.1 million, the first guy would be miserable for the next year. So it is envy, not greed, that is the dominant sin among investment bankers.

Buffett opined that envy is the least fun of the seven deadly sins because it leaves you feeling awful.

Gluttony has some upside—Buffett jested that some of his best times were with gluttony. As for lust . . . he joked that he wouldn't go there. He concluded that envy is interesting in that it is widely practiced and, yet, is the least enjoyable sin.

Munger, adding an ironic sidebar, noted that the SEC now requires CEO pay to be listed. While it was hoped this added transparency would rein in egregious compensation, the list has had the opposite effect. Envious CEOs use it as a shopping list for seeking pay raises.

Succession

Year after year, this question is unfailingly asked: "What happens after Warren is gone?"

Buffett noted that there are three obvious successors, and it will be up to the board.

He referred to Wal-Mart as an example of "personalized institutional legacy," where the company has become even stronger since the founder passed on.*

Speaking for the heirs of the Munger clan, Charlie shared, "We prefer to wring the last drop of good out of Warren."

Munger concluded rhetorically, "Do you really think Warren Buffett will blow the job of passing on the faith?"

Finding Great Managers

On the subject of great managers, Buffett and Munger again explained how they keep it simple.

---

* Unlike 20 years ago, Buffett now has a deep bench of managerial talent and a world-class board, so we're not losing any sleep over it.

Munger emphasized that Berkshire does not train executives, it *finds* them.

Buffett referenced a letter that led to the ISCAR acquisition. He said CEO Eitan Wertheimer's character and talent jumped off the page.

Munger concluded, "If a mountain like Mount Everest stands up, you don't have to be genius to see it's a high mountain."

Corporate Governance

Regarding corporate governance, Munger predicted that the current fashions in government regulations would have little effect.

Buffett asserted the real question for boards of directors to consider is, "To what extent do the managers think like owners?"

Buffett said he sees an *enormous* difference in boards based on that.

According to Buffett, the job of the board is to 1) get the right CEO, 2) keep the CEO from overreaching and 3) exercise independent judgment on acquisitions.

Based on these priorities, boards have not done too well in recent years. Meanwhile, Berkshire has assembled a first-class board. Buffett claimed proudly that no other board in America has a larger percentage of its net worth in the company purchased on the open market than Berkshire.*

In/Out/Too Hard

One of our favorite Mungerisms of the meeting was his explanation of the Berkshire idea-handling process.

There are three boxes—"in," "out" and "too hard." It is important to know what is too hard for you and stick to what you do best.

He quoted IBM CEO Tom Watson, "I'm smart in spots."

Buffett noted that if you're fast, you can run the 100 meters for the gold medal. You don't have to throw the shot put.

Munger shared that a reporter once said to him, "You don't seem smart enough to be doing so much better than everyone else." The key is knowing the edge of one's circle of competence.

Ethanol

While ethanol is a hot topic nationally, Buffett and Munger were decidedly unenthusiastic.

---

* Hence our mantra: good ownership drives good stewardship.

Buffett noted that, as a general rule, he ignores what is hot.

Furthermore, with all the government subsidies, it's not clear what the return on equity on an ethanol plant would be five years out. Historically, agricultural processing has not earned high returns on capital.

For Buffett, the key question is, "How can you gain a significant competitive advantage?" With commodities, if you get too many producers, you'll have poor returns.

Munger was even more of a wet blanket, suspecting that more fossil fuel energy is used than is created in the ethanol process.

Ever the diplomat, Munger concluded that "ethanol is a stupid way to solve an energy issue."*

Pumpkins to Mice

Buffett noted that any asset class that has had a big move will eventually attract speculation. That is now the case with copper and a number of other commodities.

In a startling admission, Buffett informed the crowd that he sold his much-heralded silver position some time ago for a modest profit.

Munger contributed two gems to this discussion.

Regarding Buffett's admission of selling silver too soon, Munger said, "It's a good habit to trumpet your failures and be quiet about your successes."

Regarding future speculation, Munger noted, "We have failed to profit from one of the biggest commodity booms in history. And in that way, we will probably continue to fail."

Buffett summed up that speculative markets become like Cinderella at the ball. At midnight, they will turn to pumpkins and mice. Each player wants one more glass of champagne, one more dance, and then they'll get out in time. But there are no clocks on the wall.

Manufactured Housing

Berkshire became a big player in the manufactured housing industry with the acquisition of Clayton Homes several years ago.

Berkshire has made a number of expansionary moves in the industry since. At this meeting, they let shareholders know why.

Costing around $45 per square foot, manufactured homes offer good value.

---

* The Renewable Fuels Association reports there are 101 ethanol plants in the U.S. and 32 more under construction. An estimated 20% of the corn crop is now going to ethanol production. There are three IPOs of ethanol producers coming in the very near future.

With 130,000 units produced last year, the industry accounted for just 6% of all homes built. In better years, the industry has produced 20% of all homes.

The industry got oversold five years ago after years of abuse. This hangover phase included working through a lot of "dumb" financing. The aftermath produced numerous bankruptcies and a capital markets squeeze.

Buffett chortled that "Clayton is so good, it's hard to find No. 2."

While it will take a few years, Munger sees manufactured housing eventually taking a much larger share—"it's so logical."

Buffett predicted that the industry will get to 200,000 units or more and that Clayton could easily be the biggest homebuilder in the U.S. someday.

Stick-Built Housing Bubble

Munger sees the same sins that collapsed the manufactured housing industry five years ago resurfacing in the stick-built industry.

Buffett noted that loose lending has run amuck. He cited with particular interest how some lenders are counting as income interest accrued but not paid.

Munger concluded that it's yet another case of "dumb lending assisted by corrupt accounting." Buffett quipped, "Our auditing bill just went up."

Buffett noted that in some coastal markets, the day-traders of the Internet bubble became the day-traders of condos. Now he believes that the speculative bubble has clearly turned and that a significant downward adjustment from the peak is underway.

Coca-Cola

When asked about Coca-Cola, Buffett marveled that it now sells 21 billion cases of product and sells more units every year.

In 1997, the stock was 80 with $1.50 per share of low-quality earnings. Today, the stock is 44 with $2.17 a share of better-quality earnings.

Every year, the company gets a little greater share of the liquids consumed around the world and earns fabulous returns doing it.

Coca-Cola earns 100% pre-tax on tangible assets.

If Coke annually sells 5% more units and global population grows 2% annually, Coke will necessarily be selling evermore liquids to go down evermore throats. And that has been happening since 1886.

Buffett summed up, "Coke has been and will be a great business. We'll own it 10 years from now."

Insurance and Hurricanes

Buffett offered a fascinating glimpse of how he looks at risk and reward.

Buffett noted that Berkshire is the No. 1 mega-catastrophe underwriter in the world. Prices are up a lot. But are the exposures up even more? Which is more meaningful—the last 100 years of hurricanes or the last two years of hurricanes? The water temperatures have changed. Nobody really knows what will happen.

At this point, you and I might choose the "too hard" box. Not Buffett and Munger. Buffett announced his mega-bet: "We're in. If the last two years hold, we're not getting enough. If the last 100 years hold, we're getting paid plenty."

Buffett then thought even bigger. Katrina was a $60 billion event. Berkshire took a $3.4 billion hit.

Buffett theorized that there could be a disaster as great as four times Katrina, or $250 billion. In that event, Buffett estimated that Berkshire's exposure would be 4%, or $10 billion.

For that reason, Buffett wants to maintain at least a $10 billion cash position. Buffett asserted, "We can play bigger than anyone and still pay."

Perhaps sensing some shareholder shock at these big numbers, Munger summed up, "Why shouldn't we use our capital strength when others are frightened?"*

Media

Long a favorite Buffett area of investment, the world of media now offers a huge variety of sources, many of them free.

Meanwhile, there has been no corresponding expansion of time for humans to acquire information and entertainment.

So media economics will continue to deteriorate as competition increases. For newspapers, TV and cable, the future will be less attractive than the past.

---

* Some more thoughts: Berkshire has float of $48 billion to 49 billion, or about 10% of the property casualty industry. Yet when the Katrina losses were tabulated, Berkshire's share of the $60 billion disaster was $3.4 billion, or just 5.7%. In Buffett's monster disaster scenario, he has Berkshire tallying just 4% of the total loss.

Question: How can Buffett occasionally be "all in," yet be so much less exposed percentage-wise than the general industry? Shrewd people, yes?

Derivatives

Buffett was early in warning of the potential dangers of the widespread use of derivatives.

He said it is hard to predict what might happen, but strange things do happen—like the Long-Term Capital Management debacle in 1998.

In a riveting digression, Buffett said Salomon Brothers in 1991 was within 30 minutes of bankruptcy. The lawyers were drawing up the papers for it. However, Nick Brady, the Treasury secretary, knew Berkshire and trusted Warren. At the last minute, the Treasury reversed itself.

It could have been absolute chaos with Salomon's $700 million book of derivatives.

Of course, those numbers are peanuts today. Buffett concluded, saying derivatives are much bigger now, though better collateralized.

Weaker Dollar: Hard Landing

Buffett disagrees with those pundits that are predicting a "soft landing."

Buffett feels "stronger than ever" about his weak dollar view. He called it a very high probability that the U.S. currency will weaken over the years given our current policies.

Buffett noted that Greenspan said in 2002 that the current account deficit—then $350 billion—must be restrained. It has doubled since then. The U.S. is a net debtor to the world to the tune of $3 trillion.

Buffett mused about how portfolio insurance led to a 22% decline in the stock market in one day (1987's Black Monday).

Like with portfolio insurance two decades ago, Buffett predicted currency markets will be a catalyst for some future decline.

Buffett believes our eventual comeuppance will almost surely be painful, and when "fire" is yelled, the currency market will play a part in the rush for the door.

Inflation

Buffett noted that the CPI (Consumer Price Index) is not a particularly good measure of inflation.

First, "core" inflation excludes food and energy. "Not much is more core!" Buffett exclaimed. Second, since CPI uses a rent equivalent factor for living costs, it hasn't captured the rising cost of housing. In sum, the CPI understates inflation.

Munger noted that inflation is where you look.

A Costco board member, Munger reported that Costco has seen almost no inflation in its composite flow of goods. LIFO (last in, first out) adjustments for both Costco and Wal-mart have been peanuts. Meanwhile, such adjustments have been big for the jewelry, carpet and steel businesses.

Buffett noted that one possible side effect of the weaker dollar could be significant inflation. It is tempting for governments to devalue what they owe to reduce the burden of debt repayment

Opportunity Cost

Munger summed up this key concept as succinctly as ever: "To measure opportunity cost, take your best available opportunity versus all other options." Concentrate in your best one or two ideas.

He went on to say in his understated way, "That's why modern portfolio theory is so asinine."

Buffett noted that often the best opportunities come in the midst of some convulsion. The key is to buy when others are paralyzed. Stocks in 1974. Junk bonds in 2002. Several years ago, numerous Korean companies sold for three times earnings.

The key is to follow logic rather than emotion. Focus on what is important and knowable rather than on public opinion.

One fascinating side note, Buffett observed, "Any calls you get on Sunday, you're going to make money." Those rare calls are the best since they are inevitably from seriously distressed sellers.

He concluded that if you buy convulsion and remember that the market is there to serve you, not instruct you, then you cannot miss.

Munger corrected his partner, "Some of you probably can miss."

Terrorism: Ultimate Challenge

Buffett labeled terrorism as "the ultimate challenge of mankind," noting it is a worst-case problem.

Out of a global population of six billion, there will always be a small percentage of crazy people bent on doing others harm. Technology enables the unbalanced few to do unprecedented damage. Where 1,000 years ago, they might have thrown rocks or shot arrows, now there are nuclear, biological and chemical weapons in the mix.

Munger noted that the chance of going 60 years with no nuclear events was close to zero.

Buffett somberly noted that the best we can do is to keep the leaders awake to minimizing the threat.

Low Turnover = Owner Attitude

Buffett threw in a chart measuring Berkshire's annual share turnover, so here's another point he really wanted to make.

Berkshire had 14%, Exxon Mobil 76%, GE 48%, and Wal-Mart 79%.

Buffett asserted that Berkshire has the lowest turnover of any major company, and that is attributable to the owner attitude of Berkshire's shareholders.

Venue: Qwest Center

Attendance: 27,000

Details About This Year:

- This year features Corey's notes exclusively as Daniel attended another institutional learning event that day—his son John's graduation from Iowa State University.

Fortune 500 Ranking: 12th

Stock Price: $110,089

One dollar invested in 1964 would now be worth **$8,900**.

Berkshire's per-share book value has grown from $19.46 to **$78,008** (a rate of **21.1%** compounded annually).

The S&P 500 compounded at **10.4%** annually for the same period.

HIGHLIGHTS FROM 2007's NOTES

Good First Quarter

Buffett announced that Berkshire had a good first quarter (with net earnings of $2.6 billion, or $1,682 per A share).

He noted that insurance earnings will go down with a lag effect. After an extraordinary period with no major disasters, the insurance businesses have booked huge profits. However, competition has caused premium rates to go down, so insurance profits will follow suit.

Buffett warned that when hurricanes occur, Berkshire will have losses, so look at last year's profit as an offset to future losses.

He noted that most of the non-insurance businesses did fine. The exception would be in the residential-construction-related businesses like Shaw and Acme Brick, which were hit hard by the housing slowdown.

Buffett guessed that weakness there could continue for quite a while.

Overall, Buffett believes his managers continue to do a sensational job. He proudly declared, "We have the best managers and shareholders of any company."

Berkshire CIO Hunt

Buffett caused a stir by announcing in the annual report that he is looking for an investment manager to succeed him.

He noted he wants someone who not only learns from what has happened but can also envision things that have never happened, especially in regard to risks.

He shared that they've received about 700 applications, including one from a man recommending his 4-year old son.

Buffett reminisced that he undertook a similar process in 1969 when he closed the Buffett Partnership and had to recommend to his investors where they should put 100% of their money.

He chose Charlie Munger, Sandy Gottesman and Bill Ruane. Charlie wasn't interested in more partners. Sandy took separate accounts and has done very well for his clients. Bill Ruane set up a separate mutual fund (the Sequoia Fund), which has also done very well.

Stewardship: Brains Plus Caution

Later in the meeting, when asked about some sort of managed futures fund, Buffett noted that it isn't the investment structure that makes an opportunity. "It's brains that make an area of opportunity."

At the same time, Buffett noted his concern several times during the meeting that some very smart people have lost a lot of money. The problem is that anything times zero is zero. No matter how good the record was in every other year, if there is just one year with a zero, it's all over.

Buffett noted that he and Charlie have seen guys go broke or close to it because 99 of 100 of their decisions were good, but the 100th did them in.*

Derivatives and the Crowded Trade

Buffett claimed that derivatives introduce invisible leverage into the system and have made any regulation of margin requirements a joke.

We may not know when it becomes a super danger or when it will end precisely, but he believes it will go on and increase until very unpleasant things happen because of it.

As one example of what can happen under forced sales, Buffett reviewed October 19, 1987: The infamous Black Monday when the Dow Jones Average dropped 23% in a single day.

It was driven by portfolio insurance, which was a joke. It was a bunch of stop/loss orders, but done automatically, and the concept was heavily marketed. People paid a lot of money for people to teach them how to put in a stop/loss order.

When a lot of institutions do this, the effect is like pouring gas on a fire. They created a doomsday machine that kept selling and selling.

You can have the same thing today because you have fund operators with billions of dollars—in aggregate, trillions of dollars—who will all respond to the same stimulus. It's a crowded trade, but they don't know it. And it's not formal. They will sell for the same reasons. Someday, you will get a very chaotic situation.

As for what could trigger this and when, who knows? Who had any idea that shooting an archduke would start World War I?

Munger asserted that enormously deficient accounting contributes to the risk. If you get paid enormous bonuses based on profits that don't exist, you'll keep going. What makes it difficult to stop is that most of the accounting profession doesn't realize how stupidly it's behaving.

One person told Munger that the accounting is better because positions are marked to market and said, "Don't you want real-time information?"

---

* A current example is the Bear Stearns High-Grade Structured Credit Fund, which, as we related in our Market Update, boasted 30 consecutive months of profits but is now facing heavy losses due to its combination of extreme leverage and illiquid mortgage securities.

Munger replied that if you can mark to market to report any level of profits you want, you'll get terrible human behavior. The person replied, "You just don't understand accounting."

Buffett said that when he went to close out Gen Re's derivatives book, Berkshire took a $400 million loss on a portfolio that was "marked to market" by the prior management and auditors.

Buffett joked that he wished he could have sold to the auditors instead!

Munger concluded, "As sure as God made little green apples, this will cause a lot of trouble. This will go on and on, but eventually will cause a big denouement."

The Electronic Herd

One element contributing to the crowded trade risk is the rise of what Buffett calls "the electronic herd."

Buffett observed that the percentage of securities that can be sold at the touch of a button has gone up a lot. There's nothing necessarily evil about it. But it's a different game, and there are consequences. If you're trying to beat the other fellow on a daily basis, you're looking to push the button quicker and quicker.

Buffett shared that when he and Charlie were at Salomon, they talked about five or six sigma events, but that doesn't mean anything when you're talking about real markets and human behavior. Look at what happened in 1998 and in 2002. You'll see it when people try to beat the markets day by day.

Credit Contractions

Buffett observed that we have had major credit contractions in the past. One occurred during the junk bond crisis in 2002 and another with equities in 1974.

Buffett doesn't think a contraction of credit will come from the Fed stepping on the brakes.

More likely, he believes, would be an exogenous event to shock the system. That, in turn, could cause a huge widening of credit spreads and a cheapening of equities. That would be good for Berkshire because it has the money to take advantage of such an event.

Buffett reminisced that in the old days, when credit contracted, there was *no* money around.

He mentioned trying to buy a bank in Chicago 30 or 40 years ago, and the only people willing to lend to Berkshire were in Kuwait and would only lend in dinars. Now that was a credit contraction!

He cited Jon Alter's book, *The Defining Moment: FDR's Hundred Days and the Triumph of Hope*, for describing how the country was close to the brink and how FDR got laws passed as fast as he could write them. In this case, that was a good thing because banks were closing, and people were dealing in scrip.

While he doesn't see the Fed orchestrating a contraction, he noted that the Long-Term Capital Management blowup in 1998 seized-up world markets. People panicked about even the safest of instruments.

He concluded, "History doesn't repeat itself, but it rhymes. We'll have something that rhymes."

The Declining Dollar

Buffett believes the dollar will likely decline against most major currencies over time unless current policies change in a major way.

When the carry trade made it expensive to own foreign currencies directly (at one point Berkshire had over $20 billion in foreign exchange contracts), Buffett shifted his focus to buying companies that earn a lot in foreign currencies.

Berkshire does have positions in foreign companies in its portfolio, listing Petro China, POSCO and Tesco in the 2007 annual report.

In addition, Berkshire owns U.S. based companies that have global operations.

He noted he would own Coca-Cola whether it was based in the U.S. or in Amsterdam.

He admitted that Berkshire is not well-known outside of the U.S. But that is changing since Eitan Wertheimer (CEO of ISCAR) entered the Berkshire fold. Wertheimer is going through a procedure to get Berkshire better-known abroad.

Buffett assured shareholders that the entire world is on his radar screen and that Berkshire hopes to be on the world's radar screen in the future.

Buffett surmised that Berkshire has a pretty good group of businesses for the world we face. While we may not know which will be super-winners, a significant number will do okay.

Buffett said he doesn't buy businesses with much thought of world trends, but he does think about whether businesses are subject to foreign competition, have high labor content and/or have products that can be shipped in.

He noted that oil went from $30 to $60 a barrel while the euro went from 83 cents per dollar to $1.35. Thus, the price of oil for Europeans rose only 25%, while for Americans, it rose 100%.

He concluded that it is easy to get anchored in your own currency. He also teased that Berkshire owns one currency position right now that will surprise us when we hear about it next year.

The Subprime Mortgage Mess

We have expressed great concerns about the subprime mortgage meltdown.

However, Buffett does not see that this will be "a huge anchor on the economy."

Especially if unemployment and interest rates do not go up, Buffett believes it unlikely this factor alone will trigger anything major in the general economy.

However, that's not to say Buffett didn't find anything wrong with what happened.

He called it "dumb lending" for lenders to make a high percentage of loans where people make tiny payments early on and hope to make it up with higher payments later. Someone who can only make 20–30% of a full payment now isn't going to be able to make 110% payments in the future.

The real bet was that housing prices would keep going up. Now that has stopped, and there is plenty of misery in the field, especially on the coasts.

Munger chimed in that much of the sin and folly was due to accountants who let lenders book profits when no one in their right mind would have allowed them to do so. If accountants lie down on the job, you see huge folly.

Buffett concluded that it will be at least a couple of years before real estate recovers. The people who were counting on flipping the homes are going to get flipped, but in a different way.

Executive Compensation

While there have been some remarkable examples of outrageous executive compensation, Buffett asserted the larger problem is having the wrong manager rather than the wrong compensation system.

It's an enormously difficult thing to run a big company, so the greater sin is having the wrong person.

As he's pointed out in prior years, what really drives the compensation insanity is envy, not greed. Someone getting paid $2 million might be quite happy until they hear about someone else that got $2.1 million.

In addition, compensation consultants know that getting hired in the future depends on a recommendation from the CEO, so they are not interested in low-balling what the compensation should be.

If the boards do not negotiate with some intensity, there is really no one to represent the shareholders. Buffett concludes that under those circumstances, it's an unfair fight.

Boards of Directors

Buffett's view is that the most important job of the board is to pick the right CEO.

The second most important job is to prevent the CEO from over-reaching, which often happens in acquisitions.

The CEO often stacks the deck before he proposes the deal and, with all the focus on the acquired value to be gained, seldom carefully considers how much value is being given away.

Buffett used himself as an example, noting that when he gave away 2% of Berkshire to acquire Dexter shoes, it was a dumb move, especially considering what 2% of Berkshire is worth today.

At Berkshire, Buffett has compiled a superb board and has encouraged ownership.

He noted that everyone on the board at Berkshire has a lot of Berkshire stock. Thus, they are in the same position as shareholders. They don't have directors and officers insurance, and they have purchased the stock in the open market. It's a real owner's board.[*]

Modest Expectations

Buffett's *Fortune* article in 1999 was right on, suggesting that future market returns were bound to be much more modest after 17 years of well-above-average returns in the 1980s and 1990s.

He shared that if he were writing today, he would expect equities to do better than the 4.75% being paid by Treasury securities—not necessarily high expectations for equities but higher than that for

---

[*] Note to regulators—here's a corporate governance model worth examining.

bonds for sure. And to the extent he does own bonds, he's 100% in short-term maturities.*

Buffett has clearly acted on his views, increasing the percentage of Berkshire's investment portfolio allocated to stocks from 41% to over 51% over the last 15 months.

Munger summed up that Warren was right in 1999 that the experience from owning equities from that point would be pretty lean, so he suspects Warren is right again to have modest expectations now.

Corporate Profits

U.S. corporations have been earning record profits with record profit margins.

Buffett said he's been amazed. Corporate profits as a percentage of GDP have been higher only two or three years out of the past 75. Historically, when corporate profits get to around 8% of GDP, there's a reaction, such as higher taxes.

Buffett noted that to have lots of businesses earning 20% on tangible equity in a world where corporate bonds are yielding 4–5% is astonishing.

He suspects Congress may do something to change this.

Buffett concluded that Corporate America is living in a great time, but history shows that this is not sustainable.

Munger noted that the extreme expansion of consumer credit has played a role. There's been a huge flow of profits to banks and investment banks. Other countries with extreme consumer credit have suffered bad consequences, such as South Korea.

He surmised that this is not a good time to swing for the fences.

Buffett added that the bust in South Korea produced some of the cheapest stock prices he's ever seen.

Private Equity Bubble

Unlike other bubbles, Buffett doesn't see this one popping anytime soon but perhaps slowly deflating over a number of years.

Since the money is locked up for 5–10 years, it's not like people can or will leave in a panic. More likely is a gradual slow down, especially if the spread between high-yield bonds and safe bonds widens.†

---

* Which is identical to the view of FPA's Bob Rodriguez, who sees "no value in bond land."
† Which is happening right now.

Another factor driving the boom is that if you have a $20 billion fund and get a 2% fee, you take in fees of $400 million a year. But you can't raise another fund until you get the first one invested, so there is a great rush to get all these funds invested quickly so that you can go raise money for the next fund.

Buffett allowed that Berkshire cannot compete against these buyers and that it might be some time before disillusion sets in.

Munger concluded that things like this can continue for a long time after you're in a state of total revulsion.

Buffett quipped, "The voice of total optimism has spoken."

Newspapers

Buffett had a great thought picture to explain the long-term fate of the newspaper industry.

Suppose Johannes Gutenberg, the inventor of modern printing, had been a day trader or hedge fund manager instead so that printing was never invented. Then along came the Internet and cable TV.

Now imagine someone coming up with this idea to chop down trees, buy expensive printing presses and a fleet of trucks, all to get pieces of paper to people to read about what happened yesterday.

It wouldn't happen.

It just turned out that newspapers came first, so they have some momentum. But you're not going to reverse the decline.

Buffett noted that earnings at the *Buffalo News* are down 40% from the peak.

Similarly, the shift to the digital world has decimated World Book Encyclopedia, where unit sales have dropped from 300,000 to 22,000.

Gambling: A Tax on Ignorance

Buffett noted that people simply like to gamble. And as more states legalize it, it gets easier for people to do so.

He shared that he had a slot machine in his house and taught his children a good lesson with it. He'd give his children any allowance that they wanted, and he'd have it all back by nightfall. He joked that his slot machine had a terrible pay-out ratio.

Buffett asserted that to a large extent, gambling is a tax on ignorance. You put it in, and it ends up taxing many that are least able to pay while relieving taxes on those who don't gamble.

He finds it socially revolting when a government preys on its citizens rather than serving them. A government shouldn't make it easy for people to take their Social Security checks and waste them by pulling a handle. In addition, other negative social things can flow from gambling over time.

Buying Businesses

Buffett favors great businesses, which he defines as those having a high return on capital for a long period of time, where he thinks management will treat shareholders right.

Ideally, Buffett buys these businesses for 40 cents on the dollar, but he'll pay closer to a dollar for a really great business.

Munger piped in that margin of safety means getting more value than you're paying. It's applied high school algebra. However, there is no one easy mechanical formula to determine intrinsic value and margin of safety. You have to apply lots of models. So it takes time to get good at it. You don't become a great investor rapidly any more than you become a bone-tumor specialist quickly.

He added that he has no system for estimating the correct value of all businesses and, in fact, puts almost all in the "too hard" pile and sifts through the few easy ones.

Buffett broke it down into an example:

Let's say you want to buy a farm, and you calculate that you can make $70/acre as the owner. How much will you pay for that farm?

You might decide you wanted a 7% return, so you'd pay $1000/acre.

If it's for sale at $800/acre, you buy, but if it's for sale for $1200/acre, you don't.

You wouldn't base this decision on what you saw on TV or what a friend said. You would do your own homework.

It's the same with stocks.

Buffett emphasized that the ability to generate cash and reinvest is critical. He noted that it is the ability to generate cash that gives Berkshire its value. In addition, it is important to understand the competitive position and dynamics of the business and look into the future.

If you were thinking about paying $900,000 or $1.3 million for a McDonald's stand, you'd better think about things like whether people will keep eating hamburgers and whether McDonald's could change the franchise agreement.

Buffett has taught in past years that it is important to know the one or two key factors in each business you own. This year, he mentioned that when he bought into USAir, an airline with high seat-mile costs of 12 cents, it was protected. However, trouble ensued when Southwest showed up with 8-cent costs.

Buffett also noted that with evaluating oil and gas managers, he believes the key variable should be finding costs.

Finally, Buffett stressed the importance of staying within one's circle of competence. Buffett said a large part of his success has come from knowing how to recognize and step over one-foot bars and to recognize and avoid the seven-foot bars.

Become a Learning Machine

Munger has often extolled Buffett's relentless thirst for learning, calling him a "learning machine."

Buffett agreed that he is big on reading everything in sight and recommended good investors should read everything they can.

In his case, he said that by the age of 10, he'd read every book in the Omaha public library on investing, some twice! Fill your mind with competing ideas, and see what makes sense to you.

Then you have to jump in the water—take a small amount of money, and do it yourself. He joked that investing on paper is like reading a romance novel versus doing something else.

Munger shared that Berkshire Director Sandy Gottesman, who runs a large, successful investment firm (First Manhattan), asks interviewees, "What do you own, and why do you own it?" If you're not interested enough to own something, then he'd tell you to find something else to do.

Buffett noted that he and Charlie have made money a lot of different ways, some of which could not be anticipated 40 years ago.

Rather than a defined road map, what's called for is a reservoir of thinking and experience built by looking at markets in different places, different securities, etc.

One good place to look is where there are few other players. The RTC, Resolution Trust Corp, was a great example of a chance to make a lot of money with relatively few competing players. Here was a seller (the government) with hundreds of billions of dollars of real estate and no money in the game, who wanted to wrap it up quickly, while many buyers had no money and had been burned.*

---

* One of our favorites, Leucadia National Corp, was a very profitable player in the RTC process.

At age 19, Buffett read *The Intelligent Investor.* He shared that at age 76, he's still running through the same thought processes he learned from the book at age 19.

In an interesting point, Buffett again noted that you need something in your programming so that you don't lose a lot of money.

He claimed that his best ideas haven't done better than others' best ideas, but he's lost less on his worst ideas.

Comments on Risk

In modern portfolio theory, beta is a measure of volatility, which, in turn, is seen as a measure of risk. The higher the beta, the higher the risk. At least that's how the theory goes.

Buffett begs to differ, asserting volatility does *not* measure risk. Beta is nice and mathematical, but it's wrong.

For example, a couple decades ago, farmland in Nebraska went from $2,000 to $600 per acre. The theory would say the "beta" of farms went way up, so you would be taking far more risk buying it at $600 (as Buffett did) than at $2,000/acre.

That, of course, is nonsense. But stocks do trade, and math types like the ability of computers to model all those jiggles in prices.

Buffett concluded, "This concept of volatility is useful for people whose career is teaching, but it's useless to us."

Buffett believes that real risk comes from the nature of certain kinds of businesses, by the simple economics of the business and from not knowing what you're doing. If you understand the economics and you know the people, then you're not taking much risk.

For example, Buffett noted that he's willing to lose $6 billion in one catastrophe, but Berkshire's insurance business over time is not very risky. Given time, the probabilities will play out. Similarly, if you own a roulette wheel, you sometimes have to pay 35 to 1, but that's okay. He'd love to own a lot of roulette wheels.

Munger put in his two cents, "At least 50% of what is taught is twaddle, but these people have very high IQs. We recognized early on that very smart people do very dumb things, and we wanted to know why and who so we could avoid them."

Ethanol

Munger, ever the diplomat, weighed in on ethanol: "I think the idea of running vehicles on corn is one of the dumbest ideas I've ever seen. Governments under pressure do crazy things, but this is among the craziest. Raise the cost of food so you can run these autos around? You use up just about as much hydrocarbons making ethanol as it produces, and its cost doesn't even factor in the permanent loss of topsoil. I love Nebraska to the core, but this was not my home state's finest moment."*

Giving His Fortune Away

Buffett provided a very interesting summary of his $30 billion (and growing) gift to the Bill and Melinda Gates Foundation and to some other foundations run by his children.

Buffett said he always felt that he would compound money at a rate higher than average, and it would have been foolish to give away a significant portion of that capital. He also thought his wife would have been the one giving it away, but things didn't work out that way.

The idea of finding talented people to do what they do best is one of Buffett's driving principles.

He noted that when he and Suzie had a baby, they hired an obstetrician—he didn't try to do it himself. When his tooth hurts, he doesn't turn to Charlie.

Similarly, when it came time to giving his money away sensibly, he turned to Bill and Melinda Gates, people who are smart, energetic and passionate. He wanted to give the claim checks to someone who could follow generally what he would do himself if he were to do it.

Buffett added that as far as he's concerned, he hasn't given up anything. He hasn't changed his life. He couldn't eat any better or sleep any better, so he really hasn't given up anything. Someone giving up a trip to Disneyland to make a donation is the one making a real sacrifice.

More Wisdom from Charlie

We have often recommended to our friends and clients George Clason's classic, *The Richest Man in Babylon,* so we were delighted to hear Charlie speak of it.

He said that he read the book when he was young and that the book taught him to under-spend his income and invest the difference.

Lo and behold, he did this, and it worked.

---

* Munger is not alone in questioning the wisdom of the ethanol program. The July 15, 2007, *Des Moines Register* featured a headline story debating the future of ethanol subsidies.

He got the idea to add a mental compound interest as well. So he decided he would sell himself the best hour of the day to improving his own mind, and the world could buy the rest of his time.

He said it may sound selfish, but it worked.

He also noted that if you become very reliable and stay that way, it will be very hard to fail in doing anything you want.

Venue: Qwest Center

Attendance: 31,000

Details About This Year:

- The Qwest Center on the Berkshire weekend has become part meeting, part circus. There were country western singers, live bulls, speed boats, antique cars and an entire manufactured home from Clayton Homes.

- Some 25 Berkshire companies, from Justin Boots to Fruit of the Loom to GEICO insurance, sold their wares in the show room.

- Nebraska Furniture Mart had record sales of $7.5 million during the event.

Fortune 500 Ranking: 11th

Stock Price: $141,685

One dollar invested in 1964 would now be worth **$14,454**.

Berkshire's per-share book value has grown from $19.46 to **$70,530** (a rate of **20.3%** compounded annually).

The S&P 500 compounded at **10.3%** annually for the same period.

HIGHLIGHTS FROM 2008's NOTES

Buy the Business

Asked how not to be an investment lemming, Buffett suggested reading his old standby, *The Intelligent Investor* by Benjamin Graham (especially chapters 8 and 20), which changed his life.

Always remember that when you are buying a stock, you are really buying part ownership of a business.

Buffett, after working at his grandfather's grocery store, learned the importance of hard work. However, his grandfather was very negative about the stock market. Buffett stopped listening to him at that point.*

If Buffett were teaching business school, he would make it shockingly simple. Teach 1) How to Value a Business, and 2) How to Think About Market Fluctuations—that the market is there to serve you, not influence you." That would be it. Professors fill the time with all sorts of formulas.

Just as the priesthood of Biblical scholars would not have much to do if the masses simply followed the 10 Commandments, so do business school professors need something to teach and impress the students.

On the stock market, Buffett noted that the market represents thousands of businesses. So it should not matter where the stock market goes in the short run. He would be happy with his stocks if the market were closed several years.

If you were buying a farm, for example, you would look at the farm's production over time versus the purchase price. You would not be trading farms based on short-term swings in agricultural prices.

Munger: "I have nothing to add."

Buffett: "He's been practicing for months."

Future Returns: Lower Expectations

Buffett noted that he will be very happy with a 10% total return on his stock portfolio.

He predicted (for the umpteenth time) that Berkshire's future returns will not even be close to the returns it has earned in the past. Given Berkshire's size, it must look at companies with $50 billion market caps to move the needle. He concluded that "we'll have decent results but not indecent results."

---

* Luckily for all Berkshire shareholders.

Munger added, "We're happy making money at a reduced rate and suggest you do the same."*†

Good Managers: We Cheat

Buffett noted that he cheats when it comes to finding good managers.

He simply buys the ones who are already running great companies.

If he were shown 100 MBAs, Buffett asserted that it would be impossible for him to rank how they will actually perform as managers.

He simply finds decades-long records of excellent performance. Then he seeks to retain them in a way that maintains their enthusiasm for the work.

Buffett asks whether the manager loves the money or loves the business. If they love the business, they'll be a good fit for Berkshire.

In sum, Buffett looks for .400 hitters that can work for decades. He joked that Mrs. B (founder of Nebraska Furniture Mart) left at age 103 and died the next year. He hopes that's a lesson for his managers.

Ethics

Buffett said he's very proud of how the Berkshire managers, as a group, have behaved over the years.

To maintain clarity, Buffett sends a letter every two years to the managers, asking who their successors would be and reminding them to be sure not to lose a shred of reputation for the company.‡

He suggests the "newspaper" standard: behave as if your actions will be on the front page of the local newspaper. Berkshire has no budgets or earning goals, which eliminates some of the perverse pressures that infect most other large companies.§

Hedging the Dollar: Going International

Buffett warned years ago that the U.S. dollar was at risk with our ever-expanding trade deficit.

---

* Note the steady increase in equities in Berkshire's Cash/Bond/Equity Ratio (See Appendix II).
† Berkshire has been active in the stock market, accumulating 8.6% (about $4 billion) of Kraft Foods and adding to its stakes in Burlington Northern, Wells Fargo, U.S. Bank, Johnson & Johnson and Carmax.
‡ We recall how Buffett famously spoke about employee ethics at the congressional hearings of the Salomon scandal: "Lose money for the firm, and I will be understanding. Lose reputation for the firm, and I will be ruthless."
§ In past meetings, Munger has referred to "earnings management" as evil as it pressures managers to do irrational things.

Given that there has been no meaningful change in U.S. economic policies, Buffett continues to be bearish about the dollar.

As a result, Buffett is happy to earn profits in currencies other than the U.S. dollar. That can happen through stock ownership (Coca-Cola earns 80% of its profits overseas) or through the direct purchase of foreign companies. He's actively looking to do more of the latter.

Buffett is heading to Europe soon to tout the virtues of family-controlled companies selling to Berkshire. ISCAR in particular has opened Buffett's eyes to the possibilities overseas. ISCAR opened a plant in China last year and its CEO, Eitan Wertheimer, is accompanying Buffett on his swing through Europe.

ISCAR, by the way, has exceeded Buffett's very high expectations. He noted that both the financial performance and the personal relationships have made it a "dream acquisition."

Buffett wants more family owners who, when they feel the need to monetize their business, will think of Berkshire Hathaway.

That was the case recently for the Pritzkers and Marmon Group. It was the case a couple of years ago with the Wertheimers and ISCAR.

Munger noted that Germany has a particularly evolved civilization, especially in terms of inventiveness and engineering. For example, in the printing business, to an amazing degree, the best equipment is German-made.

Buffett reflected how he lost big time on Dexter shoes. Twenty years ago, the U.S. made one billion pair of shoes annually.

He quipped that our shoe-wild culture made the U.S. a nation of Imelda Marcos'. Now, while we still buy shoes, the U.S. makes no shoes. All shoes are made abroad today, especially in China.

Buffett noted how China is now unleashing its potential in a more open society. The talent was always there. It was just suppressed for so long.

Municipal Bond Dislocations

In his annual shot at modern portfolio theory, which claims that markets are always efficient, Buffett described what happened in the municipal bond market in early 2008.

Once in a while, Buffett brings props, and this year's was a set of municipal bond bid sheets.

He noted that there were some $330 billion of auction rate securities (ARS) weekly. Voilà—long-term funding with short-term rates. Good as long as it works. But when credit markets seized up in February, so did the ARS market. Chaos ensued.

Buffett noted that Los Angeles County Museum bonds that yielded 4% in January suddenly were priced to yield as high as 10% in mid-February. Now, the bonds are back to a 4% yield.

He also noted that during the panic, different bonds of the same issuer yielded anywhere from 6% to 11% at the same time! So much for the efficient market. It was a short-lived but very obvious opportunity for Buffett, and Berkshire acquired $4 billion of municipal bonds during the period.

Munger noted how quickly the opportunity came and went. Hedge funds had to dump because of margin calls. If you cannot think fast and act resolutely, it does you no good. Like men spear fishing, you may wait a long time, and when opportunity comes, you must act.

Berkshire Hathaway Assurance

In a remarkable turn of events, Berkshire recently entered the municipal bond insurance industry as the mortgage crisis infected the other primary players.

Buffett provided an update, noting that Ajit Jain started up Berkshire's municipal bond insurance subsidiary at the end of last year.

Buffett proudly announced that in a matter of months, BHA (Berkshire Hathaway Assurance) already has collected premium volume of $400 million, which may be more than all other municipal bond insurers—combined! It's done 278 transactions, mostly secondaries, with just 30 people in the office. The Berkshire-insured bonds are trading at a premium to those of any other bond insurer.

Buffett said that the premiums represent coverage that only pays if the primary insurer cannot pay. And Berkshire is getting better than 2% when the original insurance cost 1%.

Munger shared that once, when he was asked what was Berkshire's single best investment, he answered, "The fee for the corporate recruiter that brought us Ajit Jain."

Succession

Buffett announced that the board has the names of several potential successors and reviews succession plans at each board meeting.

Munger noted that Berkshire still has a rising young man in one Warren Buffett.

Buffett wryly pointed out that the term "aging management," so often used to describe Berkshire's top brass, refers to *all* managers.

Furthermore, given that he and Charlie average 80 years between them, they are aging at the rate of just 1.25% per year. Meanwhile, a 50-year-old manager is aging at a 2% rate and, therefore, is a much riskier bet.

Munger, on what Warren wants said at his funeral: "That's the oldest looking corpse I've ever seen."

Concentration

Munger and Buffett were in complete agreement about the benefits for the professional investor of loading up on your best ideas.

Buffett claimed that concentration is a good thing in investing, noting that he has had 75% of his non-Berkshire net worth invested in a single idea numerous times. It would be a mistake not to have 50% of your net worth in a really good situation. The big mistake is having *500%* of your net worth in things. Long-Term Capital Management had 25 times its net worth up, so it couldn't play out its hand when things went against it.[*]

Munger rued that elite schools teach that the secret of investment management is diversification. They have it backasswards he asserted. *Non-diversification* is the key.

Oil

The danger, according to Buffett, isn't that we will run out of oil, as is sometimes heralded by the press, but that daily production will level out and then slowly decline over time.

The world now produces 87 million barrels per day, the most ever, and yet we are probably at the lowest surplus capacity ever as demand marches ever higher. If we are at peak production, and it looks like we are, the world will have to adjust.

Munger noted that it is stupid to use our limited supply of hydrocarbons as fast as we are.

Munger believed that we need to use the sun—there is no other alternative.

---

[*] Almost weekly, we are reading of blowups of hedge funds levered 10:1, 20:1, and more.

Ethanol Update

Munger weighed in with his usual sunny assessment: "Corn to motor fuel is one of the dumbest ideas for the future of the world I've ever seen. It's stunningly stupid. The idea is probably on its way out."

Investment Bank Follies

Munger observed that Enron shocked the nation with its gross folly and misbehavior. That brought us Sarbanes-Oxley, which turned out to be like trying to shoot an elephant with a pea shooter. The convulsion underway now makes Enron look like a tea party. We will have more regulation, and it won't work perfectly for everyone.

Buffett felt that the Fed did the right thing with the Bear Stearns bailout. Bear would have failed, and the sorting out of some $14.5 trillion of derivative contracts with thousands of counterparties would have been a spectacle of unprecedented proportions with another big investment bank or two folding within a few days. These firms never dreamt that the world would stop lending to them.

Buffett asserted that investment banks and big commercial banks are too big to manage the way they have been going. It works most of the time, so you don't see the risk day to day. And if you're a 62-year-old executive, you don't worry too much about the very long run. What you need is a CEO with risk aversion in his DNA and the ability to resist employees who want to copy others to make money.

OFHEO Spells Awful

Regarding the difficulty of regulating complex financial enterprises, Buffett observed that OFHEO (Office of Federal Housing Enterprise Oversight) oversees two incredibly important entities, Fannie Mae and Freddie Mac.

These two accounted for 40% of mortgage flow a few years back and perhaps some 70% today.

OFHEO, with a staff of 200, existed solely for the purpose of watching these two companies. And what happened were two of the greatest accounting misstatements in history, billions and billions of dollars, while these 200 people had their jobs. They went two for two.

Buffett concluded that when you combine "too big to manage" with a government that deems them "too big to fail," you get interesting outcomes.

Munger was more direct, calling it crazy that the government would allow the banks to get too big to fail, a product of a culture of greed and overreaching. Overconfidence in algorithms played a part as well.

Munger called it demented to let derivative trading end up this way and regretted that so few spoke against it.

GURF: Good Until Reached For

Munger noted that so much of derivative accounting was not real profits.

And he coined a new accounting term, GURF: "good until reached for." Many investment banks carried assets that went "poof" when it came time to sell them. There were no bids.

He asserted that the accounting failed us and that accounting should be more like engineering.*

Buffett recounted how, in the dark days of the Salomon Brothers scandal, its traders were doing business with Marc Rich—who had fled the country for securities fraud! Yet the traders resisted orders to stop trading with him because they were making money at it. Buffett had to issue a specific directive to stop it. This is the sort of thing that happens in a corporate culture of greed.

Munger intoned, "There is much that happens in the bowels of American business that you don't want to know about."

Thinking About Risk

Buffett noted that it's important to think about risks, including those that have never happened before. The investment banks all had models, they had weekly risk committee meetings and they still didn't have a clue.

Buffett opined that "a chief risk officer is an employee that makes you feel good while you do dumb things."

At Berkshire, Buffett is the chief risk officer, and they spend a lot of time thinking about what could hit them out of the blue.

Munger said one can see how risk adverse Berkshire is. It behaves in a way where no one will worry. There's a double layering of safety around risk.

While the crisis originated in the mortgage area, the troubles have spread to other areas. In fact, Buffett said he couldn't remember such

---

* GURF reminds us of Bob Rodriguez's "to whom" securities, as in, when it comes time to sell, "to whom" will you sell them?

shock waves and the exposure of weakness of other practices like this one. Stupid things were done, and now the price must be paid.

And he predicted, eventually, we will see it all again, just in a different form. Some combination of wanting to get rich, leverage and belief in the tooth fairy will generate another bubble in time.

Munger noted that this was a particularly foolish mess. He asked if folks remembered that Internet-based grocery delivery business, Webvan, which he thought was a simply asinine idea. Well, he asserted, that idea was a lot smarter than the ideas cooked up in the mortgage industry.

Buffett summed up that he could have more leverage at Berkshire, but for what? Why expose the company to ruin and disgrace for an extra percentage point of return? You cannot farm-out risk management. Buffett willingly accepts lower returns for being able to sleep well, whatever may come.*

Fair Value Accounting

Buffett allowed that accounting for asset values is a tough thing, though he still strongly favors fair value versus cost.

The trouble with fair value can occur when the market produces prices that makes no sense.

He talked about CDOs (collateralized debt obligations), which were aggregations of tranches of thousands of different mortgage claims.

They were so complicated that there could be 15,000 pages to read to understand all the mortgages and tranches involved.

As if that wasn't complicated enough, there are also CDOs squared, which might be a security that comprises 50 CDOs. At 15,000 pages per CDO, one would have to read some 750,000 pages to understand one CDO squared.

When you start buying securities made of tranches of other instruments, nobody knows what they're doing. It was madness. Forcing people to mark things to market ("fair value"), valuing things like these CDOs at a 10 cent market price versus the cost of 100 cents, helps to keep management a little more honest.

Munger also took a shot at Alan Greenspan, suggesting Greenspan had overdosed on Ayn Rand—adopting the belief that if things happen in a free market, they must be okay.

---

* Ironically, this is the mindset that has produced among the very highest average rates of compounding over the past four decades.

Munger emphatically disagreed, saying that some things should be forbidden: "If we had just banned the phrase 'this a financial innovation that reduces risk,' we would have prevented a lot of trouble."

CDS Trouble?

When asked about CDS (credit default swaps), a $60 trillion national market, Buffett felt the CDS market was not a big risk to tumble into chaos.

A CDS is insurance against a company going bankrupt. While corporate default rates will rise, most of the CDS market is a zero-sum game. The losses of some will be matched by the gains of others.

In contrast, when the subprime mortgages went south, real dollars were lost.

With the Fed stepping in to bail out Bear Stearns, Buffett believed the odds for a CDS calamity now are low.

Munger concurred. Could we have a big time mess out of CDS? Yes. But the stupidity is not as bad as in the mortgage market where skid-row bums were swept up and given easy term mortgages.

What Munger did believe was bizarre was that CDS contract holders actually have a perverse incentive: they make money when corporations fail. So there could be manipulation to create corporate failures to collect on contracts.

Munger believed it was insane for regulators to allow this. It is illegal to buy life insurance on people you don't know as it creates a moral hazard (if they die, you get rich). He concluded that the CDS market is the product of a major nutcase bunch of proprietors and regulators.

Buffett tallied, "Charlie 1, Invisible Hand 0."

Keep It Simple

Munger asserted that Berkshire has lower due diligence expense than any other large corporation. And they have less trouble than any other large corporation.

At Berkshire, they think like engineers, looking for big margins of safety. If you need an accountant to tell you about a deal, you should be the accountant and let him run the business.

Buffett noted that this simplicity is a big advantage. Mars came to Berkshire because they knew no lawyers were needed. The folks at Mars knew that at Berkshire, a deal's a deal, and the check will clear.

Branded Food Companies

Berkshire has long been invested in branded food companies and recently took a more than 8% stake in Kraft Foods.

Buffett observed that big food companies are good businesses. They earn good returns on tangible assets.

Good brands like See's, Coke, Mars, Wrigley's are tough to compete with.

Coke now provides 1.5 billion servings a day worldwide. Since 1886, Coke has been delivering "happiness" and "refreshing" associations. These associations get implanted in people's minds.

Good branded products are often a good investment.

Keep It Simple II

Buffett allowed that one of their success secrets has been to focus only on those things that they figure out.

If it's a "no go," Buffett will cut off a proposal in mid-sentence (a technique he says he learned from Charlie). If he can figure it out, he can make a decision in five minutes.

A fascinating point: Buffett claims he could spend five months more on the idea, and it wouldn't add value to his decision.

Munger chimed in that they have a good "blotter out" system. They don't waste time on certain things.*

China Olympics

Buffett was in favor of going ahead with the Olympics, believing it is a mistake to start deciding which of the 200 countries are worthy to participate.

He noted that the U.S. didn't allow women to vote for 120 years and that blacks, at one time, were considered three-fifths of a person.

Munger was even more pointed, saying that distressed persons should ask themselves, "Is China more or less imperfect over the decades?"

He believes China is clearly on the right track and that it is a mistake to take what you like least about something and then obsess about it.

---

* Less information, when it's the *right* information, is a key to good decision-making.

Bargains in Banks?

Buffett noted that the size of a bank means little to him. What really counts is the culture.

He wants a bank CEO who has risk controls in his DNA.

While places like Wells Fargo, U.S. Bancorp and M&T Bank are not immune from problems, they are immune from institutional stupidity.

Too many banks do crazy things by trying to do what is popular. As Maury Cohen once said, "There are more banks than bankers."

Munger noted that smaller banks are probably a good place to prospect for investment value.

Buffett feigned great excitement: "That's wildly bullish coming from Charlie! I'm gonna buy that stuff as soon as I get out of here."

Nuclear Proliferation

Buffett noted that one of the greatest risks to civilization continues to be nuclear proliferation.

A given percentage of the world's 6.5 billion people will be psychotic.

Thousands of years ago, the worst the demented few could do was to throw rocks. With the advance of technology came bows and arrows, then guns and cannons and, today, nuclear devices.

He believes it is paramount to minimize the risk and that not much progress has been made. We should do everything possible to reduce access to materials.

As Albert Einstein warned in 1945 with the advent of the A bomb, "This changes everything in the world except how men think."

Buffett said he hoped that this issue will be at the top of the next U.S. administration's agenda.

Savings Rate

Somewhat surprisingly to us, Buffett suggested that the fact that the U.S. savings rate has turned negative is not necessarily a big negative for the economy.

He noted that the economic value of the United States has been increasing for decades even without a high savings rate. With a per capita GDP of $47,000, we're so rich we may not need to save as much.

With imports exceeding exports, the world is doing the savings for us. China, with a much higher savings rate, will grow faster than us, and it probably needs to do so.

Dividends

No meeting would be complete without the perennial "When are you going to pay a dividend?" question.

Buffett noted it has been better to retain the cash at Berkshire, where it can automatically compound. If you need cash, you can sell stock and pay capital gains tax at a lower rate than a dividend would be taxed.

Munger kidded that Warren has always planned to pay a dividend in the manner of St. Augustine: "God give me chastity, but not yet."

Corporate Compensation

Buffett admitted that there isn't much the individual investor can do.

What is needed is for the half-dozen largest institutional owners, in egregious cases, to withhold their votes and make statements about excessive compensation. Big shots do not like to be embarrassed. The press can help, too. An effective pressure is needed to check the self-interest of management.

Munger reflected that in England, class warfare resulted in a 90% income tax rate. While it proved to be totally counterproductive, it showed how the politics of envy can ruin an economic system.

Munger believes CEOs taking compensation have a moral duty not to take the last dollar. Like Supreme Court justices, they should *choose to be underpaid*.

Buffett noted, "Envy is the worst of the seven deadly sins. It's the only one that makes you feel worse, and the other party feels nothing. Gluttony—that has at least some temporary upside. As for lust—I'll let Charlie speak to that."

Pharma

Berkshire expanded its position in Johnson & Johnson and added shares of Sanofi in 2007.

Buffett admitted that he doesn't know much about the drug pipelines, and in five years it will all be different anyhow.

In aggregate, he believes pharma is doing something enormously important, and overall, the group should have decent profits. A group approach should provide a reasonable result over five years.

Munger deferred, "You have a monopoly on our joint knowledge of pharmacology."

Buffett quipped, "He gets cranky late in the day."

Keys to Good Health

Buffett joked that good health starts with a balanced diet: some Coca-Cola, some See's Candy, some Wrigley's gum and a Mars bar.

Seriously, he noted the importance of a good mental attitude, to love what you do and to do it with other people who love what they do. He said he feels blessed in so many ways, especially with great partners and great managers. It would be crazy to focus on the minuses.

He also noted that he was lucky to find his passion so early in life. He recalled reading his dad's books on investing as a boy and how that turned him on. (He joked that was before *Playboy* was invented.)

He pointed out that it is a terrible mistake to sleepwalk through life, to just go through the motions. Ideally, you have a job that you would do for free.

Surprisingly, he claimed that when he went to work for Ben Graham at the age of 24, he never even asked what his salary would be.

He also noted that getting the right spouse is essential.

He told the story of the man who spent 20 years looking for the perfect woman before he finally found her. Unfortunately, she was looking for the perfect man.

Benefits of Public Speaking

In a revealing aside, Buffett admitted that years ago he was terrified of public speaking. He got physically ill at the thought.

He said he even signed up for a $100 Dale Carnegie course but cancelled the check when he got home.

Later, he did a communication course in Omaha. Doing it with others in the same boat helped him to "get outside of himself." He's very glad he did it, noting that effective communication is under taught, and recommended that many could benefit by forcing themselves to learn public speaking at an early age.*

Number One Investment

As he has counseled on numerous occasions, Buffett suggested the best investment one can make is in oneself.

He noted that few people get the maximum horsepower out of life. Potential exceeds realization for so many.

---

* Throwing a party for 31,000 . . . yes, it is clear that young Warren has come a long, long way with his stage fright.

When he speaks to students, he suggests they adopt the mindset of someone who is picking one car for the rest of their lives. How would they treat it? They would read the manual carefully, change the oil twice as often and clean up the rust spots. Well, each of us gets one mind and one body for life. How will you treat yours?

Buffett admitted that the focus has been on the mind at Berkshire. He and Charlie didn't bother to work too hard on the body.

Munger also suggested that it is very important to learn how to avoid being manipulated by lenders and vendors.

He strongly recommended Robert Cialdini's book, *Influence*, for the task. He also recommended Cialdini's newest book, *Yes*, noting that Cialdini is the rare social psychologist who can connect the world of theory and daily life.

Read

Buffett reflected that he devoured books from an early age. He spends much of his day reading books, annual reports and newspapers.

Munger noted that different people learn in different ways. He too has always been an avid reader. With books, he likes that you can learn just what you want to learn and at the speed of your choosing.

Buffett concluded that if you read 20 books on a subject you are interested in, you are bound to learn a lot.

Legacy

Buffett hopes that in the long run, Berkshire will provide decent performance for shareholders and maintain its unique culture.

Buffett hopes it will be seen as the best home in the world for family businesses.

Munger sees Berkshire deserving to be even more of an exemplar and sees it having even more influence on other corporations.

Buffett concluded with this quip: "We also hope that Berkshire will have the oldest living managers in America."

2009

Venue: Qwest Center

Attendance: 35,000 or so

Details About This Year:

- The highlight of this year's movie was a tongue-in-cheek skit where Buffett becomes a floor salesman for Nebraska Furniture Mart. After a miserable year of investing in 2008, the board suggests Buffett might help the company more by selling a few more mattresses. The new best-selling mattress is the "Nervous Nellie" with a special "night deposit" compartment under the mattress for storing important items. A shopper tries out the mattress and notes that "it bounces back slow." Once the sale is made, Buffett hurries to remove his valuables from under the mattress, including some vintage Playboys.

Fortune 500 Ranking: 13th

Stock Price: $96,629

One dollar invested in 1964 would now be worth **$7,812**.

Berkshire's per-share book value has grown from $19.46 to **$84,487** (a rate of **20.3%** compounded annually).

The S&P 500 compounded at **8.9%** annually for the same period.

HIGHLIGHTS FROM 2009's NOTES

Negative Treasury Yields

Buffett opened the meeting with an overhead.* The overhead was of a trade ticket dated December 18, 2008, where Berkshire sold a $5 million Treasury bill due in April of 2009 for more than its maturity value: $5,000,090.97.

This means the buyer was willing to accept a *negative* yield.

Extraordinary.

Buffett quipped that the ticket was, in effect, an ad for the Nervous Nellie mattress and added that we may not see such a thing again in our lifetimes.

First Quarter Earnings

Buffett gave a heads up on first quarter earnings, sharing that Berkshire operating earnings were $1.7 billion down from $1.9 billion a year ago.

He sees Berkshire's insurance and utility operations doing well for 2009 as they are not all that economically sensitive. The retail and manufacturing subsidiaries have been hit hard by the recession.

He noted that MidAmerican Energy's $1 billion of operating earnings would be reinvested in utility operations.

Float bumped up from $58 billion to $60 billion due to a deal with Swiss Re.

Cash ended the quarter at $23 billion, though cash has since dropped to $20 billion as Berkshire invested $3 billion in a Dow Chemical convertible preferred.

Debt? Equity? How About Both?

You want yield? How about something in the double digits?

You want appreciation? How about equity participation in some of the biggest companies in the world?

Well, that's what Buffett has done with his special deals.

Buffett upped his "other" category in investments with deals combining both yields and equity kickers with Goldman Sachs ($5 billion of

---

* We always take special note when Buffett goes to visuals.

a 10% preferred and warrants to buy 43 million shares at $115/share), General Electric ($3 billion of a 10% preferred and warrants to buy 135 million shares at $22.25/share) and Wrigley ($6.5 billion total—$4.4 billion in 11.45% notes and $2.1 billion of 5% preferred).

We note also that preferred dividends are tax-preferenced for corporations, so in the case of Goldman and GE, that 10% preferred dividend is equal to nearly a 14% interest coupon on an after-tax basis to Berkshire.*

This is why we would guess that while Buffett and Munger agreed that the opportunities of 2008 were great, though not as compelling as the 1974–75 bear market when PEs were 4 (though interest rates were higher then), they were referring to the general market, not the unique opportunities Buffett was able to create during this meltdown.

Summarizing 1974, Munger declared, "I knew I'd never get another trip to the counter like that."

Buffett said, as with hamburger, he'd rather pay ½ X than X, so he liked the lower prices.

With stocks down 40% and interest rates down, stocks and bonds had to be more attractive.

He noted that the corporate bond market was very disorganized.

For Berkshire's life insurance companies, they barreled into good quality corporate bonds yielding 10% or better with great call protection.

Financial Literacy

Buffett allowed that financial literacy is a tough sell in a world of calculators. Few can actually do the math anymore. Add in credit cards, and you've made it easy for people to do silly things.

Munger chimed in with an anecdote about going to Vegas for his honeymoon back in 1952 at the Flamingo. There, he saw very well-dressed people who had traveled for miles to do something dumb with negative probabilities, and he thought to himself, "What a world of opportunity!"

Munger added that states legalize gambling with lotteries, effectively *encouraging* the populace to bet against the odds.

---

* Again, this is the best of all worlds—double-digit yields AND equity participation rights. And Buffett isn't done yet. Subsequent to year-end, Berkshire acquired $3 billion Swiss francs worth of a 12% convertible note with Swiss Re and invested $3 billion in an 8.5% convertible preferred of Dow Chemical. All in, that's over $20 billion in high yield securities with equity kickers. Amazing.

Banks

Buffett and Munger were both complimentary of the government's actions in the midst of crisis and are optimistic for the recovery of the banking system.

Buffett asserted that mid-September, we were at the brink of a total meltdown throughout the financial system. There was that one weekend where Lehman went down, AIG went down and Merrill Lynch would have gone down if not acquired by the Bank of America.

Under such pressure, overall, he believed the government did a good job, particularly in guaranteeing the safety of bank deposits and money market funds.

Buffett spoke especially well of Wells Fargo, calling it a fabulous bank with advantages that the other large banks do not have. In particular, Wells Fargo has the lowest cost deposit base, making it the low-cost producer in the business.

Buffett provided that Wells Fargo will come out of this way stronger than it went in.

In a fascinating aside, Buffett shared that he was teaching a class the day Wells Fargo went under 9. Usually, he refuses to answer the old "name a stock to buy" question, but on that day, he said that "if I had to put all my net worth in one stock, I'd buy Wells Fargo."

Wells Fargo has a fabulous business model. With Wachovia, it picked up the fourth largest deposit base in America.

Wells Fargo will be much better off in a couple of years because this debacle happened.

Efficient Market Jab

Buffett and Munger do their level best each year to debunk the efficient market hypothesis that dominates academic thinking.

Buffett noted that investing is really all about laying out cash now to get more back later.

Buffett joked that in 600 B.C., Aesop, who was a very smart man, though he didn't know it was 600 B.C., he couldn't know everything— said, "A bird in the hand is worth two in the bush." That's really it.

Munger noted that a lot of spreadsheets and fancy math can lead to false precision and worse decisions.

He allowed, "They teach the fancy math in business schools because ... well, they gotta do something."

Buffett chimed in that if you taught the "bird in the hand" maxim, you would not get tenure. Rising in the priesthood requires complexity.

Buffett added that this false precision only arises with very high IQs. You only need an IQ of 120 or so to be a good investor. In fact, he suggested, if you have a high IQ, keep your 120 and sell the rest. Higher math can lead you astray.

The Housing Bubble

Buffett noted that housing prices had risen for so long that there became an almost total belief that housing prices would never fall. They could only go up. Thus, a $20 trillion asset class, housing, out of the nation's $50 trillion in assets, became increasingly levered up. And the blame is shared by all players.

Buffett pointed out that it was Congress that presided over the two largest mortgage entities in the world, Fannie Mac and Freddie Mac, and both are in receivership.

As for the rating agencies, especially Moody's, in which Berkshire owns a 20% stake, Munger noted that they are good at fancy math and, as with the man with the hammer, treated each problem like a nail.

Going forward, Buffett believed the rating agencies are good businesses: there are few competitors, they affect a large segment of the economy and they don't require much capital (though they are still very much attackable).

Buffett noted that the biggest surprise may have been that so many of these AAA toxic creations ended up in the hands of the creators themselves. They drank their own Kool-Aid. Stupidity ran wild, and "everyone else was doing it" became the primary rationale. It's hard to stop once there is such widespread industry acceptance.

Real Estate

California volumes are up for real estate transactions, especially in the lower to mid-priced homes, so Buffett sees some stability coming to parts of the real estate market.

The new mortgages going on the books each day are much better in quality than the old ones they are replacing. Low interest rates are helping.

Buffett laid out the big picture brilliantly:

There are about 1.3 million new households created each year. Maybe a bit less right now with the recession.

During the bubble, we were building two million new homes annually, which far outstripped the household formation rate.

The current total excess in homes is about 1.5 million. The building rate has plunged to about 500,000 units annually.

So if we continue to build homes at that reduced rate, we can sop up about 800,000 of the excess housing inventory annually for a couple years, and supply and demand will roughly come back into balance.

Buffett quipped that we could take care of the overhang tomorrow by blowing up 1.5 million homes or accelerate household formation by having 14 year olds start marrying.

However, what is happening is that we're producing less, and eventually, the excess inventory will get absorbed.

In sum, housing is more affordable, mortgage rates are low, payment terms are more sound . . . we're on the road to healing.

Four Investment Managers

Buffett has four investment managers, inside and/or outside Berkshire, and each of the four did no better than the S&P 500's 37% decline in 2008.

Buffett added that he's tolerant of that as "I didn't cover myself with glory."

Munger added that practically every investment manager he regards highly got creamed last year.

Furthermore, they don't want a manager at Berkshire that thinks he can jump into cash and back into the market. They have excluded those types.[*]

Warrenomics 101

Buffett loves to teach college students.

Buffett noted that he had eight sessions last year with students from 49 different universities.

His two courses, if he were to run a business school, would be 1) How to Value a Business, and 2) How to Think About Markets. That would be it.

In valuing businesses, it is important to understand the language of accounting, to stay within your circle of competence, and to focus on what is meaningful and sustainable.

---

[*] For Corey and me, this news was a nice balm for our bruised egos.

In thinking about markets, it is important to remember that markets are there to serve you, not instruct you. The key here is emotional stability, to have an inner peace about your decisions. It is important to think for yourself and to make good decisions over time.*

It is simple, but not easy.

The key with markets is that you cannot allow yourself to be forced to sell (from using too much leverage) and that you must not sell in a panic mode, emotionally pulling the rug out from under yourself.

Munger added that there is so much that is false and nutty in modern banking, investing and academia that the most one can hope for is to reduce the nonsense. If someone has an IQ of 150 but thinks it is 160, it leads to disaster.

Buffett imagined himself an economics teacher, professing the efficient market hypothesis: "Everything is priced properly." And mused, "What do you do for the rest of the hour?" And this is the stuff of Nobel Prizes!

Buffett concluded with Max Planck's observation of the inexorable evolution of science despite the strong resistance to new ideas by even the best and brightest of his peers: "Science advances one funeral at a time."

Replace Ajit?

Ajit Jain heads up BH Reinsurance and has done wonders, building float to an incredible $24 billion as of year-end 2008. What would Berkshire do without him?

Buffett noted that the authority here goes with the person, not the position.

While he's happy to give his pen to Ajit, signing for major deals, he would not do so with anyone else.

He recounted the story of how Mutual of Omaha back in the 1980s, the largest health and accident association at the time, got into property and casualty insurance. By handing its pen to insurance brokers, Mutual of Omaha lost half of its net worth in a very short time—a huge scandal.

In sum, if Ajit were gone, some of what BH Reinsurance does would not be replaced.

Munger added that Berkshire is not looking for mismanagement. While they like businesses that can withstand some folly, some fabulous things are one off. That's the case with Ajit.

---

* So focus on the *process*, not the outcome.

What Matters at Berkshire

Buffett asserted that Berkshire was cheaper at the end of 2008 than it was at the end of 2007. The investments are worth more than what they are carried for. And the non-insurance operating earnings may suffer for a bit but long term will do very well.

Munger noted that 2008 was a bad year for a float business.*

However, long term, the fact that Berkshire can have so much float at a cost of less than zero is a great advantage. The key is to focus on what matters.

According to Munger, what matters at Berkshire is that the property and casualty business is probably the best in the world, the utility subsidiary is the best, ISCAR is the best at what it does, etc.

Munger emphasized that it is not easy to get into these positions.

GEICO

Perhaps no world-beating subsidiary is hotter right now than GEICO, the low-cost provider of auto insurance.

Buffett noted that the economic downturn changed consumer behavior like ringing a bell. Everyone is a bargain shopper now.

That has hurt at American Express, where the average ticket is down 10%. It has helped at GEICO, where the phone is ringing off the hook. Thousands are coming to the website every day to see if they can save money.

In the first four months of 2009, GEICO has added 505,000 policyholders. The competitive advantage GEICO has built over the past decade is paying off hugely.

Buffett sees market share going to 8.5% by year-end. That's up from 7.2% at the beginning of 2007.

Incredible!

And each policyholder has significant value—effectively an annuity paying, on average, around $1,500 annually for a policy they must have if they want to drive—and Americans love to drive.

Buffett quoted Marshall Fields: "We waste half of the money we spend on advertising . . . the problem is we just don't know which half."

---

* We believe he's referring to that 15:1 leverage factor—just as it has turbo-charged Berkshire's up-market returns, it leverages the losses incurred in a down market.

From a paltry $20 million ad budget when Berkshire took full control of GEICO in 1995, Buffett has amped up the annual ad budget to $800 million—far more than State Farm or Allstate.*

He wants everyone in the U.S. to have in mind that there's a good chance to save money at GEICO.

He related that to Coca-Cola, which, since 1886, has advertised to associate Coke with moments of pleasure and happiness all around the world.

And that share of mind is paying off for GEICO—with the economic downturn, thousands more are checking to see if they can save even $100 with GEICO.

Munger noted that in effect, GEICO is earning $800 million pre-tax (the ad spend) that never shows in the earnings.

Buffett agreed, saying GEICO could probably go to a maintenance advertising level of, say, $100 million and maintain the present policy-holder count for many years.

Infrastructure: Build the Grid

Munger nearly elbowed Buffett out of the way to answer a question on whether the U.S. should be spending more on infrastructure. "YES" was his answer.

He went on to say that there is one big no brainer that would hugely improve U.S. industry and commerce, and that is to build a nationwide electricity grid. We have the technology and know-how, and it would be 100% likely to make the system better.†

Derivatives

Buffett asserted that the use of derivatives caused leverage to run wild, straining an already fragile economic system and causing problems to pop up in unexpected places.

After 1929, Congress decided it was very dangerous to let people borrow against their securities. The Federal Reserve instituted margin requirements of 50%. Derivatives totally went around these regulations of the markets.

---

* We haven't seen recent numbers, but GEICO outspent the entire rest of the auto insurance industry *combined* on advertising for most of the past decade.
† Munger said much about the grid at the Wesco Financial meeting as well.

In addition, while normal securities settle in three days or less, keeping counterparty risk to minimum, derivative contracts can have very long settlements. These unsettled contracts pile up over time, adding to the risk in the system. (Buffett recommended reading John Kenneth Galbreath's *The Crash.*)

Munger believed the deeper problem was that the derivatives dealer was not only the croupier at the gambling table, but was also playing the game itself against his clients with an informational advantage.

He concluded that society does not need this sort of thing.

Berkshire Derivatives

Buffett has written derivative contracts on both equity markets and on high yield bond markets, which has caused quite a stir.

The equity puts raised $4.9 billion in cash, which Berkshire will hold for the duration of the contracts, and the contracts do not require Berkshire to post much (if any) collateral.

In effect, it's much like writing long tail catastrophe reinsurance where Berkshire creates that much coveted "float."

The high yield bond contracts are experiencing higher than expected default rates, so Buffett is not doing so well with those and may end up losing some money.

The Berkshire Advantage

Buffett noted that the Berkshire culture and business model are very difficult to copy.

Shareholders are high grade with an average turnover of 20% a year, versus 100% for the average publicly traded large company.

They run the business without teams of lawyers and bankers. Management is decentralized and incentives are rational. The culture is constantly reinforced as the managers see that it works.

In contrast, Munger opined that many corporations are run stupidly, forcing things down from headquarters, worrying about quarterly profits.

For companies selling to Berkshire, Buffett noted that it is important that "it is known that we like allocating cash flows. Our reputation is that we buy to keep, and people can trust us on that."

Buffett noted one of his standard management questions is, "What would you do differently if you owned 100% of the company?"

Answering the question for himself, he said he wouldn't change a thing at Berkshire.

Copy Berkshire

Buffett noted there are things that Berkshire does that the average investor cannot copy.

1. Float—Berkshire has that $58 billion interest-free loan.

2. Berkshire makes direct purchases and deals of its own design.

3. Berkshire sometimes buys whole companies.

Beyond that, Buffett shared that he did copy Ben Graham by studying Graham Newman reports years ago. "Coat-tailing" was the term.

Munger concluded that it is quite smart to follow very good investors around.

Inflation

Buffett said it is certain we will have some inflation over time. For the U.S. and governments throughout history, this is the classic way of reducing the cost of external debt. Inflate and pay the world back with cheaper dollars.

Buffett noted that the Chinese, the largest holder of government bonds, will suffer the most with devaluation as it is fixed-dollar investors whose notes are worth less at maturity.

Buffett also chided politicians who constantly refer to how much all of this government bailing-out is costing the taxpayers. The taxpayers have yet to pay one cent more than in years past!

Buffett guaranteed that the dollar will buy less over time, and that is happening with all other currencies as well. All major nations are electing to run major deficits in the face of the economic crisis.

Buffett was emphatic: "You can bet on inflation."

Munger reflected that when he was growing up in Omaha, a postage stamp was 2 cents and a hamburger was a nickel. And yet, he has lived in the most privileged era of history.

Buffett added that a Coke was 5 cents with a 2-cent deposit—so it really hasn't gone up that much. Meanwhile, a newspaper was a penny, but now costs a $1 and loses money.

The best protection against inflation, according to Buffett, is your own earning power. If you constantly increase your earning power, you'll be sure to get your share of the economic pie.

The next best thing is to own wonderful businesses, especially those that have low capital requirements. For example, Coca-Cola requires little capital to grow and is sure to get its percentage of income, however it is measured, whatever the currency.

Munger summed up, "A young man should become a brain surgeon and invest in Coke instead of government bonds."

Newspapers

Buffett loves newspapers, reading at least five a day. However, he said that most newspaper companies today are not a buy at any price. What was an absolutely essential business 30 years ago is now a business looking at unending losses.

Buffett said Walter Annenberg invented a term, "essentiality," and that newspapers once had that for advertisers and customers. Over time, that essentiality has eroded, and there appears to be no end to that erosion.

At Berkshire's *Buffalo News*, Buffett said the unions have been very cooperative, and it can still make a little money. At the *Washington Post*, there is a good cable business and a very good education business but no answers yet for the newspaper.

Munger said it was a national tragedy to lose such an important sinew of the civilization. The newspaper, with its desirable editorial influence, kept government honest.

Retail and Manufacturing

Buffett again said he looks for housing supply and demand to return to equilibrium in a couple of years. Business for Berkshire's housing-related products will recover at that point.

As for retail, Buffett sees a big change in consumer behavior going for the low-priced products, and he suspects it will last quite a long time.

He wryly noted that for years, government has asked people to save more while the savings rate drifted down to zero. Now, government wants people to *spend* more, and the savings rate has jumped up to about 4%–5%.

In commercial real estate, the 5% cap rates of recent years look silly now. Vacancies are up. Shopping centers are suffering. Real estate could be tough for quite a period. South Florida in particular he expects to be flat for a long time due to huge oversupply.

Share Repurchases

Buffett noted that corporate America as a whole has not added value with its stock repurchases.

Back in the 1970s and 1980s, stocks were cheap—clearly well-below intrinsic value—and very few corporations repurchased shares.

Then, during the last 10 years, buying stock became the thing to do. Many companies had stock buyback programs at high to even silly prices.

Buffett estimated that 90% of the buyback activity in the last five years was mostly herd behavior.

Now, with stock prices dramatically marked down, many at less than half the prices at which repurchases were made, there are few buybacks going on.

Opportunity Cost

Buffett noted that calibrating opportunity costs last year got a little crazy with prices and intrinsic values changing so fast.

He shared that Berkshire got lots of calls and ignored most of them, but interestingly, even the calls he chose to ignore were helpful in calibrating the more promising ones.*

For example, Goldman Sachs called on a Wednesday. The time for that transaction was NOW—it wouldn't be there a week later. So in a chaotic market, Berkshire was able to put large sums to work fast.

The Constellation Energy offer (which "failed," though Berkshire took home a $1 billion profit), $5 billion in Goldman Sachs preferred and warrants, $3 billion in GE preferred and warrants, etc.

Buffett noted that he hadn't had a flurry of activity like this in a long time.

The New PE at BYD

Munger was very excited about Berkshire's attempt to acquire 10% of BYD, a Chinese manufacturer.

He noted that BYD is no startup, with $4 billion of revenue and having already pulled off miracles in becoming a world leader in lithium batteries and a major player in cellphone components.

Now, the company aims to take on the auto world from a standing start by building electric cars. It already has the best-selling car model in China and makes each of the parts itself.

Munger seems especially excited by the fact that BYD has 17,000 engineering graduates—the top of the class in a country of 1.3 billion people.†

---

* Who can match Buffett's flow of information?
† The thought occurs to us that Munger may be on the verge of a new analytic device—the PE ratio—that is, Price to Engineers. We noted last year that Munger gave us the "GURF" asset accounting idea—"good until reached for."

Lithium batteries are needed in every utility function. To harness the power of the sun, we will need batteries. BYD is the sweet spot, Munger concluded.

Buffett quipped, the Irish banks were my big idea and BYD was Charlie's. He's the winner![*]

Moody's Downgrade

Buffett admitted to being irritated with the Moody's downgrade of Berkshire from AAA to AA.

Buffett claimed it makes little difference in Berkshire's borrowing costs, and there remains no stronger credit than Berkshire, having always conducted its affairs so that no one worries about getting their insurance checks well into the future.

Munger noted that at least Moody's showed considerable independence in making the change.[†] And he predicted the next change by Moody's in the Berkshire rating will be in the other direction.

Buffett quipped that as Charlie has told him before, "In the end, you'll see it my way because you're smart and I'm right."

Utility Investments

MEC is now the largest wind utility in the nation.

Iowa is No. 1 in wind power with some 20% of its power wind-generated. The wind blows 35% of the time, so this is not base capacity.

Overall, MEC is a net exporter of energy for Iowa. Berkshire is a big taxpayer, so it can use the 1.8 cents per kilowatt/hour tax credit. They are putting in wind power in the Pacific Northwest and are looking to do more.

Munger noted that he's very proud that MEC is a leader in the field.

Buffett noted that he wished that he had been able to purchase Constellation Energy.

The day David Sokol heard CEG was in trouble, facing bankruptcy, he called Buffett with an idea to make an offer. That very evening, Sokol and Greg Abel were in Baltimore with an all-cash offer. So Berkshire went from an 11 a.m. phone call by Sokol to an in-person bid that night!

---

[*] Berkshire lost a few hundred million dollars on Irish banks last year.
[†] Berkshire owns 20% of Moody's.

Munger added that Berkshire once bought a pipeline in two hours. Dynergy had purchased the Northern Natural Gas pipeline from Enron, and then Dynergy itself went down. To close the deal, Berkshire needed FERC approval, so Buffett agreed to do whatever FERC said to do post-deal.

Buffett noted that while it's the shareholders you need to please in most deals, it's the *regulators* you need to please in utility transactions.

China

Munger weighed in with praise for Chinese economic policy:

China has one of the most successful economic policies in the world. Growth is so significant and important to China that it amounts to just a trifle if the dollar declines. Their goal has been to make it very hard to compete with them all over the world. That's exactly what they've done and what they should do.

Gen Re

Buffett announced that Gen Re is working well after a terrible start.

When Berkshire bought it in 1998, Gen Re's premier reputation was not reality. It was an enormous mess.

Thanks to Tad Montross and Joe Brandon, the operations have been turned around. Now Buffett feels terrific about its future.

Munger noted that it is important sometimes to turn lemons into lemonade, and while it wasn't pretty or pleasant, Joe Brandon was the one brilliant hero in the transaction.

Insurance

Buffett said they have marvelous insurance businesses.

His worst-case estimate was that Berkshire could lose 3%–4% of a major industry loss.

For example, Hurricane Katrina amounted to about a $60 billion loss, while Berkshire lost less than $3 billion.

In a $100 billion event, Buffett guessed Berkshire would now pay around $3 billion to $4 billion.*

---

* Again, we wonder how Berkshire can have 6%–7% market share in reinsurance and yet have only 3–4% exposure in a catastrophe.

Swiss Re: A Four-Course Meal

In another exciting tale of fast action, Buffett related how Swiss Re was under extreme pressure last year during the crisis.

Buffett met with them in Washington D.C. to hammer out a deal that met their needs and that was good for Berkshire.

Buffett emphasized that Swiss Re's problems were ones of capital adequacy, not underwriting standards.

Berkshire agreed to a quota share arrangement where it will receive 20% of Swiss Re's property casualty reinsurance business over five years.

Earlier in 2008, Berkshire had purchased 3% of Swiss Re. Then, in February of this year, Berkshire invested $3 billion Swiss francs in a 12% note that is callable at 120% of par for two years and in three years is convertible at $25 francs/share. The notes are senior to Swiss Re equity of $20 billion.

Buffett said the odds are good that the note will get called, which would not make him happy.

Then, in addition to all that, Berkshire did a $2 billion Swiss franc adverse loss cover with Swiss Re. That pushed Berkshire's float to just over $60 billion at quarter end.

So to summarize, Berkshire bought shares of Swiss Re, wrote a 20% quota share contract, invested in a 12% convertible note, and provided an adverse loss cover. That's a lot of bites from one apple!

Hope for the World

Buffett offered that there is always a lot wrong with the world, but it's the only world we got. Fortunately, over time, people do better and better.

For all its flaws, the capitalist system works, unleashing human potential. Consider that there were 35,000 people at the Berkshire meeting— that would have been 10% of the entire population of the U.S. in 1790.

Buffett allowed that we'll have bad years in capitalism. There were six panics in the 19th century. While we have had these interruptions, we have grown at a great clip overall.

The standard of living increased 7 to 1 in the 20th century. At one time, a black man was considered three-fifths of a person, and women couldn't vote for our first 130 years. We were wasting human potential. Our kids and grandkids will live better and better.

Buffett repeated that he hopes to grow 2% or so faster than the S&P 500 in intrinsic business value. And that's a far cry from outperforming the market by 10% annually in his partnership days.

However, Munger beamed that Berkshire's best days of contributing to civilization are ahead.

He noted that mankind is getting close to solving the technical problem of our time—solar power. Cheap, clean, storable power will change the world.

Munger said, "As I get closer and closer to my death, I get more cheerful about the future I won't see."

He talked about the potential of solar power as the final breakthrough. It would solve the main technical problems of humankind. He's excited that MEC and BYD will participate. If we have enough clean energy, we can do all sorts of things.

2010

Venue: Qwest Center

Attendance: 40,000

Details About This Year:

- Munger and Buffett answered shareholder questions for nearly six hours.

- Highlights from this year's movie included:
    - An extended Burlington Northern Santa Fe tribute.
    - The annual GEICO employee rock video featuring Buffett doing an Axl Rose impersonation.
    - "Warren the Whip" coming in from the bullpen (wearing number "$\frac{1}{16}$") to bail out the Red Sox in the bottom of the ninth against the Yankees—a spoof where they squeezed in a mention of nearly every one of the 70 some companies that Berkshire owns.

- Corey and Daniel also attended the Wesco Financial annual meeting. We have added some comments of Munger's from that meeting as well.

Fortune 500 Ranking: 11th

- Berkshire now ranks in the top 10 by revenue. Adding the revenues of the recently acquired Burlington Northern, Berkshire's revenues in 2009 would have been about $126 billion. That would place Berkshire just ahead of AT&T at No. 7.

Stock Price: $99,238

One dollar invested in 1964 would now be worth **$8,022**.

Berkshire's per-share book value has grown from $19.46 to **$95,453** (a rate of **20.2%** compounded annually).

The S&P 500 compounded at **9.3%** annually for the same period.

HIGHLIGHTS FROM 2010'S NOTES

First Quarter Earnings: Recovery Picking up

Buffett opened the meeting with a slide showing Berkshire had a first quarter profit of $2.2 billion versus $1.7 billion a year ago, noting that the economic recovery has been picking up steam.

Buffett was especially pleased to see a surge in heavy industry, where there's no inventory fill.

For example, BNSF railroad cars in use have jumped significantly. ISCAR metal-working tools, which are used on assembly lines around the world, have had a sharp uptick. Marmon Group was seeing improved sales.

Buffett added that the slide did not show earnings per share as a matter of principle, noting that the practice too often leads to a fudging of the numbers.

He cited a *Wall Street Journal* article, where a Stanford study looked at nearly half a million earnings reports to the tenth of a penny over a 27-year period.*

What they found is that the earnings numbers seldom ended in a fourth of a cent. The study concluded that the vast majority of companies were gaming the numbers, so they could round up!†

The study went on to suggest that this fudging was a good leading indicator for companies that would later have accounting problems.

Buffett concluded that this is not good for enterprise.

Asked if he had anything to add, Munger said, "I agree with you."

Buffett quipped, "He is the perfect vice chairman."

Goldman Sachs

Anticipating a round of questions about the SEC's investigation of Goldman Sachs, Buffett had an extensive reply ready to go.

He noted that as he understood the transaction in question (called "Abacus"). It was no different from many transactions Berkshire has done over the years. For every buyer, there is a seller on the other side.

In particular, one of the parties in the transaction, ACA, was a bond insurer, so it was active in the business of handling these mortgage packages. These were hardly innocent parties.‡

---

*"Quadraphobia" from February 13, 2010.
† Hence the article's title.
‡ A *Wall Street Journal* story on Jan. 8, 2008, indicated ACA had capital of $425 million and credit default swaps outstanding of $69 billion—hardly a risk-averse group.

Buffett displayed a slide showing an $8 billion municipal bond package with bonds from a number of different states that Berkshire had agreed to insure for a $160 million premium.

Buffett noted that he came to that conclusion with his own analysis. He did not care who was on the other side of the transaction. If it makes sense and the premium is high enough, he'll take the deal. And he wouldn't dream of coming back later to cry "unfair" if he took a loss on the deal.

Regarding Goldman, Buffett lavished praise on Goldman CEO Lloyd Blankfein.

Munger agreed, saying, "There are plenty of CEOs I'd like to see gone—Blankfein is not one of them."

However, Munger also noted that every business should decline some business—that we should aspire to a higher standard than merely what is legal.

Buffett did have advice for Blankfein on how to handle crisis: "Get it right. Get it fast. Get it out. Get it over."

He added that the SEC suit is actually a plus for Berkshire because it most likely delays the point at which Goldman can call Berkshire's $5 billion 10% preferred at 110% of par. That preferred pays Berkshire $500 million a year, or $15 every second. Every extra "tick" between now and the calling of the preferred is another $15 for Berkshire. Tick, tick—while he sleeps—tick, tick on weekends—tick, tick . . .

Buffett loves this investment.

Buffett threw in another slide of the tombstone of a 1967 $5.5 million 8% bond due November 1, 1985, of Diversified Retailing (though it only had one store!).

He noted that two of the most important underwriters were not listed—Gus Levy of Goldman Sachs and Al Gordon of Kidder Peabody. Each agreed to take $350,000 of the deal on the condition that they be left out of the tombstone!

Buffett was grateful for their help 43 years ago.[*]

Financial Regulation

Munger doubted that anyone in Congress has actually read the 1,550-page bill for financial regulation.

However, he sees a clear need to make the investment banking system less permissive. Reduce the allowed activities. Reduce the complexity. Reinstitute Glass Steagall.

---

[*] And he clearly has a long memory when it comes to his friends.

Similarly, the savings and loan industry stayed out of trouble for years with its narrow charter. As soon as the charter was loosened, major trouble ensued.

He lamented, "Give humans a chance and they'll go plum crazy."

At the Wesco Financial meeting, Munger used the analogy of a soccer referee. If one team has an extraordinarily good soccer player, it's in the best interests of the other team to knock the crap out of him to slow him down. You need the referee to keep things civil.

Likewise in the competitive world of investment banking, with everyone so aggressively trying to outdo everyone else, it creates a system where eventually everyone goes blooey.

He added that the investment banks will push back hard. Like a diver with an air hose, they do not want anyone stepping on their air hose. They will defend it as if their lives depend upon it. So it will take stern measures.

He concluded that if he were a benevolent despot, he would make Paul Volker look like a sissy.

Derivative Reform

Buffett clarified some lobbying he had recently done to have one element of the financial regulation bill revised regarding collateral for existing derivative contracts.

It appeared the bill might retroactively require hundreds of companies to post additional collateral without proper compensation.

As Buffett put it, "If I sell you my house unfurnished, that's one price. If you later want it furnished, well, then you need to pay me more."

He noted that Berkshire had just been shown a contract that had two prices, $7.5 million with no collateral and $11 million fully collateralized.

Munger concluded that the provision in the bill was of dubious constitutionality and was both unfair and stupid.

Greece and the Dollar

Currencies worldwide appear to be in a race to the bottom.

Buffett noted that events in the world over the last few years make him more bearish on all currencies holding their value over time.

He emphasized that there is no possibility of U.S. default—because it prints its own currency and can simply print more money. Greece, however, is in a more awkward spot. While Greece is sovereign in terms of its own budget, it cannot print its own money as it is part of the euro-zone. This is a test case for the durability of the euro.

Munger noted that in the past, the U.S. was conservative, which gave it wonderful credit.

Munger pointed out that credit status helped us fund World War II and, then, in one of the greatest foreign policy decisions in all history, funded the Marshall Plan to help reconstruct Germany and Japan. Now, our government has pushed credit too hard for too long. Greece is just the start of an interesting period where we see what happens when government blows it by pushing too hard for too long.

Buffett chimed in that running a budget deficit of 10% of GDP is not sustainable. How the world weans itself off of huge deficits in country after country will be an interesting movie.

Munger added that unfunded promises are miles bigger than the reported problem. It can work out as long as the economy grows. If growth stops, you have a very difficult problem.

Higher Inflation

With the above observations, it follows that it is likely we will have higher inflation in our future.

Buffett noted that since 1930, the dollar has depreciated by over 90%, yet the U.S. has done okay. Prospects for significant inflation have increased around the world. The medicine for the crisis—massive doses of debt—was okay, but continuing to run high deficits as a percentage of GDP diminishes the value of the currency over time.

Both Buffett and Munger are betting on higher, and maybe a lot higher inflation in the years to come.*

Biggest Global Challenge

As in years past, Buffett noted that the biggest challenge to civilization is a massive nuclear or bio-chemical attack.

Over 50 years, the probability of such an attack occurring is high. Over one year, the probability is low.

Buffett noted that throughout history, there has been incredible progress, with lots of hiccups, in the state of mankind. The U.S. has been remarkable in unleashing human potential like no other country.

* We note how Buffett has responded to this situation. He's fully invested in businesses and equities.

Buffett imagined that a farmer in 1790 probably dreamed of a tool that would shorten the work day from 12 hours to 10. At that time, the U.S. had a fraction of the population that China had, and look how well we have done.

He noted that the Berkshire crowd was probably no smarter than folks 200 years ago, but boy do we live better.

Succession

Buffett once again assured shareholders that succession plans are in order. A new CEO would be ready at any time on short notice.

Munger assured shareholders that he is quite optimistic that the culture of Berkshire will last a long, long time after the founder is gone.

Buffett noted that the culture at Berkshire now is strongly self-reinforcing.

He added that it's really tough to change an existing culture. A plus for Berkshire is that the culture has been engrained, evolving since 1965 as Buffett added more and more complementary companies.

Capital-Intensive Businesses

Buffett said this is the number one question he would ask of himself: why is Berkshire investing in capital-intensive businesses?

Berkshire's hallmark has been to find companies that gushed cash and required little or no capital reinvestment—companies like See's Candy.

As that cash flow got funneled to Omaha, it was then Buffett's job to reinvest in the next cash machine.

However, as Berkshire grew, Buffett found it more and more difficult to put those billions of dollars of cash flow to work. So Buffett shifted gears.

Starting with MidAmerican Energy in 1999, Buffett saw the appeal of companies that could reinvest all the cash they generated, assuming they could do so at decent returns.

Owning a utility like MEC fit the bill. MEC has invested every dime of its cash generation back into its utility businesses, mostly at regulated rates of return in the 11%–12% range. Not brilliant, but the investment has worked out very decently.

With that experience in his pocket, Buffett was ready for another.

Berkshire recently closed on the acquisition of Burlington Northern Santa Fe, another highly capital-intensive business where he expects low double-digit rates of return on investment.

In the first quarter 10-Q, Berkshire estimates that the two subsidiaries will have capital expenditures of $3.9 billion for 2010.

Debt versus Equity

Buffett noted that the analytical hurdle for buying a bond requires answering the question, "Will the company go out of business?" while buying an equity requires answering the more difficult question, "Will the company prosper?"

This is why Berkshire bought the 15% notes of Harley Davidson rather than the stock.

He had no question the company would stay in business, quipping, "You have to like a business where the customers tattoo your name on their chests!"

But gauging Harley's long-term prosperity was much more difficult, especially during the throes of the crisis.

Surprisingly (to us, anyway), Buffett added that had Goldman offered him a non-callable 12% instead of a callable 10% plus warrants, he would have taken the 12%.

Buffett added that Berkshire has some $60 billion of liability in insurance with some exposures lasting as long as 50 years, so Berkshire will never have all its money in stocks.

Munger piped in that Berkshire is investing as a fiduciary, so it is constrained in how aggressively it buys equities.

Though, Munger added, investing in the equities of distressed companies can be a very promising area.

Ajit

Buffett annually sings the praises of Ajit Jain, who heads up Berkshire's National Indemnity reinsurance unit.

In the annual report, Buffett joked, "If Charlie and I and Ajit are ever in a sinking boat—and you can only save one of us—swim to Ajit."

Jain has been a key player in expanding Berkshire's insurance float far beyond what Buffett thought possible many years ago.

Three years ago, Ajit took over huge liabilities from Lloyds, a contract that brought Berkshire a $7.1 billion premium.

Last year, Ajit negotiated a life insurance contract that could produce $50 billion of premium for Berkshire over the next 50 years.

So while Buffett doubted that Berkshire's $63 billion of float will grow much in the years to come, he allowed that there could always be the float-expanding deal.

Buffett shared that Ajit runs a staff of 30 in a way that makes the Jesuits look liberal in what they allow the members to do. It's one disciplined operation.

If Ajit weren't there, it would be a huge loss for Berkshire, but Berkshire could still do some of the large deals it has become famous for.

Learning Money Lessons

Buffett noted that people do crazy things from time to time, and it is not a function of IQ. You cannot modify the madness of mankind.

On a personal basis, Buffett emphasized how important it is to form good financial habits early in life.

He noted that he and Charlie got lucky. They grew up in households that taught the basic money lessons. It is far more important to get the elementary ideas than those that come with an advanced degree.

Munger added that McDonald's has been a great educator for the American workforce. It teaches folks to show up on time, do their work efficiently and so on. It's had an enormous effect on training the country.

Buffett also plugged a cartoon series seeking to train kids about money called "The Secret Millionaires Club."

Taxes

Buffett has been criticized for suggesting higher taxes are in order for the wealthy while he has avoided estate taxes by gifting his Berkshire shares to charity.

Buffett welcomed people to follow his example. It does avoid taxes, and likely, the money will do a lot of good.

Munger added that Warren, as will we all, will ultimately pay a tax of 100%—when we die we leave it all.

On a national scale, the government budget equals some 25%–26% of GDP, with roughly 15% from tax revenues and 10% from deficit financing.

Buffett said that reducing the deficit will need to involve some balance of lower expenditures and higher taxes.

NetJets

Buffett admitted making a mistake with NetJets, buying too many planes at too high a price.

He gave Davis Sokol enormous credit for turning things around and getting the operating costs more in-line with revenue.

He added, this isn't the first mistake he's made.

Berkshire was in textiles for 20 years even though he knew it was a bad business. He joked, "I finally woke up. I was Rip Van Winkle."

Munger gave the episode some context.

He said, if you have 30 businesses with historically successful managers and that works 95% of the time, then you will have one case that doesn't work so well.

And in the case of NetJets, the franchise is fine—what was lost were past profits. Overall, this is a very good system.

BYD

At the Wesco Financial meeting, Munger gushed that he'll be surprised if they ever find another business as good as BYD. He noted that David Sokol was key in enrolling him into looking at it.

BYD had a track record of rare accomplishment, so this was no startup.

He was especially impressed with the founder, Wang Chuanfu (who was recently crowned China's richest man due to the sharp rise in BYD's stock price). Munger asserted that BYD will work out well as it solves significant world problems with its batteries and electric cars.

He added that with Burlington Northern, MidAmerican and now BYD, that adds a fair amount of engineering to Berkshire, which he likes.

In his younger days, Munger shared how he lost a bundle in a venture capital investment—they lost their main inventor to another company, and then their oscilloscope was obsolesced by the new technology of magnetic tape. And that soured him on technology ventures ever since. Until BYD.

Munger suggested that BYD illustrates their ability to keep learning at Berkshire.

Compensation

Buffett shared that Berkshire owns more than 70 different businesses, so it needs a variety of compensation arrangements.

For example, Burlington Northern requires lots of capital and See's Candy requires none.

Each business has its own key measures of building business value. What Buffett wants to pay for is widening the moat.

Munger noted that GE and many other large companies have centralized personnel departments for such things. Imposing policy from headquarters can build resentment. Berkshire is the opposite— totally decentralized management.

Munger mused that it is amazing how simple it's been, how well it has worked and how little time it takes.

Allowable Returns

Utility returns are based on returns on equity averaging between 11%– 12%, depending on the state regulators. Berkshire is almost certain to earn that rate as demand for power is unlikely to fall off much.

Railroads are riskier as they are more sensitive to the economy. However, it serves society to have railroad investment exceed depreciation.

That common interest suggests Berkshire will earn decent returns on Burlington Northern, and there will be much needed investment in the railroad over the next 30 years.

Munger observed that the railroads have been hugely successful in a regulated system. They've been totally rebuilt over the past 50 years, and the average train has doubled in both length and weight.

Insurance Risks

Buffett shared that earthquakes and hurricanes are the two biggest catastrophe risks.

Currently, rates are soft, so Berkshire has been doing less business. Berkshire is willing to take on a maximum risk of $5 billion. Katrina was $3 billion, and 9/11 was $2 billion.

Berkshire is deliberately seeking big overall losses on occasion when everyone else is trying to avoid them. That's a big competitive advantage.

Buffett said it's actually close to a permanent advantage that gets wider every year.

By taking the other guy's desire to smooth earnings, Berkshire gets big premiums up front and books larger, though lumpier, earnings over time.

Speculation

"Speculators may do no harm as bubbles on a steady stream of enterprise. But the position is serious when enterprise becomes the bubble on a

whirlpool of speculation. When the capital development of a country becomes a by-product of the activities of a casino, the job is likely to be ill-done."

Buffett kicked off an extended discussion on the nature of speculation with this quote from chapter 12 of John Maynard Keynes' *The General Theory of Employment, Interest and Money.* (Buffett added that he thought Keynes' chapter 12 was the *best* description of the way capital markets function.)

Wall Street has always been partly a casino operation, as well as a socially important operation in the raising and allocating of capital. However, this casino element became unbalanced with the advent of options and derivatives.

According to Buffett, Pandora's box was opened in 1982 when Congress approved the creation of S&P 500 contracts.

It changed the game.

Now anyone could buy the index and ignore real companies. The casino was then officially opened to all.

In addition, the contracts received preferred tax treatment, 60% long-term gain and 40% short-term gain, regardless of the holding period.

Buffett wrote Congressman Dingell that year, suggesting that 95% of the trading in these contracts would be gambling.

Munger noted how it was crazy and that Warren was the only one to write in opposition of the bill. Munger concluded, quoting Bismarck, "You shouldn't watch two things—sausage making and legislation making."

Municipal Bonds

Asked about the possibility of municipal bond defaults, Buffett noted that Harrisburg, PA had recently defaulted.

The real key, according to Buffett, was *correlation*—could a contagion break out where many municipalities defaulted at the same time? For bond insurers, the amount of liabilities is extraordinary relative to the capital backing them.

Buffett also noted that the government bailed out GM, so how could it not also come to the aid of a troubled state? The problem is a moral hazard: if the undisciplined are not punished for it, then why should others be disciplined?

Munger concluded that it is wise to invest in places that are prosperous and disciplined—integrity still matters.

Buy American Update

Buffett was asked about his famous *New York Times* article from October 2008 entitled "Buy American. I Am."

Buffett noted that he writes very seldom, and he was pretty premature on that one. Yet he knew that stocks would be better than bonds or cash over the long run.

Even after the market rally, he said he would rather own stocks than bonds for the next 10 or 20 years.

Munger was less sanguine, saying that equities were the best of a bad lot of opportunities and that he sees a long period of dull returns ahead.

Energy

Buffett observed that there are 500,000 producing wells in the U.S. and that we've really exploited what took millions of years to create. It has contributed significantly to the world's prosperity.

Buffett said not to give up on humans' abilities to solve problems. In fact, leaving aside the nuclear and bio-chemical threats, this is a great time in history to be born.

Munger noted that the world is less dependent on oil than in the past. In the 1850s, the technology of the day needed oil to get ahead. Today, oil is not so essential.

He cited physicist Freeman Dyson (the Templeton Prize winner in 2000), who points out that the world going off oil is not that dire—we may go from 85 million barrels/day to 55 million barrels/day over the next 50 years. Munger concluded that if it doesn't bother Freeman Dyson, then it shouldn't bother you.

Munger asserted that solar power is coming because it is so obviously needed. However, he wouldn't buy solar panels yet as they will get cheaper in the future.

He continues to be concerned about ethanol, calling the use of fossil fuel and water to grow corn to make ethanol a "stunningly stupid idea."

He is optimistic that we will build a smart electric grid eventually. Munger believes our energy problems are solvable, and that the right answer may end up being counterintuitive.

Kraft

Berkshire owns 8.8% of Kraft.

Buffett did not like the price Kraft paid to acquire Cadbury's. Nor was he happy about Kraft's tax-inefficient sale of DiGiorno Pizza to Nestlé's to raise cash for the deal.

He did say Kraft is selling for considerably less than its constituent parts. The present price is below the value of very good businesses, such as Kool-Aid and Jell-O.

Munger opined that many top U.S. business leaders think they know too much and dream of running easier businesses with less competition.

He recalled Xerox buying Crum and Foster (an insurance company)— no tough Japanese to compete with in the insurance business. It was just an awful deal.

Munger went on to add that Berkshire avoids a small subset of stupidities by not having around an army of sales folks pushing deals.

Integrity

Munger asserted that the financial crisis was formed by a lack of integrity in management.

Munger poignantly quoted Pope Urban about Cardinal Richelieu: "If there is a god, he has much to answer for. If there is no god, he has done rather well."

Buffett added that the "everyone is doing it" factor is tough to handle.

For example, when the Accounting Standards Board (as instructed by the Senate) allowed options to be treated otherwise, 498 of the S&P 500 opted for otherwise. CEOs surrendered, "I have to do it if everyone else is doing it." The situational ethics problem is huge.

Buffett recommended that the key to handling it is to create a structure that minimizes the weaknesses in human nature.

Munger added that much bad behavior is subconscious, and the cure is to have folks bear the consequences of their decisions. Seen from this perspective, Wall Street is an irresponsible and immoral system.

Munger lamented, "Who do you see apologizing? People think they did fine."

Fear and Opportunity

Buffett repeated his old mantra that successful investing requires the right temperament—to be greedy when others are fearful. If you get scared yourself, then you won't make a lot of money in securities.

Munger shared that he developed courage after hardship. Maybe it's a good idea to get your feet wet in some failure.

Buffett suggested that most people would invest better with no daily quotations. Buy a good business, and hold it for a long, long time.

Munger concluded with a joke. The man says, "Would you still love me if I lost all our money?" The wife replies, "Yes, I will love you always, and I would miss you terribly."

The Electronic Record

Asked why he is on TV so much, Buffett responded that he likes having the electronic record, so there is no chance of him being misquoted or misunderstood.*

If he's on Charlie Rose, he knows the record will be permanent and will be exactly what he said.

0% Interest Rates

Buffett wryly noted that while it is called an easy money policy, it isn't so easy on the people that have the money. It has been tough on savers. Meanwhile, purchasing power is being eaten away by inflation.

He asserted that it won't work forever to have huge budget deficits and 0% rates.

By the way, he added that if this goes badly, don't blame the Fed, blame Congress.

Munger agreed that it is enormously depressing. Stocks are up, in part, because the savings rates are so low. It cannot last.

Making It In Business

Buffett quoted Emerson, "The power that resides within you is new in nature."

He shared how Rose Blumkin, who never went to school, was a force of nature, turning a $500 investment into a $400 million business sitting on 78 acres called the Nebraska Furniture Mart.

He remembered visiting Mrs. B at her home once, and she had green sales tags hanging on the furniture. Buffett quipped that he said to himself, "Forget Sophia Loren, this is my kind of woman!"

---

* In this year's Berkshire annual report, Buffett cited how badly misquoted he was by the media after last year's annual meeting.

Buffett shared that there's nothing like following your passion. That's the common factor with all of Berkshire's excellent managers—they love what they do.

Buffett also shared some of his classic bits of wisdom about growing wealth. Spend less than what you make. Know and stay within your circle of competence. The only businesses that matter are the ones you put your money in. Keep learning over time. Don't lose. Insist on a margin of safety.

Munger suggested making it your practice that you go to bed each night wiser than when you got up. You may rise slowly, but you are sure to rise.

Munger reminisced that the only business course he ever took was accounting.

As a little boy he saw a man who hung out at the club all day. He asked his dad why. His dad explained that the man was very successful in business because he had no competition—he rendered dead horses. Munger said he has been interested in business ever since.

In Omaha, many businesses have come and gone, but he said you could predict that Kiewit would be a success because they worked hard and were disciplined.

Causes for Optimism

Long noted for being a bit of curmudgeon, Munger may have surprised the crowd with a list of things he is quite optimistic about:

1. The main problems of civilization are technical and solvable, all with energy, with huge benefits for civilization.

2. Berkshire's culture will continue to work for years to come.

3. He likes to see people rising rapidly from poverty, and that is happening in China and India.

4. Maintain low expectations—that is the key to happiness.

Munger finished with a flourish, "Seeing as I'll be optimistic when I'm nearly dead, surely the rest of you can handle a little inflation."

Pragmatism

Asked about their theory for life, Munger seized the microphone and said, "Pragmatism! Do what suits your temperament. Do what works better with experience. Do what works and keep doing it. That's the fundamental algorithm of life—REPEAT WHAT WORKS."

Venue: Qwest Center

Attendance: 40,000

Details About This Year:

- This year's movie included a GEICO employee rock video featuring Buffett rapping and break-dancing (obviously, a stunt double). There was a hilarious special edition of "The Office," featuring both Buffett and Munger, where one Office employee said, "I'm just like Buffett. I save. I invest. And my kids ain't gettin' diddly-squat."

- Munger and Buffett handled questions from the throng of shareholders for six hours.

- It is an impressive learning experience—even more so when one considers that "Professors" Buffett and Munger (ages 80 and 87, respectively) are as sharp as ever.

Fortune 500 Ranking: 7th

Stock Price: $120,475

One dollar invested in 1964 would now be worth **$9,739**.

Berkshire's per-share book value has grown from $19.46 to **$99,860** (a rate of **19.8%** compounded annually).

The S&P 500 compounded at **9.4%** annually for the same period.

HIGHLIGHTS FROM 2011'S NOTES

First Quarter Earnings: A Look at What the Numbers Mean

Buffett has long been the accounting teacher.

In four decades of annual reports, Buffett has covered many nuances of accounting convention versus a practical picture of business reality.

The message throughout: Look not what at the numbers are but what the numbers mean.

So we took it as highly significant that "Professor" Buffett opened this year's meeting with no less than four overhead slide projections.

The first of which showed Berkshire's first quarter net operating profit of $1.6 billion versus $2.2 billion a year ago—$821 million of insurance underwriting losses obscured a decent increase in operating profits ex-insurance.

Other than the residential construction area, Buffett was positive about the slow but steady improvement in the economy. In particular, Berkshire's purchase of the BNSF railroad was proving to be a real winner with its competitive advantages becoming more and more evident as fuel prices increase.

What the numbers mean: With the exception of residential construction and some catastrophe losses, Berkshire's businesses are rolling.

Slide two showed Berkshire's estimate of its losses incurred from the recent catastrophes of flooding in Australia ($195 million), the earthquake in New Zealand ($412 million) and the earthquake in Japan ($1,066 million) which came to $1,673 million.

Berkshire estimates that $700 million of that total came from its 25% quota share arrangement with Swiss Re.

Buffett noted that historically, Berkshire experiences losses totaling some 3%–5% of total catastrophe losses (which was true with Katrina).[*]

For perspective, Buffett noted that the New Zealand quake caused $12 billion in insured damages. Thus, New Zealand, with a population of five million people—just one-sixtieth of that of the U.S.—suffered a catastrophe on a per capita basis that was *10 times Katrina* in scale.

Buffett warned that the third quarter (hurricane season) is usually the worst for catastrophe losses, so 2011 might well go down as one of the worst years in history for such losses.

---

[*] So here's a really good unasked question: how can Berkshire have some 10% of the world reinsurance market and yet consistently participate in only a fraction of that percentage of the losses when catastrophe strikes?

Slide three showed the phenomenal policy growth ongoing at GEICO, which added 218,422 policies in the first quarter of 2010 and added another 319,676 policies the first quarter of 2011.

Buffett values each policyholder at $1,500 (about 1x premiums), so GEICO added nearly $500 million of value in the first quarter. Goodwill accounting does not reflect this increase in value.

Buffett noted that GEICO's intrinsic value has grown to over $14 billion now, and GEICO continues to gain market share every day.

Buffett joked that if just 66 shareholders would sign up with GEICO in the convention hall, that would add $100,000 of value for Berkshire and help pay for the annual meeting.[*]

What the numbers mean: GEICO's growing intrinsic value is much greater than what the accounting reports.

Slide four touched on an accounting convention called "other than temporary impairment." It makes little sense, but the fact was that Berkshire took a mark down of Wells Fargo stock purchased at higher prices and a deduction of $337 million on the income statement due to this convention. Meanwhile, Berkshire's $3.7 billion of unrealized gain on its other shares of Wells Fargo was ignored.

What the numbers mean: Ignore income or losses from investments in calculating Berkshire's operating earnings.

Buffett summed up the slides, decrying the news headlines that report the "all important number," which could easily be the "all deceptive number." Instead, investors should focus on gains in operating earnings, gains in book value and gains in intrinsic value.

For the first quarter of 2011, Berkshire showed progress by each measurement.

The Sokol Issue: Inexcusable and Inexplicable

As widely reported, David Sokol resigned from Berkshire recently and left controversy in his wake.

At the center of the storm were questions about Sokol's purchases of shares of Lubrizol, contact with Citigroup—Lubrizol's investment

---

* Here's another area of inquiry. Advertising does more than bring in new policyholders, building advantages in customer retention, brand and share of mind. So this is oversimplified. However, we note that GEICO is spending $225 million per quarter in advertising—so that's about $700 per new policyholder for the first quarter. If GEICO can average a 94 combined ratio (6% margin) on a $1,500 average premium, that's $90 profit per year per shareholder.

That means it may take Berkshire about eight years to get its money back *just on the ad spend*. So what are the features (which no doubt include float creation) that make this business so darn valuable?

banker, and a meeting with Buffett where Sokol pitched the idea that Berkshire should buy Lubrizol.

Buffett reminisced that it was 20 years ago that he endured the Salomon Brothers scandal. That scandal, even after all these years, Buffett still describes as "inexcusable" and "inexplicable." His guess is that he may well say the same about this one 20 years from now.

Buffett noted that Sokol did nothing to hide the trades he made, so there was no deception there.

He also noted that a decade ago, he offered an incentive bonus plan to Sokol where, if certain extreme goals were met, Sokol would get $50 million, and his junior partner, Greg Abel, would get $25 million.

Sokol agreed with the proviso that the bonus be split equally, $37.5 million each.

So here was part of what Buffett found so inexplicable—here's a man of such great integrity voluntarily giving up $12.5 million of bonus and then, with Lubrizol, the same man acting in a seemingly suspect way for a profit of a mere $3 million.

Munger's one word explanation for Sokol's actions, "hubris."

There was anger from some shareholders about a lack of outrage in Berkshire's initial press release, which conveyed praises for Sokol's contributions as well as regrets for his resignation.

Munger conceded that the press release was not the most cleverly written in the history of the world.

At the same time, he held firm that it doesn't serve to make decisions in anger. He quoted Berkshire board member Tom Murphy: "You can always tell a man to go to hell tomorrow if it's such a good idea."

The Lubrizol Deal

Buffett noted that Lubrizol is a low-cost provider of fuel additives, a $10 billion market.

It has a good-sized, sustainable moat with lots of patents, number-one market share and regularly works with customers (primarily the major oil companies) to develop new additives.

Buffett compared it to ISCAR, which "shines up tungsten into tools and a durable competitive advantage."

Munger noted that Lubrizol and ISCAR are sister companies where their markets are small enough that they were not worth attacking.

Buffett also noted that by spending $9 billion on the Lubrizol acquisition, Berkshire had used up a good chunk of the estimated $12 billion after-tax earnings he expects to come in this year.

Succession: Independent Chairman

Buffett shared that on his demise, Howard Buffett will likely become the independent chairman as he will represent a large block of stock and receive little or no compensation.

By separating the chairman and the CEO positions, Berkshire can more easily correct mistakes with CEOs that don't work out. Fire one, hire another if need be.

Buffett quoted the Bible, "The meek will inherit the earth," but then noted the next question is, "Will they stay meek?" Thus, it is critical to separate the chairman and CEO positions.

1776–2011

One longtime shareholder asked Warren how he can be so infernally happy when we have so many problems.

Buffett answered that he is indeed enthused about America. Since 1776, America has been the most extraordinary economic story in the world.

If you had been told that following Aug. 30, 1930, the day Warren was born, the market would crash, 4,000 banks would fail, the Dow would sink to 32 (32!!!), there would be 25% unemployment, a dust bowl, the grasshoppers would take over . . . you might think we were in big trouble.

Instead, despite all those problems, since 1930, the average standard of living in America has increased 6 for 1.

In contrast, Buffett observed that you can look at entire centuries in world history where nothing happened. The economic growth of America has been an incredible achievement.

Many have underestimated the resilience of our republic.

Buffett said his father-in-law-to-be, Doc Thompson, was very anti-New Deal. He called young Warren over for a pre-marital talk, which made Buffett very nervous.

He said that Doc went on for a two-hour rant about the certain failure of the politics of the day and then concluded with this advice for young Warren: "You're going to fail, but it's not your fault. Susie would have starved anyway. The Democrats are taking us to communism."

In 1951, the two men Warren admired most, his father and Ben Graham, both advised him against starting in the investment business at that time. The Dow at 200 (200!!!) was much too high. Better to park yourself on the sidelines for a while.

We've had the Civil War . . . 15 recessions . . . it certainly has not been a straight line of progress, but the power of capitalism has been amazing. Stimulus has helped our recent problems, but what will really bring us out of recession is capitalism. And the world has caught on.

Buffett predicted that in the next 100 years, we will have 15 to 20 lousy years and that we'll be so far ahead of where we are now that it will be beyond belief.

Munger, in his characteristically sunny way, concluded that "Europe had the Black Death where one-third of the population died. The world will go on."

Inflation Hedges

Buffett declared the best inflation hedge is a company with a wonderful product that requires little capital to grow.

As a test, he invited each of us to look at our own earning ability. In inflation, your compensation can go up without any additional investment.

As a business example, Buffett noted that when See's Candy was purchased in 1971, it had the revenues of $25 million and sold 16 million pounds of candy annually with $9 million in tangible assets. Today, See's sells $300 million of candy with $40 million of tangible assets. Berkshire needed to invest only $31 million to generate a more than 10-fold increase in revenues.

In aggregate, Buffett noted that Berkshire has earned $1.5 billion in profits at See's over the years.

See's inventory turns fast, has no receivables and has little fixed investment—a perfect inflation hedge.

Buffett allowed that if you have tons of receivables and inventory, that's a lousy business in inflation.

The railroad and MidAmerican Energy both have these undesirable characteristics, but that is offset by their utility to the economy and subsequent allowable returns.

Buffett rued that there simply aren't enough "See's Candys" to buy.

Buffett added that being an investor has made him a better businessman and that being a businessman has made him a better investor.*

Munger noted that they didn't always know this inflation-business element, which shows how continuous learning is so important.

---

* We concur.

Well Fargo/U.S. Bancorp

Buffett asserted that both banks are among the best, if not the best, large banks in the country, with Wells Fargo being about four times larger than U.S. Bancorp.

Buffett predicted that banking profitability will be less than it was in the early part of this century due to reduced leverage, which is good for society.

Significantly, Buffett said he thought that, by far, we've seen the worst of the banking crisis. Loan losses will continue to come down. Banks should be conservatively run given that they get very cheap money with an implicit federal guarantee.

Buffett noted that the FDIC since 1934 has bailed out 3,800 banks, 250 of which were in the last couple years, and all the money came from other banks. The FDIC has been a well-designed mutual insurance company.

The Three Categories of Investment

Asked about commodities, Buffett noted that when he took over Berkshire, the stock traded for three-quarters of an ounce of gold. At $1,500 an ounce, gold has a long ways to go to catch up to Berkshire's $120,000 per share stock price.

Then he outlined three categories of investment:

Category 1—Investments denominated in a currency.

Buffett pulled out his wallet, took out a one dollar bill and read out loud, "In God We Trust." He noted this is false advertising. What it should say is, "In Government We Trust." God isn't going to do anything about that dollar.

The point is that *any currency investment is a bet on how government will behave.* Almost all currencies have declined over time. Unless you get paid really well, these investments don't make much sense.

Category 2—Investments that don't produce anything but you hope to sell at a higher price.

Gold, for example. Buffett reprised his gold thought experiment, where if you took all the gold in the world, you could make a 67-foot cube weighing 175,000 metric tons. You could then get a ladder and sit on top of it, fondle it, polish it. But that cube isn't going to do anything. You are simply betting someone will buy it higher.

He cited Keynes Chapter 12—"The State of Long Term Expectation" from *The General Theory of Employment, Interest and Money*—that such investing amounts to a beauty contest where you are betting not on whom you believe to be the prettiest contestant, but who others will believe is beautiful.

The self-effacing Buffett reminded us that he tried to do that with silver and proved to be 13 years too early.

Category 3—Investments in assets that produce something.

This is a play on what you think that asset will produce over time.

For example, with a farm, one can make a rational calculation on its value. Success will be determined on cash produced. You don't care about the quote the next day or month. You are looking to the business for your return.

This is the basis for Berkshire's investments in ISCAR and Lubrizol.

Buffett noted that rising prices create their own excitement. The neighbor gets rich. He owns gold. You know the neighbor's not that smart . . . yet he's doing better than you. Pretty soon, you own gold.

Munger added that gold is a peculiar investment in that it only works if everything goes to hell.

Buffett joked that $100 billion of gold is produced annually, much of it taken out of the ground in South Africa to be shipped to the New York Fed, where it will be put back into the ground.

All the gold in the world is currently worth about $8 trillion. With that amount of money, you could buy all the farmland in America, 10 Exxon Mobils and still have $1 trillion to $2 trillion of walking-around money.

Buffett concluded that he will bet on good businesses to outperform gold.

Conglomerates

Buffett conceded that Berkshire is, indeed, a conglomerate. At their best, *conglomerates enable the tax efficient transfer of cash from businesses that cannot use the money intelligently to those that can.* Berkshire is a very rational conglomerate.

The word "conglomerate" got a bad rap from the 1960s Ponzi schemes of Gulf and Western (Charles Bluhdorn), LTV (Jimmy Ling), etc., where there was an unspoken conspiracy and where stock was issued like confetti to buy real assets. It ended badly, and the word "conglomerate" left a bad taste.

Legacy

When asked what he'd like to be known for, Buffett quipped, "Old age."

Munger said that what Warren most wanted to be said at his funeral was, "That's the oldest looking corpse I ever saw."

In a more serious vein, Munger mused that he'd like something like, "Fairly won, wisely used," on his tombstone.

Buffett thought perhaps he'd go with "Teacher."

He acknowledged that he loves teaching, and he's grateful for the great teachers he's had, including his father, Ben Graham, and Tom Murphy, among others.

Currency Debasement

Buffett noted that from his birth in 1930 to today, the dollar has depreciated by 16 to 1 (i.e., $1 today buys what 6 cents bought then). Yet inflation did not destroy us.

Some subsidiaries of Berkshire earn their money in other currencies. Coca-Cola receives 80% of its profits in non-dollar earnings.

Munger observed that Greece is an awful situation. People there, while wonderful in many respects, do not want to work or to pay taxes. He quoted Adam Smith, "A great civilization has a good deal of ruin in it."

Despite these concerns, Buffett concluded that if he had a choice, he would be born in the U.S. today over any other place in the world.

Lower Expectations

Buffett shared his usual advice that the average investor would do fine to simply buy shares of an index fund over time.

Munger asserted that he'd definitely rather own Berkshire over an index fund.

He also predicted that the next 50 years will not be as good as the last 50 years for skilled investors.

Buffett averred that Berkshire's mission was to increase earning power and intrinsic value with 100% alignment with shareholders. That is what they think about each day. Luck has helped, but there is no way Berkshire will compound at rates anywhere close to when it was working with smaller sums.

Munger said he was confident Berkshire will outperform U.S. industry in aggregate.

He suggested that reduced expectations are the best defense for the investor. He added that lowering expectations was how he got married— "My wife lowered her expectations."

Buffett immediately quipped, "And he lived up to them!"

Trust

Given the Sokol situation, Buffett had a number of questions around rules and compliance.

Buffett reiterated his desire that employees honor both the spirit and letter of the law. However, with 260,000 employees at Berkshire, a number roughly equal to the households in Omaha, not all will match the rules.

Buffett noted that you can have all the rules and records in the world, and someone can still go off and trade in some cousin's name.

Munger shared that it is fun to be trusted and to have much self-respect. In his view, an attitude of trust was the best compliance.

He noted that you can find huge compliance departments on Wall Street, and that is where the biggest scandals occur.

The Economy

Buffett observed that we have had the foot to the floor with both monetary and fiscal policy in America, and this will go on for an extended period.

He noted that many people think of our "fiscal policy" as having passed a "stimulus bill."

Buffett suggested we look past the words. Forget the "stimulus bill." What is really happening is that we have a 10% deficit, which is gigantic. We're taking in 15% of GDP and spending 25% of GDP. That is huge stimulus.

Residential construction has flattened to 500,000 units per year, so the crazy excesses of the boom are getting worked out.*

When that ends, we'll see employment pick up much more than most people think. Construction has a ripple effect through many ancillary businesses.

Buffett stuck with the prediction he made in the annual report, that we'll see improvement in residential construction by year-end.

Munger added that one advantage of buying into cyclical industries is that many people don't like them because the earnings are so unpredictable. At Berkshire, they don't mind having lumpy earnings over a business cycle.

For example, Berkshire just bought the largest brick company in Alabama. Nobody's bidding on Alabama brick when there are no customers. Buffett chimed in that See's Candy loses money eight months of the year. Yet we know that Christmas will come, so there's no reason to look at one losing month and panic. Over the next 20 years, there will be some lousy years, some great ones and plenty of okay ones.

As for Berkshire's other businesses, he says that steady improvement is widespread. Railcar loadings peaked at 219,000, bottomed at 150,000 and are now running at 190,000. ISCAR has seen month-by-month improvement.

Financial Reform: Or the Lack of It

Munger felt it was a huge mistake not to learn more from the subprime mortgage debacle.

In his view, we haven't throttled the sin and the folly of asinine and greedy behavior. He would take an ax to the financial sector, whittling it down to a more constructive size. He would change the tax system to discourage trading, so that securities would trade more like real estate.

He asserted that the lack of contrition on Wall Street for the debacle makes Sokol look like a hero.

Buffett piped in, "He's warming up!"

Then Buffett noted the inanity of a tax system where a six-second trade in an S&P 500 futures contract results in 60% of the profit being taxed as long-term capital gain.

Munger concluded that having a system where hedge funds are taxed at rates less than those for professors of physics or taxi-cab drivers is demented.

---

* Average construction runs around 1.2 million units per year. Bubble year construction ran around two million units per year.

Munger noted that past panics and the depression started on Wall Street with great waves of speculation and bad behavior. This last mess should have caused a 1930s-type reaction (like the Securities Act of 1934). It hasn't, so Munger confidently predicted that we'll have another debacle.

Munger asserted that it was really stupid not to have done more, that part of the stupidity was in the way finance and economics are taught at the universities and that finance attracts the same sort of people who are attracted to snake charming.

Buffett quipped, "If there's anyone else we forgot to insult, just pass their names up."

BYD

While BYD trades roughly double Berkshire's cost in the shares, the stock is down some 80% from its high.

Munger was unconcerned, noting that a company trying to move as fast as BYD will have delays and glitches. In trying to double auto sales each for six years, BYD did it for five years and then had a glitch.

Overall, Munger asserted that he's quite encouraged.

In a rare and sweet role reversal, Buffett muttered, "I have nothing to add."

Too Big to Fail

Buffett acknowledged that there are institutions in the world that governments should properly save. Europe is in the process of deciding whether whole countries are "too big to fail."

Buffett suggested that this problem will always be with us, so our best tactic is to reduce the propensity to fail.

One measure he proposed was that those institutions that put society at risk and fail should leave the CEO and spouse dead broke. The board should also suffer severe penalties. If society needs to save you, you should have very painful penalties.

Musing on the miserable case of Fannie Mae and Freddie Mac, Buffett called them "too big to figure out!"

Great Insurance Companies

Buffett got quite enthusiastic discussing Berkshire's insurance empire. He called GEICO, now the third largest auto insurer, a fabulous company.

GEICO debuted the idea of selling direct (without an agent) way back in 1936, and few have been able to copy it.

Meanwhile, Ajit Jain built Berkshire's reinsurance business from scratch.

Buffett loves Ajit, claiming that he cannot think of any decision Ajit has made that he'd have done any better. Ajit is as rational as anyone Buffett has met, loves what he does, is very creative and unfailingly thinks of Berkshire first.

Interestingly, Buffett claimed later in the meeting that Berkshire spent its first 15 years in reinsurance not making money. It wasn't until Ajit came along that reinsurance became a real profit center for Berkshire.

Berkshire's Gen Re unit, with Tad Montross, runs a disciplined business, and Berkshire's smaller insurance units have unusual franchises.

And it all started when Berkshire bought National Indemnity for $7 million in 1970. Now, in that same building, they run an insurance company with the largest net worth of any in the world and some $66 billion of float.

Munger noted that Berkshire has a number of best-in-class companies. BNSF is certainly one of the best railroads in the world. MidAmerican Energy is top-ranked among utilities.

Munger concluded that it's not all bad to be world-class in your main businesses.

Buffett noted that the high-speed rail proposal in California came with an estimated cost of $43 billion, a cost that would be sure to go up.

Meanwhile, Berkshire paid about $43 billion for BNSF and got 22,000 miles of track, 6,000 locomotives, 13,000 bridges (anyone want to buy a bridge?). So the replacement value of BNSF is huge. The country will always need railroads. It's a terrific asset to own.

Costco

Munger, a board member of Costco, made his annual assertion that Costco (the $80 billion membership warehouse club retailer) is the best in the world in its industry.

It's a meritocracy that takes it as its extreme ethical duty to pass along savings to its customers, which, in turn, creates ferocious customer loyalty.

Costco has a store in Korea that will do $400 million in revenue— something that one would think cannot exist in retail, yet there it is.

Costco has the right ethics, diligence and management to continue its winning ways—quite rare.

Munger observed that it's a problem to prevent success and wealth from creating your demise. General Motors was the most successful company in the world at one time and then became a victim of its success with large unionization and very tough competition eventually wiping out the shareholders.

Munger asserted that if he taught business school, he would do the full sweep of the history of a business.

Buffett joked that he and Charlie were hijacked by terrorists who decided to shoot the capitalists. They allowed them one last request. Charlie said, "I would like to give once more my presentation on the virtues of Costco with slides." The terrorists reluctantly agreed. Then they asked Warren for his last request. Buffett said, "Shoot me first."

Cash in Treasures

Buffett agreed that investment choices for short-term money are lousy right now. However, he emphasized that he doesn't mess around with short-term money.

Basically, at Berkshire, cash is always in Treasuries. While it may be irritating that they pay virtually nothing, Berkshire will not reach for another 10–20 basis points.

"It's a parking place, and we want our car back when we're done parking," Buffett declared.

Buffett shared how critical it was when panic hit in 2008 that Berkshire has the money to do deals. It was not in a money market fund or commercial paper.

Munger noted that he's seen a lot of people struggle stupidly to reach for an extra 10 basis points.

He noted that they were able to buy pipelines because they could agree to a deal on Friday and produce the cash on Monday.

Buffett added that the seller was worried about going bankrupt the next week. Buffett concluded that "if panic breaks because Ben Bernanke has run off with Paris Hilton, we're ready."

Learning

Munger noted that we're here to go to sleep each day smarter than when we woke up.

Buffett shared how he lived in the Omaha Public Library for four years.*

---

* Buffett is reported to have read every investment book in the library.

He also noted that his Dale Carnegie course in 1951 cost him $100, and the value was incalculable as the value of good communication skills so dramatically enhanced his life.

So Buffett's big point was to develop yourself. Find your passion, and improve your skills.

2012

Venue: CenturyLink Center (renamed from "Qwest")

Attendance: 35,000

Details About This Year:

- The meeting lasted six hours. It was an impressive accomplishment that "Professors" Buffett and Munger (ages 81 and 88, respectively) were still going strong.

- After the weekend, Buffett was pleased to announce that Berkshire shareholders spent $35 million at "The Berkshire Mall" on everything from See's Candy to Borsheim's jewelry. That was an average of $1,000 per attendee.

Fortune 500 Ranking: 7th

Stock Price: $114,813

One dollar invested in 1964 would now be worth **$9,282**.

Berkshire's per-share book value has grown from $19.46 to **$114,214** (a rate of **19.7%** compounded annually).

The S&P 500 compounded at **9.2%** annually for the same period.

HIGHLIGHTS FROM 2012's NOTES

Sovereign Debt Crisis

Munger and Buffett agreed that the sovereign debt mess is the big question of the moment and tough to answer. There have been many failures throughout history.

Buffett noted that the wealth doesn't go away—the farms, the factories and labor remain. Rather, the wealth gets reallocated. It's a big reallocation of wealth. He compared the ECB's trillion euro bailout to giving a guy with a margin account more debt.

Munger observed that it is dangerous to go low on fiscal virtue, paraphrasing St. Augustine, "Everyone wants fiscal virtue but not quite yet."

He recommended we follow the Roman example where two-thirds of the Punic Wars were paid off before the war was over.

He concluded that we need more sacrifice, more patriotism and more civilized politics.

Banks

Buffett asserted that American banks are in far better position than European banks. They have taken most of the abnormal losses, buttressed capital in a big way and have "liquidity coming out of their ears."

Munger noted that we have a full federal union, so we can print money. He's comfortable with the U.S. system.

Buffett agreed, noting that it's night and day. The U.S. Fed and Treasury had the power to do whatever it took. In contrast, 17 countries in Europe surrendered their sovereignty with respect to currency. As Henry Kissinger once said, "When I want to call Europe, what number do I dial?"

Regarding European banks, Buffett called the ECB coming up with 1 trillion euro ($1.3 trillion in U.S. dollars—an amount equal to one-sixth of all bank deposits in the U.S.) a huge act. Because European banks have less in deposits and rely more on wholesale funding, they needed to build more capital but have done little to do so. He noted one Italian bank had at least had a rights offering.

Munger noted that Canada kept to the old standards and had almost no trouble. We departed from sound decency and participated in folly with lots of disgraceful behavior and suffered enormous damage. Similar things happened in Ireland and Spain. Greenspan was wrong with his laissez-faire policies. It is the duty of government to step on bad behavior. Once we were in it, we had to nationalize.

Buffett admitted buying some JP Morgan for his own account. His favorite bank is Wells Fargo, which he buys exclusively for Berkshire, which now owns over 400 million shares.*

Chief Risk Officer

Buffett noted that the role of the chief risk officer (CRO) must not be delegated. He has seen risk management group reports ignored too many times.

Buffett noted that he is the CRO at Berkshire and that role along with capital allocation and the selection of managers, are his primary duties. The two basic risks he analyzes are excessive leverage and insurance risk.

Munger averred that not only has risk management been delegated, it has been stupidly done.

He characterized "value at risk" as one of the dumbest ideas ever put forward.

Buffett agreed that PhDs who should know better got hooked on their fancy math, which may not be applicable to human behavior.

Munger related the story of how Sandy Gottesman (who founded the investment advisory firm First Manhattan and joined the Berkshire board in 2003) fired a man who was his top producer. The man said, "How can you fire me?" Gottesman replied, "I'm a rich old man, and you make me nervous."

Buffett assured shareholders that no one at Berkshire makes him nervous.

Special Deals

Buffett acknowledged that he cold-called Bank of America CEO Brian Moynihan to offer the preferred with warrants deal ($5 billion of 6% preferred with 700 million 10-year warrants to buy common stock at $7.14 a share).

They had never talked before. However, Moynihan knew Buffett had 1) the ability to commit and 2) large sums available.

Buffett asserted that Berkshire will still have this advantage after he is gone.

---

* Wells Fargo is now Berkshire's largest position after Coca-Cola and is becoming just as dominant as Coke in its own way. Wells made 34% of the mortgages originated in the first quarter, more than triple the share of the closest competitor.

While the next CEO might not have Warren's Rolodex, he will still have these unique Berkshire deal advantages.

Buffett emphasized that the impact of special deals is peanuts compared with the long-term impact of buying great businesses for Berkshire.

Insurance

A question on surprisingly higher than expected mortality on Berkshire's Swiss Re life insurance business got Buffett going on one of his favorite topics.

Buffett noted that surprises like this are why Berkshire's overriding principle is to reserve conservatively. GEICO is short tail business and has had redundancies in reserves year after year. While Gen Re was under-reserved when Berkshire bought it in 1998, reserves are developing well now under the management of Tad Montross.

Munger inserted, "It's inevitable that some contracts work out worse than expected. Why would anyone buy insurance if that weren't the case?"

Buffett noted that after 9/11, it was very difficult to assess insurance damages. For example, what counts as business interruption?

Similarly, with the tsunami in Japan, does a U.S. auto parts company have a case for business interruption? These sorts of issues take years to sort out and argue, again, for reserving conservatively.

Pricing the reinsurance of catastrophes is very difficult. It's hard to detect a series of random events from what might constitute a long-term trend.

Buffett's tactic is to assume the worst and price from there.

In the last few months, Berkshire has written far more business in Asia, New Zealand, Australia, Thailand, etc.

As he noted last year, Buffett pointed out that the second quake in New Zealand caused $12 billion of insured damage in a country of five million people. On a per capita basis, this was the equivalent devastation of 10 Hurricane Katrina's.

Events like this are why Buffett insists that Berkshire keep at least $20 billion in cash.

Buffett is very pleased with GEICO's continued success, asserting that GEICO is worth $15 billion more than what it is carried for on the books.*

---

* Buffett said last year that he would value GEICO at $1,500 per policyholder. With over 10 million policyholders now times $1,500 per, that would equal $15 billion.

GEICO is hitting on all cylinders. In 1995, GEICO had 2% of the market. Under Tony Nicely's superb management, GEICO now has nearly 10% of the market.

Buffett admitted, "Gen Re was off the tracks when we bought it—lots of 'accommodation business' emphasizing growth over profitability."

Joe Brandon refocused the underwriting discipline, and Tad Montross has followed through. Now, the business is right-sized, and the culture is good, as are prospects for decent long-term growth, creating a terrific asset for Berkshire.

In valuing Gen Re, Buffett would calculate intrinsic value as a combination of net worth and float.

In valuing GEICO, he would also include its significant underwriting profits for the next 10–20 years and its significant growth prospects.

Float

When Berkshire's float reached $40 billion, Buffett started talking about how it was unlikely float would grow much more. Now, float is $70 billion.

Ajit Jain has found innovative ways to create more float. However, some of the business, such as retroactive insurance, runs off by nature.

He credited Ajit Jain for working miracles for Berkshire over the years and doing a spectacular job of managing the "melting ice cube" that is Berkshire's float.

In addition, because Berkshire's companies write profitably, Berkshire gets the economics of float at a bargain rate. As long as Berkshire underwrites at a profit, *people are actually paying Berkshire* to hold this $70 billion of float.

Munger concluded that property casualty insurance is not a terribly good business. You have to be in the top 10% to do well. Berkshire probably has the best in the world. To have something that is very good and not growing much is okay.

Running Berkshire

Munger suggests that it's an illusion that there is vast control at the average corporate headquarters. One of the beauties of Berkshire, he contends, is that it doesn't require much control from headquarters.

Buffett's key to motivating Berkshire's managers is giving them room to paint their own paintings.

Buffett joked that if someone told him to use more red than blue, he'd likely tell them where to stick the paintbrush.

He likes painting his own canvas and getting applause for doing well. So he seeks managers who are wired in the same way, giving them the paintbrushes and compensating them well for good performance.

In addition, Berkshire managers don't have to talk to shareholders, lawyers, reporters, etc., so they can focus on their businesses.

Buffett concluded that his focus is on not taking away something that's already good, a sort of negative art.

Munger noted how rational this approach is versus the percentages and quota arrangements dreamed up by human resource departments. Regarding compensation consultants, he suggested prostitution would be a step up for them.

Buffett quipped, "Charlie's in charge of diplomacy at Berkshire."

Valuation

Buffett confessed that he'd prefer that Berkshire would trade just once a year at a fair value that he and Charlie would come up with. This is how some private companies do it.

However, public markets can do strange things.

Buffett reminded us that Berkshire issued stock in the mid-1990s when it was overpriced. Surely a first for any public offering, on the prospectus Buffett and Munger stated that they would not buy the stock at the price, nor would they recommend that their families buy shares.

Buffett confirmed that the intrinsic value of Berkshire is significantly higher than the book value, so he is very comfortable about the idea of buying in shares at 1.1 times book. He would love to buy tens of billions of dollars in at 110% of book, consistent with maintaining his cash cushion of $20 billion. Such a move would be certain to increase intrinsic value per share, so doing it on a big scale would be an obvious winner.

Buffett noted that Berkshire nearly completed a $22 billion deal recently, suggesting there is plenty to do in the world of adding value in ways other than buying in shares.

Buffett noted he has seen the stock cut in half four times and that the beauty of stocks is that they can sell at silly prices sometimes.

Buffett was definitive, "It's how we got rich."

As he has in years past, Buffett asserted that *The Intelligent Investor* chapters 8 (Mr. Market) and 20 (Margin of Safety) give you all you need to know. Build into your system that stocks get mispriced.

In the next 20 years, Berkshire will be significantly overvalued and undervalued at different points. The stock market is the most obliging of money-making entities. Armed with the right system, the rules are stacked in your favor.

In valuing the operating businesses, Buffett said he would love to buy the group for 10 times pre-tax earnings or maybe even more.

Natural Resources

Buffett observed that cheap natural gas has been a huge plus for the trade deficit. The U.S. energy picture has changed a lot in three years.

Buffett noted that there has been a remarkable decrease in electricity usage as kilowatt hours used declined 4.7% in the first quarter. In addition, with natural gas at $2 per mcf (thousand cubic feet) and oil at $100 a barrel, that creates a 50/1 ratio of oil to gas pricing, something he didn't think was possible. Now natural gas is supplanting coal at these low prices.

Munger called the using up of our natural gas reserves "idiotic." He would use up our less precious thermal coal first. That would be rational and exactly the opposite of what we are doing.

He asserted that we would have been better off to keep oil and gas, the hydrocarbons that are the single most precious resource of the U.S., in the ground over the last 50 years.

In his usual understated manner, Munger summed up his point: "Energy independence is stupid. We want to *conserve* it and use the other fellow's resources."

Buffett joked, "This is Charlie's version of saving up sex for old age."

Munger retorted, "But we're going to use the oil!"

Business School

Buffett and Munger took their annual shot at modern portfolio theory and the business schools that teach it.

Buffett noted that business schools focus on one fad after another, usually mathematically based.

Buffett said if he ran a business school he would have just two courses: 1) How to Value a Business and 2) How to Think About Markets.

He noted that Ray Kroc had no need to know the option value of McDonald's, but thought long and hard about how to make better fries.

Buffett concluded, "If you think about business and buy businesses for less than they're worth, you're going to make money."

Munger added that valuing a very long-term option on a business you understand does not fit the Black Sholes option pricing model.

It makes no sense. However, the accounting profession wanted some standardized way of valuing them. And they got one.

The Buffett Rule

Buffett took pains to note that his idea of having the rich pay more taxes applied to only the 400 largest incomes, which now average $270 million each—131 of that group paid taxes at less than a 15% rate.

This compares to 1992, where the 400 largest income earners averaged $45 million and just 16 paid less than a 15% rate.

Buffett's point is that a group that has done so well over the last two decades should be paying taxes at least at the same rate they did 20 years ago.

For himself, Buffett said he has no tax planning, no gimmicks.

He earned between $25 million and $65 million the last few years. And he had the lowest tax rate in his office at about 17%.

MidAmerican Energy

Buffett said MEC has done a lot with wind power, thanks to a 10-year subsidy of 2.2 cents per kilowatt hour. Otherwise, the economics would not work.

MEC owns half of two large solar projects as well. Both solar and wind need subsidies to develop. In addition, given that wind is unpredictable, you can never count on wind power for your base load. Wind will always be supplementary.

MEC CEO Greg Abel noted that with solar incentives, they will recover 30% of the construction cost. Since Berkshire is a full tax payer, it derives full benefit from these tax incentives.

In contrast, Buffett asserted that 80% of utilities cannot reap full tax benefits because they wipe out their taxable income with depreciation.

Buffett noted the MEC is capital intensive, and a reasonable expectation for return on investment with this utility would be 12%.

Buffett surprised us a bit, saying that MEC may have enormous opportunities in the next 15 years to invest, perhaps as much as $100 billion.

Systemic Risk

With regard to systemic risk, Buffett noted that his first rule is to play tomorrow. That means not going broke no matter what happens. So keep plenty in reserves, and go low on debt.*

---

* Again, at Berkshire, that reserve number is now $20 billion in cash.

If that is handled, then you can invest.

Buffett claimed that in 53 years, he and Charlie had never had a discussion about buying a business that included a talk about macro affairs. "If it's a good business at a good price, we buy it. There is always going to be bad news out there."

He said he bought his first stock in 1942, when we were losing the war!

Buffett reminded attendees that it was during the swoon in 2008 that he wrote his "buy stocks" op-ed piece for the *New York Times*.

Buffett concisely summed up, "We look to buy value. We don't look to headlines."

Railroads

Buffett noted that railroads have improved their position over the last 15–20 years.

Railroads are an extremely efficient and environmentally friendly way to move goods. The assets cannot be duplicated for probably six times what they are selling for.

Buffett noted that he expects BNSF to spend far more than its depreciation over the next 10 years and anticipates a good return.

With the sums Berkshire is working with, he's satisfied to earn a 12% return on capital, especially with Berkshire's low cost (or no cost) float. It takes the railroad one gallon of diesel fuel to move one ton 500 miles. Trucks cost three times more. Railroads move 42% of all intercity traffic now, offering very powerful economics compared to the cost, congestion and emissions of moving by roads. BNSF will spend $3.9 billion to improve and expand its systems, all this year and without a check from the government.

Munger allowed that BNSF has had some breaks with technology and the oil boom in North Dakota. And while it will have some bad breaks, too, averaged out, BNSF is a terrific business with terrific management.

Berkshire Investment Managers

Buffett has been pleased with Todd Combs and Ted Wechsler, the two hedge fund managers hired to manage a portion of Berkshire's portfolio. He feels he hit a homerun with both.

Buffett allowed that each could make more money elsewhere—though, he joked, they do have access to the free Coke machine in the office.

They receive $1 million a year plus 10% of the amount by which their portfolio beats the S&P on a three-year rolling basis. To encourage teamwork, 80% of the bonus is each man's own effort and 20% is on that of the other.

Berkshire had a similar arrangement with Lou Simpson, who ran the portfolio at GEICO for many years.

Buffett reported that the arrangement is working better than he hoped, and he added $1 billion to each portfolio. So they are each managing $2.75 billion now.

Newspapers

Asked about Berkshire's acquisition of the *Omaha World Herald*, Buffett noted that 50 years ago, newspapers were the primary source. Now, so much information is free and immediately online. To survive, newspapers must be primary in something. In addition, newspapers need to shift to paid subscriptions on the web, so they don't give their products away.

One strategy Buffett put forward was for newspapers to focus on being a primary source for the local community market. In this way, Berkshire is making some money in Buffalo with *Buffalo News*.

Buffett shared that Berkshire may buy more newspapers.[*]

While the economics are not as good as they once were, newspapers still have a role to play.[†]

Shrinking Businesses

Talk of newspapers led to a discussion of how it is more profitable to own growing businesses, though shrinking businesses can generate a lot of cash. Berkshire has owned its share of them.

In fact, Buffett noted, Berkshire started as a New England textile mall. Then Berkshire got into retail with Diversified Retailing, a Baltimore department store, with Sandy Gottesman in 1966. And Charlie presided over a company[‡], whose sales went from $120 million in 1967 to $20,000 today.

Buffett concluded that they were "masochistic" in those days. Munger added, "Ignorant, too."

---

[*] Berkshire bought 63 newspaper properties this week from Media General.
[†] In April, it was reported that Berkshire bought $85 million of Lee Enterprises debt for 65 cents on the dollar from Goldman Sachs. Lee is a premier publisher of local news through 49 daily newspapers and 300 weekly papers.
[‡] Probably Blue Chip Stamps.

Avoiding Mistakes

Buffett suggested that investors stay away from businesses they don't understand well.

You want to be able to have a decent idea of what the business will look like in 5–10 years—then wait for a crazy price.

Avoid new issues—the insiders are selling their company, so it's ridiculous to think that an IPO will be the cheapest thing to buy in a world of thousands of stocks. The IPO sellers pick the time to sell. So don't waste five seconds on it.

Use filters so that you don't waste time on unproductive ideas. Avoid big losses.

Munger said to avoid issues with a large commission attached. Instead, look at things other smart people are buying.

Buffett recalled eagerly reading the Graham Newman reports years ago just for that reason.

Think about playing tomorrow. Avoid the worst-case mistakes.

On the other hand, Buffett admitted that he and Munger both have instincts to do big things.

Don't dwell too much on mistakes. Learn from other people's mistakes.

Buffett noted their constant study of others' disasters has helped them enormously. Read the stories of financial follies.

No Dividend

Buffett noted that as long as each dollar retained creates a dollar or more of value, retaining profits is the way for Berkshire to go.

If people need income, Buffett suggested just selling off a few shares each year.

Buffett concluded, "We paid out 10 cents a share in the 1960s, and it was a big mistake. We'll think about a dividend when we're older."

Remembering What Can Go Wrong

An interesting aside, Buffett said that in 1962, with an art budget of $7, he made copies of seven financial days of crisis.

One was in May 1901—the Northern Pacific Corner. E.H. Harriman of the Union Pacific Railroad and JP Morgan each owned over 50% of the stock. Harriman was trying to take control of Northern Pacific to get railroad access to Chicago. The stock went from 170 to 1,000 in one day, squeezing the shorts. Margin calls ensued. A brewer committed suicide by diving into a vat of beer.

Buffett concluded that he never wanted to die in a vat of beer.

Munger added that there's a lot of false confidence on Wall Street. Risk on Wall Street may be measured with Gaussian curves, but the fat tails are not fat enough!

Barriers to Entry

"We buy barriers to entry. We don't build them," declared Munger.

Buffett concurred, noting that some industries just don't have them—you just have to keep running really fast.

However, if he had $30 billion to knock the Coca-Cola brand off the shelf, he couldn't do it.

To further his point, Buffett took note of how Richard Branson's Virgin Cola came and went, joking that a brand is a promise, but he's not sure what the promise was with Branson's product.

Buffett also declared that no one will ever build another railroad.

Munger noted that all it takes is one competitor to ruin a business.

Buffett remembered owning a gas station at 30th and Ruddick in Omaha that suffered from the daily competition of a Phillips 66 station across the street.

Plutocracy

With $48,000 in per capita GDP, America is a rich nation. However, far too much compensation has gone to the top executives over the last 20 years. The tax code has encouraged this trend.

Buffett mused that this could be the natural progression in democracy, to move toward plutocracy.*

Society needs some mitigating factors.

Munger recalled that when he went to Boston for the first time, Mayor Curley was running the city . . . from the penitentiary! Boston politics have been littered with egregious behavior.

Taxes and Tapeworms

Asked about the U.S. corporate tax rate, Buffett replied that the top rate is 35%, while 13% is the average rate actually paid. You can write off 100% of most fixed asset purchases.

* "Plutocracy"—from the Ancient Greek "ploutos" (meaning "wealth") and "kratos" (meaning "power").

However, he asserted, corporate profits, balance sheets and liquidity are not the problem.

Corporate taxes equal just 1.2% of GDP.

Meanwhile, medical costs equal 17% of GDP, a seven-point disadvantage to the rest of the world. Medical costs are the tapeworm of American industry.

Munger opined that it is time for a value-added tax. It is logical to tax consumption to equalize the trade deficit, and it creates a steadier income stream.

How Are You Feeling?

With the recent announcement of his prostate cancer, Buffett answered the inevitable question: "I feel terrific. I love what I do. I work with people I love. I have more fun every day. And I have a good immune system."

Munger joked, "I resent all this sympathy for Warren. I probably have more prostate cancer than he does. I just don't know it because I don't let them test for it."

Long-Term Outlook

Buffett declared that if the population grows 1% per year and GDP grows 2.5% per year, by the standard of 1,000 years ago, this would be a remarkable achievement. We would quadruple real GDP per century, remarkable for a country that already has such a high standard of living.

Buffett noted that in his lifetime, real per capita GDP has increased *six-fold*. We are unbelievably rich, hugely abundant. Folks in the 1930s would have thought such growth nearly impossible. The country is not a mess. The outlook is terrific. The system still works. Even after the incredible crash 2008/2009, business has proven to be extraordinarily resilient.

Munger was less bullish. He said he'd settle for 1% real (net of inflation) growth in GDP with a mature economy such as ours with a big social safety net and emerging competition. Expectations are too high.

Berkshire's Future

Munger noted that the first $200 billion was hard. The next $200 billion will be easy now that Berkshire has momentum, people and culture in place. Munger said that he hopes the Munger family will stay with this heirloom.

Venue: CenturyLink Center

Attendance: 45,000

Details About This Year:

- During the six-hour shareholder meeting, "Professors" Buffett and Munger (ages 82 and 89, respectively) were still going strong.

- The quality of questions in the Q&A was significantly improved by having a panel of three journalists and a panel of three analysts (including short seller Doug Kass) ask a majority of the questions.

Fortune 500 Ranking: 5th

- In terms of market value, Berkshire now trails only Apple, Exxon Mobil and Google for the title of America's most valuable company.

Stock Price: $134,102

One dollar invested in 1964 would now be worth **$10,841**.

Berkshire's per-share book value has grown from $19.46 to **$134,973** (a rate of **19.7%** compounded annually).

The S&P 500 compounded at **9.4%** annually for the same period.

HIGHLIGHTS FROM 2013'S NOTES

GEICO

We have talked often of the big getting bigger and the strong getting stronger with the way the global economy is unfolding.

Well-run companies with winning business models are taking market share from the less well-run. Those companies with scale can more easily deal with the increasing regulation and complexity of modern society.

We love the little guy, but the way to bet has been on the big. GEICO is getting big fast.

GEICO has always had a winning business model—selling auto insurance direct. By cutting out agents, GEICO has a lower cost delivery system, and low-cost providers usually win in commodity-type businesses.

Buffett wrote his Columbia grad school thesis on the company.

In the 1970s, GEICO got into trouble, and Buffett took advantage of a weak stock price to buy a lot of the stock.

Berkshire's percentage ownership of GEICO continued to grow as CEO Jack Byrne bought in the shares aggressively. Then, in 1995, Berkshire bought in the portion of GEICO it didn't already own at around three times book value.

At the time, the price seemed rich. However, Buffett realized that GEICO, as a public company, was limited in how aggressively it could grow the business. With GEICO fully owned by Berkshire, Buffett could put the pedal to the metal. GEICO's advertising budget soon exceeded the ad spend of *the rest of the auto insurance industry combined.* That nationwide branding created a share of mind that has led to exceptional growth in market share.

Since 1995, GEICO's share of the personal-auto market has grown from 2.5% to 9.7%. And business is accelerating.

At the annual meeting, Buffett was virtually giddy with delight about the gains at GEICO in both the closure rate and the persistency (renewal) rate.

High and rising closure rates add significant value as GEICO already added over 470,000 new policyholders for the year and might exceed one million new policyholders to date, which Buffett estimated would account for *two-thirds of all new auto policies written in 2013.* This is astonishing.

In addition, GEICO has enjoyed a meaningful increase in its renewal rate for existing policyholders ("persistency") as well. Buffett called this "pure gold." Any business where people send you a check year after year certainly has appeal.

Buffett went on to say that each policy has a mathematical value of about $1,500. So if GEICO does add one million new policyholders this year, that would create an additional $1.5 billion of intrinsic value for Berkshire—none of which shows up directly on the income statement or the balance sheet, but clearly increases the value of GEICO over what it is carried for on the books.*

Auto Insurance Primer

Asked about Progressive's new "Snapshot" product, Buffett launched into a lecture on the essentials of the business.

He noted that insurance underwriting involves figuring out the probability of a person generating a claim—i.e., having an accident.

GEICO asks a lot of questions to help it calculate this probability, and Progressive uses its Snapshot tool to help them assess the same thing.

To help explain, he used an example from the life insurance industry, noting that someone who is 100 years old is more likely to die next year than someone who is 20. With auto insurance, figuring out who's more likely to have an accident involves looking at many more variables and that every company does it its own way.

He went on to explain that if you're a 16-year-old male, you are more likely to have an accident than he is. This isn't because he's a better driver but because the 16 year old will drive a lot more and also will be trying to impress his girlfriend.

"That doesn't work for me anymore, so I've given up."

Effectively if your risk-selection process treats 16 year olds like 82 year olds, you're going to get horrible underwriting results.

Buffett added a story that Progressive's Peter Lewis had shared with him. When Lewis started Progressive, it was a tiny little mutual company without much capital that underwrote motorcycle policies. The first reported loss was some guy who was redheaded, so Lewis decided not to insure redheads!

GEICO's ability to sell insurance at a price considerably below the competition's, as shown by the large numbers of people moving to it,

---

* This growth suggests that GEICO will pass Allstate this year as the No. 2 auto insurer in the nation, trailing only the longtime king of auto insurance, State Farm. Quite a ride since 1995.

and write at a large underwriting profit shows that GEICO's system is working well.

He added that since it has been doing this for decades and has many policyholders, its underwriting is extremely credible.*

Buffett finished by saying that they're watching Snapshot but are quite happy with the current system.

Munger concluded in his usually understated way: "Well, obviously, we're not going to copy the oddball things every competitor does when we've got an operation that's working so well."

Berkshire Reinsurance

Ajit Jain has built a remarkable reinsurance business for Berkshire Hathaway, and recently, his operation made two important decisions.

Buffett discussed how Ajit's division signed a deal where they would participate in 7½% of all business in the entire London market. He also noted that Berkshire had a similar arrangement with Marsh on some of the business there before, but never across the board like this.

The second decision was to hire four well-known insurance people from AIG to write commercial insurance. These are people that reached out to Ajit in the past. Buffett believed this could make Berkshire a very significant factor worldwide in the commercial insurance business, perhaps in the billions.

While they have made acquisitions of insurance businesses in the past, Buffett said that it's really better to build than buy if you can find the right people and the right mindset. In effect, Berkshire will be able to build a very large commercial business at essentially book value and won't pick up any bad habits from other companies.

Munger observed that the reinsurance business is usually not very good for most people. The key to Berkshire's success with reinsurance is the unique way it is run.

Buffett concluded that they have "the right people, capital like no one else and can write business without spreading things out."

Reinsurance Primer

Buffett emphasized several times that Berkshire is "an unusually rational place." It has been a benefit that he and Charlie did not have outside influences pushing them in unwanted directions.

---

* The mantra for insurance underwriting is that data must be credible and reliable. Large amounts of data are required to achieve this.

Insurance in particular should be conducted as a rational activity. One problem some insurers have is that they have pressure from Wall Street to increase premiums every year.

In contrast, Berkshire will walk away when the pricing is inadequate. He recalled that at one time, National Indemnity contracted by 80% because pricing was inadequate.[*]

Buffett added that if Berkshire does something stupid, it's not because of outside influences.

In contrast, most managers, especially if they have little vested interest in a company they are running, would have a hard time resisting what Wall Street wanted them to do. They wouldn't want to be subjected to media criticism and other unwanted pressure.

Buffett noted that Berkshire wrote a lot of catastrophe insurance in the U.S. when prices were right. Now, the prices aren't right, so they aren't writing it. Buffett concluded, "We haven't left the market. The market left us."

He went on to compare this to refusing to buy Internet stocks in the late 1990s. Referring to it as a "social proof or bandwagon effect," he added that it's hard to resist this pressure when people around you are making a bunch of money and friends and the media are questioning why you aren't doing it.

Berkshire's advantage is that they don't have such pressures—"we just don't give a damn."

Munger added that the Bible says things like, "You can't covet your neighbor's ass," for a reason.

Borrowing from past comments, he finished with, "Even worse, envy is the one sin that's no fun."

Buffett chimed in, "Gluttony is a lot of fun (while reaching for a piece of peanut brittle). Lust has its place, too, but we won't get into that."

Buffett acknowledged that hedge funds have recently entered the reinsurance market in a big way. He opined that it is a product that is easily sold to investors.

Buffett huffed, "Anything Wall Street can sell they will. You can count on that." Munger added, "They'll throw in a lot of big words, too."

Adding a life lesson to the discussion, Buffett emphasized *"that you can't afford to go along with the crowd in investment or insurance or a lot of things."*

---

[*] We recall that National Indemnity subsequently did business hand over fist during the next hard market.

He recounted that if you own a gas station and the guy across the street sells below cost, you've got a huge problem. In insurance, if the guy across the street is selling below his cost, the standby costs are reasonable and aren't backbreaking.

Effectively, Berkshire can just wait for better days and better pricing to come along.

Buffett, once again, praised his insurance managers saying that Berkshire was very lucky to get such great people—such as Ted Montross at General Re, Ajit Jain, Don Wurster, and Tony Nicely at GEICO.

He went on to conclude that they like it at Berkshire because they are not pressured to do dumb things.

Munger agreed, "With our cranky methods, we probably have the best insurance operation in the world. So why change?"

BNSF Railroad

Buffett reported that the railroad is doing very well. Figures displayed at the start of the meeting showed gains in railcar loadings of 3.8% versus a gain for all other U.S.-based railroads combined of just 0.3%.

Buffett noted that there is a significant difference.

It's helped that a lot of oil was found close to their tracks. "What better place to find oil!" he quipped.

In fact, Buffett talked with oil producers in the Bakken oil play, and he sees increasing rail usage for a long time. He added that oil moves faster by rail than by pipeline.*

Burlington Northern Santa Fe CEO Matt Rose said that they're moving about 650,000 barrels of crude a day. He thinks it will be 750,000 by year end and could go up to 1.4 million in the years ahead.

Buffett added perspective, noting that the whole country produced just five million barrels a day not too long ago. This is a lot of oil, and it's not just the Bakken. There's shale developments and more unfolding.†

In terms of BNSF's coal franchise, they look for it to stay about where it is today. With some track dedicated to coal, there could be some loss of value over time. Business will fluctuate depending upon natural gas prices and the EPA. Some generating capacity can go in either direction.

---

* An engineer friend at MidAmerican Energy tells us oil can only move about 30 miles per hour max without causing undue corrosion. The rail can go twice as fast, though it has a bit more handling risk.

† Kinder Morgan recently proposed a pipeline from Texas to the West Coast to supply refiners there. Refiners have declined to sign up, preferring the new-found flexibility of oil by rail.

BNSF versus the New Normal

Asked about Bill Gross' concept of lower future returns dubbed "the new normal," Buffett stressed that he and Charlie don't pay any attention to macro forecasts.

He noted that people talk all the time about future and macro issues, but they don't know what they're talking about. It's not very productive.

Buffett profoundly noted, *"To ignore what you know to listen to someone else who doesn't know, doesn't make sense."*

Buffett went on to say that he does know that BNSF will be carrying more and more carloads, and there will be no substitute. There will be only two railroads in the West, so BNSF has incredible replacement value.

He suggested that people will do very well owning good businesses if they don't pay too much for them.

Munger demurred, saying that he believes that it's conceivable that the next 10 years may be no better than the last 10.

ISCAR

Just prior to the meeting, it was announced that Berkshire would buy the final 20% of ISCAR held by the Wertheimer family for about $2 billion.

Buffett noted that the relationship with the Wertheimer family would continue, comparing ISCAR to Sandvik.*

Buffett noted that Sandvik is very good, but ISCAR is much better. The advantage is in brains and incredible passion for the business. When Seth Wertheimer started the company around 1951, here was this 25 year old buying tungsten, the raw material for cutting tools, from China along with everyone else. Then he's selling to customers using machine tools all over the world, basically heavy industry.

He had no advantage doing business from Israel. Yet he's getting tungsten from miles away, selling to customers miles away, and he's competing with well-run companies like Sandvik.

How did he do it?

He had some incredibly hard-working and talented people who constantly improved the product and worked to make customers happier. And they haven't stopped doing this.

Buffett concluded that ISCAR is one of the world's greatest companies, and he feels very fortunate to be associated with its management.

---

* Sandvik is a Swedish company that owns Sandvik Tooling and Seco Tools—major ISCAR competitors.

Heinz

Buffett said the $23 billion deal came about at the airport in Boulder, Colorado, when 3G Capital Partners' Jorge Paulo Lemann asked if Buffett would be interested in joining him on a deal to buy Heinz. Since he respected both Heinz and Jorge Paulo, Buffett said, "I'm in."[*]

In a week or so, Buffett said he received a term sheet on the deal, and he didn't need to change anything on it. In all respects, Buffett said it was an absolutely fair deal to both parties.

Buffett acknowledged that they paid a bit more than they wanted to, as always, and wouldn't have done the deal without 3G. He added that they believe the people of 3G are both classy and are extraordinary managers.

While each party has invested $4.1 billion in equity, 3G wanted more leverage in the deal, so Berkshire agreed to invest $8 billion in that 9% preferred.

Too Big to Succeed?

Asked whether Berkshire was morphing into an index fund, Buffett acknowledged that as Berkshire gets bigger, it gets harder to move the needle, and returns, although satisfactory, will not be as good as in the past.

However, Berkshire's success will also depend on opportunities provided by turbulent markets like 2008, when size and a lot of capital gave them an advantage.

Thanks to Charlie's prodding, they have paid up for good businesses.

Buffett added that if you buy a great business for what appears to be a high price, it's seldom a mistake.

Munger attempted to do Buffett one better and noted that the record of holding companies that got really big is not good. He added that Standard Oil was pretty much the only one that got "monstrously big and continued to do monstrously well."

Even with that backdrop, he added that Berkshire has a better system than most others.

Buffett added that they have been buying some very good businesses, and in fact, *eight* of them would be on the Fortune 500 as standalone entities . . . 8½ counting their 50% stake in the Heinz acquisition.

---

[*] He's known Jorge Paulo for years from being on the board of Gillette together.

The Dollar

Buffett declared that he thinks the dollar will be the world's reserve currency for some decades to come.

While China and the U.S. will be the world's economic super powers, he thinks it extremely unlikely that any currency will supplant the U.S. dollar.

Munger acknowledged that having the reserve currency is an advantage. However, if the U.S. dollar were displaced as the world's reserve currency, so be it.

Munger noted that it is in the nature of things that sooner or later the leader is no longer the leader. As Keynes said, "In the long run, we're all dead."

Buffett joked, "This is the cheery part of the section."

Munger continued, "Well, if you stop to think about it, every great civilization of the past has passed the baton."

Corporate Profits as a Percentage of GDP

Buffett was reminded of a 1999 *Fortune* article where he wrote that one would have to be wildly optimistic to think that corporate profits as a percentage of GDP could be much above 6% for a sustained period. Today, corporate profits are greater than *10% of GDP*.

Buffett said that people should take with a grain of salt complaints of high corporate taxes.

He noted that business has done much better since the 2008 meltdown than private citizens and noted how employment levels have not recovered.

Buffett's best guess is that profits as a percentage of GDP will trend downward from here but that GDP will keep growing, so it's not anything terrible.

Munger noted that it is important to recognize that stocks are owned by many pension funds that support the masses in some way. So though the figures show that there is an income gap, it doesn't mean that the world has become more unequal and that the two figures aren't automatically correlated.

He said he likes Warren's idea that the rich should pay more but would prefer to see a lower corporate tax rate.

Buffett concluded, "He's the Republican, and I'm the Democrat."

The Huge Fed Experiment

Asked about the Fed buying $85 billion per month of mortgage securities and treasuries and what the long term risks might be, Munger replied, "The basic answer is I don't know." Buffett added that it really is uncharted territory.

However, as the Hunt brothers found out when they were buying silver, *it's a lot easier to buy things sometimes than to sell them.*

He noted the Fed's balance sheet is up around $3.4 trillion. This is somewhat balanced out by banks with huge reserve positions. He pointed out that Wells Fargo has $175 billion at the Fed earning effectively nothing.

Buffett noted that he has a lot of faith in Bernanke, though he does wonder if Bernanke is affected by the fact that his term is expiring.

Buffett quipped that maybe Bernanke's advice to his successor to help him bring down the Fed's balance sheet by a few trillion will be to tell him to read a few of the speeches he gave at George Washington University.

On a serious note, Buffett warned that this does have the potential to be quite inflationary. He also speculated that some of the Fed members were probably disappointed that they haven't seen more inflation.

Turning to the market, Buffett predicted that the impact on the market will not be when the Fed starts selling. It will be when the market senses that the Fed has changed course—stopped buying in securities.

He called this the shot that might be heard around the world. He speculated that this wouldn't necessarily be cataclysmic, but that this change will cause investors to reevaluate their investments—especially those that made their decisions based on low interest rates.

Munger took a shot at the field of economics, adding that the economists thought they knew the answers, but have been surprised by the outcome. He added that with their track record, maybe they should be more cautious in their behavior.

He recommended that they reevaluate their belief that they won't get us into trouble when they print lots of money.

Upon prodding by Buffett, Munger indicated that he is worried about inflation and that the next century will be harder, but that he won't be here to see it.

Buffett joked, "Charlie says he won't be here to see it. I reject such defeatism."

Effects of ZBIR

Moving into a tutorial on interest rates, Buffett observed, *"Interest rates are to asset prices sort of like gravity is to the apple."*

When there are very low interest rates, there is a not much of a gravitational pull on asset prices. People behave differently today, when money costs virtually nothing, versus the early 1980s when Volker was trying to stem inflation and rates were 15%.

Buffett continued, *"Interest rates power everything in the economic universe."*

He added that part of paying a bit more for Heinz included being able to borrow money so cheaply.

He noted that interest rates will change, but when they change cannot be predicted, as was the case in Japan for 20 plus years.

He surmised that asset prices were higher because people believe that interest rates will stay low. Relating the interest rate environment to bonds, he added that when the 30-year Treasury bond is 2.8%, it makes houses very attractive.

Noting that it's been a smart policy, Buffett ventured that selling $85 billion a month will be much more than buying $85 billion a month. He concluded that it is like watching a good movie because he doesn't know how it's going to end.

Munger noted that Berkshire has this enormous float[*] that is worth less than it used to be because of the low rates. So Berkshire would benefit in that regard if and when rates rise.

Buffett emphasized that at Berkshire, they *never stretch for yield*. At the end of first quarter, Berkshire had about $49 billion in short-term Treasuries earning basically nothing. If short-term interest rates got back up to 5%, that would bring Berkshire a couple of billion dollars of pre-tax earnings, though it would have lots of other effects on all their businesses.

Flim-Flam

A favorite meeting moment came when Buffett was comparing two multi-level marketing companies, Pampered Chef and Herbalife (which has been very publicly shorted by hedge fund manager Bill Ackman).

The claim by the short sellers is that Herbalife loads product up on unsuspecting people that they can never sell, and that is sort of the main business.

---

[*] $73 billion.

In contrast, Buffett contended that Berkshire's Pampered Chef is focused on selling to the end user through thousands of parties every week.

Munger nailed it: *"I think there is likely more flim-flam in selling magic potions than in selling pots and pans."*

Buffett joked, "At our age, we're in the market for magic potions!"

1-800-brk-deal

There is no doubt that Buffett's reputation and deal acumen have resulted in some remarkable deals for Berkshire. Will his successor be so successful?

Buffett noted that his successor will have even more capital to work with, and that will be especially valuable at turbulent times. Being able to say "yes" very quickly to large deals sets you apart from every other investor. *"Berkshire is the 800 number when there is a panic in the markets"*

Buffett further noted that this happens occasionally, as it did in 2008 and 2011. Using one of his favorite metaphors, Buffett pointed out that when the investment tide goes out, you will see who has been swimming naked. Adding dryly, "Those naked swimmers will call Berkshire."

Interestingly, Buffett was asked about what he would do when one of those quick investment decisions made in February of 2009 comes due in 2014. Berkshire invested $300 million in a five-year 15% Harley Davidson note.

Buffett joked that they would like to just not answer the mail and keep getting the 15%. He further noted that it will be a sad day when it comes due.

He indicated that they were able to make the decision quickly because he believed they would not go broke.

Concluding his thoughts on Harley Davidson, Buffett said, *"Any company that gets its customers to tattoo ads on their chests can't be all that bad."*

Munger observed that in the early days, Buffett was successful because he has no real competition. Interestingly, by moving into a field where Berkshire is a great home for businesses that don't want a home office overseeing everything they do, he has moved into an area where there isn't a lot of competition.

Buffett affirmed that Berkshire gets the calls that no one else gets because they have the money and the willingness to act immediately.

Interestingly, Buffett noted that this area becomes more and more Berkshire's own as Berkshire gets bigger and bigger.

Munger spoke about Berkshire's competitive advantages. In his mind, those include the ability to stay sane when others are crazy.

Another advantage he talked about was living by a corporate governance golden rule where they treat subsidiaries as they would want to be treated. Noting how rare that was in corporate America, he noted that it attracts businesses to Berkshire.

He opined that by Berkshire positioning itself in a less competitive space, it has become quite unusual. "This is a very good idea . . . I wish I'd done it on purpose."

Buffett shared the story of a business owner that was thinking about selling his business.

He was concerned that if he sold it to competitors, they would fire the people that helped him build the business. They would come in like Attila the Hun. If he sold to some private equity firm, they'd load it up with debt and resell it later on, at which point the Attila the Hun scenario would play itself out again.

So when he thought about it, he wasn't interested in selling to Berkshire because it was so attractive, but because Berkshire was the last man standing.

It turned out to be a wonderful acquisition for Berkshire. His people stayed, and he continues to do what he loves doing.

Buffett concluded, "Our competitive advantage is that we have no competitors."

Buffett also added that he thought one of the advantages was that Berkshire has a shareholder base that's different, where Berkshire looks at shareholders as partners. The owner/managers want shareholders to get the same result they get.

Energy Management

On the subject of their work habits, Munger offered a fascinating insight. By accident, he and Buffett have ideal habits for what they do.

For example, they didn't know when they started out about modern psychological evidence that you shouldn't make important decisions when you're tired and that difficult decisions are tiring.

He joked that they didn't know important decision-making was helped by consuming lots of caffeine and sugar.*

Munger offered up that because they both live on auto–pilot, they don't waste energy on the ordinary things that come up every day. He said this is an ideal way to do what they do.

He further commented that he has never seen Buffett tired, that he sleeps soundly and that his lifestyle works ideally for what he does.

---

* Cherry Coke and See's peanut brittle were present at the meeting.

Newspapers

Buffett stated that Berkshire has been buying papers at very low prices compared with current earnings and must do so because the earnings will go down.

In addition, Buffett noted that his recent newspaper purchases have some tax benefits. Buffett said he expects at least a 10% after-tax return with declining earnings over time. In terms of scale, it doesn't move the needle at Berkshire.

Altogether, Buffett estimated that they have $100 million in pre-tax earnings from their newspaper holdings.

Interestingly, although the group is below the threshold for reporting, he said he would report the results of the newspaper group annually.

Munger deadpanned, "I think I hear you saying that this is an exception, and you like doing it."

Biggest Threat

As in past years, Buffett asserted that health care costs are the biggest threat to American competitiveness. We're spending something like 17% of GDP on health care, while our rivals are paying around 10%.

He compared it to a raw material cost where U.S. industry pays about 7% more than global competitors. It's just like having a raw material or something of the sort that costs you more. Yet because any one company cannot control the cost, it's a big disadvantage.

Munger eagerly addressed this issue and offered up that the "grossly swollen securities and derivatives markets" don't really help competitiveness.

He added that Cal-Tech and MIT graduates doing derivative trading was a "perfectly crazy outcome in terms of the country."

He agreed with Buffett about health care, but finds this other issue more revolting.

Warren concluded, "Charlie is very Old Testament."

Advice for Life

Munger declared that he and Warren are basically old fashioned.

He thinks the key to life is that the old virtues still work, like plugging along and staying rational.

Warren recommended doing what turns you on. Munger agreed, saying he'd never done anything really well that he didn't like to do.

Buffett reminisced that he and Charlie both started at the same grocery store, and neither of them is in the grocery business today.

Munger joked that the young Buffett was in no danger of being promoted, either, even though his family owned the store.

Buffett interjected, "Grandpa was right, too!"

Buffett went on to say that he's been lucky—lucky to live in this country, lucky to find things he liked to do early in life.

He said, "It's so much fun running Berkshire. It's almost sinful."

Munger joked, "You found a way to atone for your sins from having so much fun—you're giving all the money back."

Buffett shot back, "You give it all back whether you want to or not."

Timing

Bill Gross recently made comments that his generation of investors owed a lot of their success to the timing of their birth. Buffett agreed that there was no question that being born male and in the U.S. was a huge advantage.

Spinning a story he first related in a 1979 *Fortune* article, he talked about his dad being in the securities business. And since his dad had no one to call on after the crash, he stayed home in the afternoons. "And there was no television . . . so here I am. I feel lucky the crash of 1929 came along."

He related that the crash turned people off to the market for an entire decade and that business was horrible.

Buffett noted that we had a similar sort of decade up to 2010 for stocks.

He allowed that the 1950s were a favorable environment for investing, with low competition for ideas, and that he would have made more money if had he been born five years earlier and probably made less if he'd been born 15 to 20 years later.

Buffett said he envies the baby being born today in the United States. That's the luckiest individual ever. He opined that the baby will do better in all sorts of different ways than when he was born. Just as we live far better than people like John D. Rockefeller, the person born today will live far better than we do.

Munger noted that the competition for investment ideas in Buffet's early career was much weaker than it is today. However, that does not mean that there's nothing to be done ahead in the world of investing.

Buffett bragged up Charlie a bit, noting that in 2008 and 2009, there were thousands and thousands of high IQ, investment professionals.

And Charlie invested the cash at *Daily Journal* (of which Munger is chairman of the board) in equities at X that are now worth 3X-4X.*

Munger observed that Buffett was drowning in opportunities when they first met, but what he lacked was money.

Buffett finished with the punchline: "Now we've got the money and no ideas."

Solar Power

Munger confidently predicted that there will be more solar generation in deserts than on rooftops. Berkshire's big solar operations get very favorable terms and are located in the desert, so Berkshire will do fine.

However, he's skeptical about rooftop panels harming Berkshire's utilities. He suspects there's some twaddle in that area.

MidAmerican Energy CEO Greg Abel added that while the cost of installing rooftop solar has come down, there are tariffs protecting the utilities.

Banks

Asked about Dodd Frank, Buffett noted that the higher the capital ratio, the lower the return on equity. Overall, he thinks that U.S. banks are much stronger than they've been in 25 years. For the most part, the old bad loans are gone, and the new ones are much better.

He added that our banking system is far stronger than Europe's.

Buffett declared that he's not worried about the banking system or a housing boom causing the next bubble. It will be something else. He noted we will always have bubbles because it is the nature of capitalism to go to excess. That's what humans do. But the next bubble will come in some other way.

Buffett said he feels very good about investments in Wells Fargo, U.S. Bank and M&T Bank. Their earnings should be decent over time, but their returns on equity will be lower than they were seven or eight years ago because of Dodd Frank.

Munger noted that he's a little less optimistic about the banking system long term than Warren. He still does not see why massive derivative books should be mixed up with deposits that are insured by this country.

Buffett agreed.

---

* We'll brag up Warren here. As we noted earlier, Berkshire has put to work over $100 billion since 2008.

Munger concluded, "The more bankers want to be like investment bankers instead of bankers, the worse I like it. I can't say more. I'm in enough trouble on this subject already."

Buffett joked, "I can see the journalists just licking their chops waiting for Charlie to throw a thunderbolt. He's unusually restrained today."

Succession Plan: The Culture

There were yet again a number of questions concerning the succession issue. Andrew Ross Sorkin asked the question, "Is Ajit your successor"?

To which Buffett replied after pausing for a moment, "I noticed you started with the A's. You'll have just as much luck with the B's."

Buffett said he and the board think about succession all the time. He added that it is the number one thing discussed at board meetings and that the board "solidly" agrees with who the successor is.

The important thing will be to preserve the culture and that picking the right CEO will be the key to that. Buffett believes the culture has been intensified year after year and that any type of foreign behavior will be "cast out" The wrong sort of person would be rejected like "foreign tissue."

Around succession, Berkshire has thought about "what can go wrong."

When indelicately asked by the short seller Doug Kass about Howard Buffett's qualifications to be the non-executive chairman on the board, Buffett reflected that the intention of the position is to solely look after the culture of Berkshire, and no one is more committed to that than Howard.

When asked about the complexity brought on by the multiple number of companies he oversees, Buffett allowed that his successor may organize things in a somewhat different way. However, Berkshire will continue to leave its CEOs running their businesses, with capital allocation decisions being made in the home office.

Buffett joked that if his successor really went crazy, he might hire one more person at headquarters.

Munger noted that managing this structure would be unwieldy if Berkshire had an imperial headquarters that forced its will on the subsidiaries, but pointed out that Berkshire doesn't operate like that. Concluding, "If your system is decentralization to the point of abdication, what difference does it make how many subsidiaries you have?"

Munger, ever inverting the topic for insight, noted that if what they were doing was too hard, it would be impossible. But it isn't.

Buffett joked, "I'll have to think about that a little."

Munger continued, suggesting that if 50 years ago, someone would have said that Buffett would manage a huge firm like Berkshire from Omaha, Nebraska, with a tiny office staff, people would have said it could never work. But it has.

Munger concluded, "I want to say to the many Mungers out there, don't be so stupid as to sell your shares."

Buffett quipped, "That goes for the Buffetts, too."

Venue: CenturyLink Center

Attendance: 40,000

Details About This Year:

- Corey took copious notes alone this year while Daniel stayed home under the weather.

- Buffett and Munger had special edition Heinz ketchup bottles for sale. The Buffett version sold for $2.00 each, while the Munger version sold for just $1.50. They joked that they will be keeping track to see who sells more ketchup.

- Nebraska Furniture Mart did over $40 million of business during this week. That's 10% of the store's annual sales.

- The shareholder meeting was six hours long. "Professors" Buffett and Munger (ages 83 and 90, respectively) were still going strong.

Fortune 500 Ranking: 5th

Stock Price: $177,953

One dollar invested in 1964 would now be worth **$14,386**.

Berkshire's per-share book value has grown from $19.46 to **$146,386** (a rate of **19.4%** compounded annually).

The S&P 500 compounded at **9.8%** annually for the same period.

HIGHLIGHTS FROM 2014'S NOTES

Five Things You May Have Missed

We have long noticed the paradox of craziness that surrounds Warren Buffett: no investor gets more media attention, and yet so little understanding flows out of that attention.

We suppose it's a problem of the short attention span/instant gratification culture bouncing off the wisdom of the ages.

In any case, now that the media frenzy over the Berkshire meeting has died down, we check in with our observations on the annual gathering.

Here's what seems big to us and what few seem to have really noticed:

1. Berkshire is more invested in equities than any time since 1997 (and less invested in fixed income than any time since 1995).

How's that for a headline?

In all our post-meeting reading, we did not see this point made.

To all those wringing their hands about an imminent bear market, apparently Buffett didn't get the notice. This is especially noteworthy as Buffett was so cash-heavy during the "lost decade."

He most decidedly is not all in all the time. So the fact that he is leaning so decisively toward equities is worthy of note.

In addition, while the investment portfolio has shifted over the last decade from being the centerpiece of the Berkshire empire to merely a part of the whole, it still represents his thinking about the opportunity costs of various asset classes over time.

He clearly believes equities are the superior choice to bonds and cash at this time. That's a point worth noting.

2. Buffett is touting Berkshire's value.

This is a complete about-face.

For decades, we well remember Buffett and Munger downplaying Berkshire's value and low-balling expectations for future growth year after year after year. You could almost hear the violins in the background.

In recent years, Buffett has been more upfront about what makes Berkshire so remarkable and hinting at what those values might be.

This year Buffett did a "*shout out*" on Berkshire's value.

He was quite direct that Berkshire's plan to buy back shares at 120% of book value is nothing less than a not-so-subtle hint to own Berkshire from the master himself.

To put some numbers on that, first quarter equity of $230 billion equates to $93 of book value per "B" share—120% of that would be $112. With the "B" shares at $126, they are selling at just 12% above the price at which Buffett would buy in large amounts of stock—a value differential that Berkshire's growth will close within the year.

After years of low-balling Berkshire, Buffett is fairly screaming to whoever will listen to notice the value here.

3. Buffett loves banks.

It's well-known that Buffett likes Wells Fargo. It's less well-known that Buffett likes banks.

For example, what is Berkshire's fifth-largest equity holding?

Come on now, make a guess.

The Big Four get plenty of press: Wells Fargo, Coca-Cola, American Express and IBM.

What's number five?

If you don't know, don't feel bad. We asked several of our friends who study Berkshire, and they did not know.

The answer: Bank of America.

Assuming exercise of the warrants, the shares were worth $10.9 billion at year-end and $12 billion at the end of the first quarter.

Between Wells Fargo, Bank of America, U.S. Bancorp, Bank of New York Mellon and M&T Bank, Buffett has a $40 billion investment in U.S. banks.

This is a huge position and, thus, worth close inspection.

For all the hand-wringing about increased regulation, increased capital requirements, ongoing lawsuits and narrow interest rate spreads, something must be very right about banking and/or these particular banks for Buffett to have his *largest sector weighting in banks.*

We would add that Buffett knows banks, having purchased the Illinois National Bank of Rockford in 1969.

In the 1977 Berkshire report, Buffett proudly took note of Gene Abegg's able management in building a bank whose rate of earnings to assets was about three times that of most large banks.

4. Buffett is happy.

Over the years, we have found Buffett's general level of energy and enthusiasm remarkable.

However, some years are more difficult than others, and that shows up in a more somber demeanor at the meeting.[*]

This year, we report that we have seldom seen him happier.

We believe a big contributor is that *Berkshire is hitting on all cylinders.* Every one of his major investments and important hires of the last decade is working out and—in certain cases—working out very well.

The man is on a roll.

5. Berkshire is a smooth-running capital allocation machine.

Allocation of capital is *the* key to future returns in the business world. Never before has the world seen an allocation machine like Berkshire Hathaway.

Generating in the neighborhood of $20 billion a year in growing cash flow, *Berkshire will easily generate more than $230 billion of cash in the next decade, an amount equal to its current equity value.*

In other words, what Berkshire does with its excess cash over the next decade will match or exceed in scale everything Buffett has done over the last 50 years.

Buffett knows full well he may or may not be around to preside over these allocation decisions, so the more capital allocation can be mechanized or delegated in a good way,

---

[*] The Salomon scandal and the year David Sokol stepped down come to mind.

the better. And Buffett has done this to an absolutely stunning degree over the last 15 years.

Perhaps, in years to come, this transition will be seen as his greatest work.

Let's take a closer look at what he has created.

Berkshire Hathaway: Allocation Machine

There are essentially five things public corporations can do with a dollar earned: reinvest in the business, acquire other businesses or assets, pay down debt, pay dividends, and/or buy in shares.

Deciding how much to allocate to each of these five areas ideally is driven by "opportunity cost."

In other words, each extra dollar should go where it gets the best risk-adjusted return over the long run compared to all other competing opportunities.

Warren Buffett, more than anyone else we know, has brought the art of capital allocation to the forefront of American business thinking. For years, he and Charlie Munger have noted that American business managers promoted to CEOs were much like the world-renowned violinist who finally makes it to Carnegie Hall and then is told to play the piano.

After years of mastering accounting or just-in-time production or sales and marketing, the rising manager is suddenly in charge of something he's had no training for: capital allocation.

Not surprisingly, the overall record of capital allocation in American business has not been good.

Back in the 1980s, we hardly ever heard companies speak of this function. Today, it has become commonplace (though execution still can and often does leave much to be desired).

For example, according to a recent *Wall Street Journal*, corporate spending on share buybacks rose 23% last year to $477 billion and dividend payments increased 14% to $1.3 trillion, while capital spending is expected to climb 6% this year to $650 billion.

That's a great little summary and not the sort of thing one read in the paper 30 years ago.

For years, Buffett has modeled a rational, intelligent and sometimes inspired approach to capital allocation.

In this year's annual report, Buffett was quite specific as to how the allocation went for 2013 at Berkshire:

Reinvesting in the businesses

Here is where the biggest changes have occurred.

Prior to 1998, Berkshire owned little in the way of operating businesses that could reinvest large amounts of cash. In fact, Buffett distinctly preferred low-capital, high cash flow businesses, so he could reinvest the cash flow himself.

Since then, however, Berkshire has been on a buying spree of capital-heavy businesses, highlighted by his "Powerhouse Five": MidAmerican Energy, Burlington Northern Santa Fe, ISCAR, Lubrizol and Marmon Group.

Exhibiting a remarkable flexibility of mind, Buffett totally shifted gears. After years of buying low-capital, high cash flow businesses, Buffett has assembled a group of businesses that can guzzle cash.

Berkshire subsidiaries spent a record *$11 billion* on plant and equipment during 2013.

BNSF alone plans to invest $5 billion in 2014.

When current projects are completed, MidAmerican Energy will have spent $15 billion on renewable energy.

From a standing start in 2004, MidAmerican now provides 7% of the nation's wind generation capacity and, when projects are completed, an even larger share of the nation's solar capacity.

In addition, Berkshire spent $3.5 billion buying the portions of Marmon Group and ISCAR that it did not already own.

We speculate here, but note that Berkshire bought in the shares of GEICO that it didn't already own in 1995. Buffett then put the pedal to the metal on the ad budget such that GEICO outspent the rest of the auto insurance industry combined!

We cannot help but wonder if the success of that capital intensity applied at the right time with the right company informed Buffett's more recent purchases and capital investment policies.

Being able to think and invest very long term and not worry about current earnings or Wall Street analysts can be a major competitive advantage in *certain* businesses.

Acquire other businesses

Here Buffett continues to be on a tear.

- **The Basic Deal:** *Buffett has long loved to buy control of good companies.* In fact, Buffett said at the meeting that he much prefers to buy operating businesses that can add to Berkshire's earnings power versus marketable securities. Last year, Berkshire spent *$18 billion* to acquire NV Energy and a major interest in Heinz (with 3G Capital Partners). Just prior to the meeting, Berkshire announced the $2.9 billion acquisition of Alta Link, which operates power transmission services for about 85% of Alberta.

- **The Fancy Deal:** Buffett has long been famous for cutting special deals that only he and Berkshire could dream up. Debt with warrants attached. Insurance quota shares. Double-digit convertible preferred issues. Berkshire cut a couple of interesting, tax-advantaged deals last year: a swap of *Washington Post* shares for a TV station in Miami and Berkshire shares, and a swap of $1.4 billion of Phillips 66 shares for full ownership of the energy firm's pipeline-services business.

- **The Bolt-On Acquisition:** Berkshire's smaller subsidiaries have the green-light to grow by intelligent acquisition. Last year, $3.1 billion was invested in bolt-on acquisitions at Berkshire subsidiaries.

- **The Portfolio:** Once the crown jewel of Berkshire, the $211 billion portfolio of cash, bonds and equities is now merely a part of this burgeoning empire. However, Buffett added Ted Wechsler and Todd Combs to the team in recent years, with each now running portfolios of over $7 billion. Buffett clearly likes what these two are doing and hints they have also contributed to some of the other deals mentioned here.

Pay down debt

Years ago, Buffett taught that the time to borrow money is when money is cheap. Debt is cheap now, so the question really might be, "Why doesn't Berkshire borrow more?"

Buffett said he prefers to keep the balance sheet super strong (with a minimum of $20 billion in cash). This unquestionable strength creates a durable competitive advantage for the insurance subsidiaries.*

Pay dividends

Berkshire has famously not paid dividends.

However, Buffett did suggest during the meeting that in the "not too remote future," Berkshire's cash generation might be so substantial, that would be a question to revisit.

"May you live until Berkshire pays a dividend" may not be so long.

Buy in shares

Berkshire has implemented this remarkable authorization to buy in shares at 120% of book value.

While few shares have been repurchased to date, it creates a floor under the price.

Interesting note: Buffett mused during the meeting that when Berkshire bought BNSF, it paid 70% of the cost in cash and the remainder in stock. He would have been wise to have bought those shares back in on the open market.

One other point here, a number of Berkshire's investees repurchase shares, increasing Berkshire's percentage ownership over time—yet one more form of "automatic" capital allocation for Berkshire.

In Summary

There you have it. The Berkshire Hathaway Allocation Machine is no longer dependent on Buffett's next idea.

The Powerhouse Five can reinvest cash to grow their own operations for years to come. Smaller subsidiaries can do bolt-on acquisitions. Wechsler and Combs are on the hunt

---

* We note that a sly old favorite of ours, Leucadia National, did just that, raising $3.3 billion on a variety of bond issues last year. Borrow money when money is cheap, indeed.

for bargains in both the stock market and in the world of deal making.

And nearly all of this capital allocation capacity has been created by Buffett in just the last 15 years.

A remarkable achievement.

Venue: CenturyLink Center

Attendance: 40,000

Details About This Year:

- Berkshire celebrated 50 years under Buffett's management.

- Buffett joked that they expanded transportation beyond planes, trains and automobiles as Justin Boots brought two big steers and Wells Fargo brought a stagecoach to parade down to The CenturyLink Center at 6:30 a.m.

- The annual movie included Buffett as "The Berkshire Bomber" going toe-to-toe with boxer Floyd Mayweather in a Rocky-style bit. It included cameos from Steve Wynn and Charlie Rose. Buffett talked trash to Mayweather. Munger said, "Mayweather's people asked me first, but I was too busy." At the start of the fight, they ask Buffett if he's going to fight with his glasses on, to which he responds, "Damn right I will!" They both swing, and just as they're about to hit each other, the screen goes blank.

- Also in the movie was an interview with Buffett's associates from the early days, Gladys Kaiser and Bill Scott. Buffett and Scott talked about the acquiring of Berkshire and the partnership days. Kaiser remembered that 1991 was an awful year, the year of the Salomon Brothers scandal, and that Buffett was totally focused: "That was quite a responsibility. You saved their behind."

Fortune 500 Ranking: 4th

- Berkshire now trails only Wal-Mart, Exxon Mobil and Chevron.

Stock Price: $226,000

One dollar invested in 1964 would now be worth **$18,270**.

Berkshire's per-share book value has grown from $19.46 to **$146,186** (a rate of **19.4%** compounded annually).

The S&P 500 compounded at **9.9%** annually for the same period.

HIGHLIGHTS FROM 2015'S NOTES

Berkshire Hathaway: Capital Allocation Machine

"The lack of skill that many CEOs have at capital allocation is no small matter: After ten years on the job, a CEO whose company annually retains earnings equal to 10% of net worth will have been responsible for the deployment of more than 60% of all the capital at work in the business."
—1987 BERKSHIRE LETTER

Intelligent capital allocation is the essence of sound wealth-building.

In last year's review, we noted how dramatically Buffett has reshaped Berkshire into a capital allocation machine over the last 15 years. As it is now configured, the future compounding of Berkshire's value depends less on Warren Buffett than at any other time in Berkshire's history.

When considering how poorly capital gets allocated in the main, Berkshire stands out even more as one exceptional story.

What we didn't realize until this year's Berkshire Hathaway annual report is how strongly capital allocation affected Berkshire from the very beginnings.

Buffett celebrates Berkshire's 50th year under his command with a terrific annual report, including excerpts from old annual reports, buy-out term sheets and other historical notes.

In fact, Buffett notes that it was a buyback announcement that initially attracted him to Berkshire. It was not the business, but the re-allocation of capital that drew Buffett to the stock.[*]

BNSF

Buffett put up a slide of Berkshire's quarterly earnings. He noted there was nothing particularly remarkable except that BNSF did much better than last year in both earnings and other performance measures.

Buffett admitted that the railroad got behind last year early in the year, so Berkshire spent a lot of money to get things the way they should be.

Those expanded efforts have paid off. Burlington Northern has gained market share and improved earnings.

---

[*] See Appendix I for Buffett's telling of the story and our analysis of his capital allocation moves in those early days. It is really quite spectacular.

276

Clayton Homes

A question came about a *Seattle Times* story alleging predatory lending practices at Berkshire subsidiary Clayton Homes.

Buffett was prepared with his response, saying that there were some important mistakes in the article and claimed that Clayton's lending practices are exemplary.

So began an interesting lecture on lending and manufactured housing.

Buffett asserted that mortgage problems in 2008 and 2009 happened in large part because the mortgage holder and the mortgage originator became "totally divorced."

Mortgage originators sold the loans to investment bankers who sliced and diced the loans into derivative products where the eventual buyers often didn't really know what they owned.

The default rates in those years was far, far higher for $800,000 and up homes than they were for loans at Clayton. In contrast, Clayton retains nearly all of the mortgages that it originates. Clayton has retained over $12 billion of mortgages on some 300,000 homes.

It is not in Clayton's interests to sell a house where the buyer defaults since that will be loss for the company as well as for the customer.

That is not true of most mortgage originators, though there has been some talk to have originators retain 3% or so of the mortgages they originate, so they have some skin in the game.

Buffett acknowledged that manufactured housing covers the lower end of the market in terms of FICO scores (620 or below). He said 70% percent of homes that sell for $150,000 or less are manufactured and that the average payment is about $670 a month.

So the challenge is to lend to people in a way that they are likely to make the payments and keep their homes.

For Clayton, about 3% of these mortgages default.

The primary reasons for mortgage default are loss of job, divorce and death.

However, 97% don't default.

Without the financing Clayton and others make available, they wouldn't be able to own such a home.

Buffett said the Clayton home on display in the Century Link auditorium goes for $69,500. Land usually costs about $25,000. So for a total of $95,000, someone could get into a home with appliances, a couple of bedrooms, and 1,200 square feet of space.

Buffett noted that there were mistakes in the *Seattle Times* story, which alleged that Clayton's average profit was $11,600 per home sold. Buffett said he knew that was nonsense. He read the affidavit about three times, and nowhere in the affidavit was that statement made.

What was in the affidavit was a comment on gross profit, not net profit. In the case of Clayton, the gross profit is around 20%, while the net profit margin is about 3%.

An interesting aside, Buffett shared that they have had absolutely no complaints about Clayton's lending standards. However, Buffett admitted that he gets letters of complaint about other subsidiaries on a regular basis.

Buffett added that Clayton is regulated by each state in which it has financing, so it is regulated by nearly every state.

In the last three years, Clayton has had 91 compliance examinations by the state. In those 91 examinations, the largest fine Clayton paid was $5,500, and the largest refund was $110,000.*

Buffett concluded that he is proud: "Clayton put over 30,000 people, at a very low cost, into very good homes last year. And a very high percentage of those people are going to have those loans paid off in 20 years and have a home that was a real bargain."

Munger mused that while Clayton has around 50% of the manufactured housing market, he's surprised the market isn't bigger since it's such an efficient way to build houses.

3G Capital Partners

Buffett also came prepared for questions about his partnership with 3G Capital Partners.

The question was about 3G's style of reducing the number of workers at companies it takes over.

Buffett noted that the 3G people are successful business builders and buyers. They seek to run their businesses efficiently, and that includes reducing headcount when there are considerably more people in the business than are needed. After reducing expenses, 3G businesses have done well.

Buffett observed that Burger King is now outperforming its competitors by a significant margin. Burger King's most recent acquisition, Tim Horton's, is already showing marked improvement.

Munger pointed out that the alternative to having your company right-sized is what eventually happened in Russia. He quoted the Russian worker who said, "Everyone has a job, and it all works out. They pretend to pay us, and we pretend to work."

---

* Buffett did his homework.

Buffett noted that the railroad business after World War II had 1.6 million people employed in the business, and it was a lousy, undercapitalized industry. Today, the rail industry has less than 200,000 employees, and the industry is much larger, more efficient and far safer. No one is claiming today that it would be better to run the railroads with 1.6 million folks. "Efficiency is required over time in capitalism."

Buffett concluded, "I tip my hat to what the 3G people have done."

Van Tuyl

Asked about Berkshire's recent acquisition of Van Tuyl, Buffett noted that it is a very productive auto dealer.

Renamed Berkshire Hathaway Automotive, the unit is one of the largest dealership groups in America, with over $9 billion in revenue and 81 independently operated dealerships in 10 states.

Some dealers, such as Carmax, have gone to a more transparent model with less negotiation.

Buffett noted that Van Tuyl will adapt to what the customer wants. However, the negotiated model is still predominant.

Munger shared that negotiating for cars has been the primary model for his entire lifetime, and he's amazed that this hasn't changed more.

Buffett assured shareholders that Van Tuyl would be fine however things unfold, though he wouldn't be surprised if things don't change that much in 10 to 15 years. Overall, there are 17,000 dealers in the country, and Berkshire plans on buying more of them through Van Tuyl in the years to come.

Interestingly, Buffett does not see any scale advantages to owning auto dealers. Most dealerships work on local considerations.

Buffett does not see Berkshire getting into the car finance business. Wells Fargo is the largest auto finance company with a cost of funds around 12 basis points, so it has an unbeatable advantage.

Munger concluded that Van Tuyl has "a system of meritocracy, where the right people have a significant ownership." It reminds him of the Kiewit company in Omaha, another very successful culture.

Filters

Asked for five or six criteria for choosing an investment, Munger asserted that Berkshire does not have a one-size-fits-all system. Each industry is different. Also, they keep learning.

Buffett observed that they do have filters. A key one is whether they have a good idea of how the business is going to do over the next five or 10 years. That filter eliminates many businesses from consideration.

Another filter is people. Buffett wants people to run the business the same way after selling to Berkshire as they ran it before selling to Berkshire. That filter also eliminates a lot of deals.

Buffett concluded, "I can't give you five criteria. Maybe Charlie has kept them from me."

IBM

Asked whether IBM wasn't a cigar butt, similar to those textile mills of the 1960s, Munger said "no."

He noted that IBM has been rare in its ability to adapt to technological change. Munger sees IBM as "a very admirable enterprise bought at a reasonable price."

Buffett chimed in that he finds it interesting when he gets asked questions about investments Berkshire owns and that people think he would want to talk them up. Either Berkshire or the investee companies may be buying more shares in the future, so why would they want the price to go up?

Buffett concluded, "Wall Street thinks it's better if price goes up the next day even if you're planning on buying more shares in. Charlie, do you have any idea why?"

Munger replied, "Warren, if people weren't so often wrong, we wouldn't be so rich."

Building the Insurance Businesses

In building Berkshire's insurance empire, Buffett allowed that he had many pieces of luck. Three in particular: visiting Lorimar Davidson of GEICO, buying National Indemnity and hiring Ajit Jain.

Buffett claimed the education he received from just four hours with Davidson was better than any university course he could have taken. That's when he realized insurance was something that he liked and understood. That understanding prepared him to buy National Indemnity when it came up for sale and, of course, prepared Buffett to buy a major position in GEICO and eventually the entire company in the decades to follow.

Buffett has often said that Jack Ringwalt had five minutes every year when he wanted to sell his company, National Indemnity. In 1967, Buffett got that call and jumped on it. National Indemnity became the base on which Buffett would build Berkshire's insurance empire.

In the mid-1980s, Ajit Jain walked in on a Saturday volunteering his services even though he hadn't worked in the insurance business.

Buffett marveled at his good fortune for this trifecta and shared that the real key was being open to ideas as they came along.

Munger noted that the real key is that Berkshire bought wonderful businesses.

Culture

Buffett asserted that Berkshire's culture runs deep.

He shared that Berkshire had just closed on a transaction in Germany, Detlev Louis Motoradvertriebs GmbH, a motorcycle apparel and accessories retailer. Mrs. Louis and her husband lovingly built the business over 35 years. Her husband died a couple of years ago, and she came to Berkshire because she wanted to sell to Berkshire.

It is essential for Berkshire to have a culture that runs throughout the entire company as well as the shareholders.

Buffett was pleased that 97% of shareholders voted against having a dividend and in favor of having management invest the cash.

Buffett observed that the culture gets reinforced and becomes self-selecting over time. Buffett believes that this culture has become institutionalized and has no doubt that it will continue long after he and Charlie are gone.

Munger did note that Berkshire's rate of gain will slow: "There are worse tragedies in life than having Berkshire's compounding slow down—that's inevitable. "

Buffett quipped," Name one."

Culture comes from the top according to Buffett. The leader must be consistent, communicate well, and reward proper behavior and punish misbehavior. Since it takes time, it's actually easier to inherit the culture you like.

Buffett concluded that one of his core values at Berkshire is to always strive to treat people the way you would want to be treated.

Munger's insightful conclusion, "I think one thing that we have done that's worked best is that we were always dissatisfied with what we already knew, and we wanted to know more. We kept learning, and that's what made it work."

Brands

Asked about Berkshire being long on sugar consumption for the past 50 years and changing consumer tastes, Buffett countered that Coca-Cola has a very wide moat.

With 1.9 billion 8-ounce daily servings of Coca-Cola products consumed worldwide, the company is still a force. And it will need to adjust to the changing preferences of consumers.

However, much like negotiated auto sales, Buffett said he just doesn't see anything revolutionary happening here. He predicted that 20 years from now more Coke will be consumed than today.

In a startling admission, Buffett declared that he estimated one-quarter of all the calories he has consumed over the last three decades came from Coca-Cola.

He joked, "If I would've been eating broccoli and Brussels sprouts my whole life, I don't think I would've lived this long."

Buffett shared that while there are shifts in preferences over time, it's remarkable how durable some brands can be. Coke started in 1886. Heinz ketchup came out in 1870.

Buffett reiterated that a strong brand is really powerful, though you do have to build them and promote them.

He marveled that Gillette bought the rights to radio advertising for the 1939 World Series for $100,000. "Think about how many people heard those commercials."

Macro Factors & Predictions

Buffett noted that he would have never predicted five years of zero interest rates. "We're operating in a world that Charlie and I don't understand."

Munger wryly noted, "If we failed to predict what happened before, why would anybody ask us what our prediction was for the future?"

Fortunately for shareholders, macro predictions are not essential to the Berkshire process.

Buffett took pains to emphasize that he and Charlie had never, to the best of his memory, ever turned down an acquisition based on macro factors.

As examples, Buffett noted that See's Candy and BNSF were purchased during difficult times in the economy.

He said the real key is to be able to figure out what the average profitability of the business will be over the long term and how strong the business moat may be.

Buffett's punch line, "We think that any company that has an economist has one employee too many."

The Railroad

Regarding concerns about railcar safety, Buffett noted that BNSF, as a common carrier, is required to carry certain dangerous substances, such as ammonia and chlorine.

The government develops the rules for these issues, and rail is the most logical way to transport many of these substances.

BNSF leads the industry in safety, and overall, Buffett believes that rail has gotten significantly safer over the years.

Renewable Energy

Solar's cost per megawatt hour has plummeted from $315 in 2009 down to $128 today. The energy cost of wind per megawatt hour is $85.48, down from $96.09. Renewable energy costs are becoming more competitive.

Greg Abel, CEO of Berkshire Energy Group, said that by the end of 2016, 58% of power in Iowa will be from wind.

All In

Winding up, Buffett noted that all of his and his families' net worth is in BRK.

Munger noted that Berkshire is only lightly levered and that "it's crazy to sweat at night."

Buffett quickly clarified, "Over financial things."

Buffett concluded that with $60 billion in cash, Berkshire would be ready and willing to act if some economic turbulence creates an opportunity.*

Stock Market and Interest Rates

There was a very good question about valuations.

---

* True to his word, Buffett was ready to act with that $60 billion in cash. In August, Berkshire agreed to its biggest acquisition ever, buying Precision Castparts (PCP), an aerospace parts company, for $32.4 billion in cash, or $235/share. Berkshire expects to fund the deal using about $23 billion of its cash and another $10 billion of borrowed money.

Buffett wasn't shy about saying how much he likes Precision Castparts CEO Mark Donegan: "The guy is fantastic. He's as in love with his company as I am with Berkshire, and that's saying a lot."

One ratio that Buffett is known to track is the total market cap to GDP. Recently, it was at 125%, which is a level approached in 1999 during the Internet bubble.

Another number that Buffett has mentioned is the ratio of corporate profits to GDP.

From 1951 to 1999, that number ranged from 4.5% to 6%. More recently, that number has been up over 10%.

Should investors be concerned about these numbers and the market?

Buffett replied that those percentages suggest that American business is doing very well, though that might be a concern for society. The valuation picture is very much affected by our zero-based interest rate structure. Clearly, stocks are worth far more when government bonds yield 1% than when they yield 5%.

Munger noted that people have limited alternatives with bonds paying so little. This has pushed stocks to higher prices than they would reach otherwise.

Buffett added that the question is how long will these low rates continue? In Japan, this has gone on for decades. Or will we get back to normal? If rates go back to a more normal level, stock prices are high. If rates stay low, then stocks look "very cheap."

Buffett concluded, "Now I've given you the answers, and you can take your pick."

Venue: CenturyLink Center

Attendance: 40,000

Details About This Year:

- Professors Buffett and Munger presided over the first-ever live-streaming of the Berkshire meeting via Yahoo Finance, creating a global audience.

- The live streaming decreased attendance by about 10%.

Fortune 500 Ranking: 4th

- Berkshire now trails only Wal-Mart, Exxon Mobil, and Apple.

Stock Price: $197,800

One dollar invested in 1964 would now be worth **$15,983**.

Berkshire's per-share book value has grown from $19.46 to **$155,501** (a rate of **19.2%** compounded annually).

The S&P 500 compounded at **9.7%** annually for the same period.

HIGHLIGHTS FROM 2016'S NOTES

Just Getting Started

Buffett, clearly in a good mood, opened with a few quips.

Buffett claimed, "Charlie gets the girls. Every mother tells her daughter, 'If choosing between two old men, pick the older one.'"

Noting he had a great grandchild in the audience, Buffett said, "If you hear crying, it's just his mother explaining my views on inherited wealth."

Slides

Slides matter. Buffett only shows slides when he has something he wants to convey.

With the first slide, he gave a snapshot of Q1 results. With the second slide, he showed the impressive growth in Berkshire's after-tax operating earnings since 1999.

Slide One: While first quarter net earnings were up from $5.2 billion to $5.6 billion, operating earnings dipped to $3.7 billion from $4.2 billion.

Buffett added some color: Insurance underwriting profits fell by half due to hail storms and catastrophe losses. Railroad earnings were down due to lower car loadings. Manufacturing earnings were up with the addition of Precision Castparts and Duracell. Net earnings were boosted some $900 million by investment and derivative gains.

Slide Two: This was the more significant slide. Buffett showed the per-share after-tax annual operating earnings since 1999, the year of the MidAmerican Energy acquisition.

Those earnings have risen steadily from $0.67 to $17.36 for 2015. This shows how operating earnings have grown substantially. Furthermore, Berkshire has done it with no corporate budgets, no quarterly earnings projections—focusing instead on adding sustainable and growing earnings power.

The chart also shows the development of Berkshire's realized investment gains and losses. They are, of course, erratic, bumping from $0.89 in 2000 to a loss of $4.65 in 2008, to a gain of $6.73 in 2015.

Overall, realized investment gains and income totaled $32.39 for the period.

Consider this: One year's operating earnings ($17.36 for 2015) equaled 50% of the entire 17 years' worth of realized gains and income.

This slide reveals how significantly Berkshire has shifted from simply being an investment company to being an operating earnings power-house with a portfolio of investments.

Precision Castparts

The $32 billion purchase of aerospace parts maker Precision Castparts (PCP) marks the largest deal in Berkshire's history.

Buffett noted that the most important asset was CEO Mark Donegan. Buffett called Donegan one of the most extraordinary managers that he's come across—one of a kind.

In addition, Buffett saw some advantages for PCP as part of Berkshire: Donegan could now spend 100% of his time on engines versus quarterly earnings calls, bank line negotiations, and so on. Donegan wouldn't even have to come to Omaha to make a $1 billion acquisition. Buffett concluded that Berkshire had taken Precision's most valuable asset, Donegan, and made it even more valuable.

Munger stressed that operating PCP requires superior management.

This is a departure from the early years at Berkshire when they owned cheap stocks and easy-to-operate companies. Now, they've learned to find great managers, which creates an opening to own more complex businesses.

With aerospace components, quality and reliability are enormously important. The contracts run many years, so customers don't just take the low bid. PCP has an unparalleled reputation for quality.*

---

* Corey and I had a 20-minute chat with Donegan at the PCP booth in The Berkshire Mall. Donegan echoed Buffett's comments, sharing that the first thing he does every morning now is thank Berkshire for buying the company. He's more than happy to never do another earnings call. He also walked us through how he does plant inspections, constantly asking, "Why do we do this?"—always challenging his team to make processes more efficient.

What struck us most was Donegan's intensity. Our sense is that Donegan runs a hard-charging meritocracy. Those who are self-motivated, hard-working, and achievement-oriented love working for him. If you're looking for a slower-paced job, don't apply here.

We see two primary game-changers with PCP having access to Berkshire's capital: 1) PCP can now do acquisitions more aggressively, and 2) PCP can invest more readily in the long-term development of parts contracts—once a contract is won, it may pay out over seven years or more. Both uses of capital can ding short-term earnings for a public company and deter a manager from making a great long-term investment.

Donegan is thrilled to no longer have that headache.

Happiness

Buffett's formula for happiness is simple: "Do what I like with people I like." He noted that he learned early in life that his favorite employer was himself. It avoids aggravation.

Munger shared that he's as fascinated at age 92 as he's been in any period of his life.

While he wishes he had wised up sooner, Munger also saw the blessing in it: "At age 92, I still have lots of ignorance left to work on."

Reinsurance

Buffett had something of a prediction: Reinsurance will not be as good the next 10 years as the last 10 years, in part, due to ultra-low interest rates.

Europe has negative yields! The whole idea of float is to invest in *positive* returns.

However, Berkshire is better situated than most. Its capital cushion and unrelated operating income give it more flexibility with investing the float. Berkshire also has more flexibility in modifying business models. All other reinsurance companies are tied to a different business model.

Munger allowed that lots of new capacity and heavy competition will make for slower going. Additional competition has come from offshore insurance companies. He groused that such companies are really investment operations seeking friendly tax jurisdictions.

In sum: Supply is up while demand is not.

GEICO

A question: Progressive Direct had a 95.1 combined ratio, while GEICO came in at 98.0.* What gives?

Looking at the question from a bigger perspective, Buffett noted that driving has become much safer over time. In the mid-1930s, there were 32,000 fatalities per year, or 15 fatalities per 100 miles driven. Today, that ratio is down to 1 fatality per 100 miles. Last year had about 32,000 deaths—the same number as in the 1930s, but with 15x more miles driven.

After years of declines, Buffett reported that last year both frequency and severity increased suddenly and substantially. There was more driving

---

* The combined ratio is a measure of insurance profitability. Under 100 is profitable, so the lower the better.

and more *distracted driving.* GEICO needed to adjust its premiums accordingly and will do better in 2016. This accounts for the elevated combined ratio.

Buffett continues to like GEICO's model, noting that it has exceeded Progressive's market share in every state. He mused that, if he lives to 100, he might even see GEICO surpass State Farm.

Munger observed that it is not a tragedy for someone else to have a good quarter.

GEICO's market share has increased fivefold since Berkshire bought it.

Amazon

Buffett admitted that Amazon is a huge development. What it has accomplished in a relatively short time is remarkable. Amazon's created a big advantage with its intense focus on developing millions of satisfied customers. You're not going to beat them.

GEICO was slow to change to the Internet because the phone worked so well. However, Buffett has been amazed how fast inquiries for GEICO migrated from the phone to online. Adaptation to the Internet by the American public has been amazing.

If you have a good business, plenty of folks will try to take it from you. Overall, Buffett sees Berkshire as well-situated with its diversified collection of businesses.

Munger suggested that, on balance, Berkshire has been helped by the Internet.

Coca-Cola

Challenged with being "long sugar," Buffett responded that he consumes 700 Coca-Cola calories per day of his daily target of roughly 2,800 calories. He elects to get 700 calories per day in a way that makes him feel good when he consumes them.

Coca-Cola delivers over 1.9 billion 8-ounce servings per day. That's 693 billion servings a year. That's 100 8-ounce servings per capita for 7.4 billion people.

Buffett finds it spurious to lay obesity all on Coke. The key lies in making the choice not to consume more calories than you can use.

Buffett likes fudge, peanut brittle. He said that he wished he had a twin who only ate broccoli. He knew he'd be happier than that twin.

Talking about health, Buffett spoke about life expectancy, noting there are now 10,000 men and over 45,000 women over age 100.

Buffett joked that, if he really wants to live longer, he should get a sex change—he'd be 4.5 times more likely to get to 100.

In an effort to improve public discourse, Munger weighed in with Munger's Law: *You can't list the detriments without listings the benefits.*

Munger suggested it would be like cancelling air travel because 100 people died in a crash. Buffett likes peanut brittle and flavored drinks. People should be free to choose to do what they like.

In classic understated Munger fashion, he asserted, "To say the detriments without including the benefits is immature and stupid."

Later, Munger went even further by suggesting that if you disagree with someone, you should understand their side better than they do before you open your mouth.

Renewables

Buffett explained that the federal government has encouraged the development of renewable energy with a 2.3 cents/kilowatt hour producer tax credit.

This subsidy has the benefit of reducing carbon emissions worldwide. The cost of the tax credit is borne by the citizenry in the form of lower tax revenues. To the degree renewables replace coal and natural gas, the benefits accrue not only to the citizenry but also to the whole world.

Since Berkshire has large taxable income and lots of capital, Berkshire will continue to have a large appetite for renewable energy development.

Buffett noted that Berkshire Energy also features very low utility rates. In Iowa, where competitor Alliant (which hasn't pursued renewables) will need a rate increase, Berkshire won't need one until 2029. He added that Iowa regulators have been marvelous to work with and very encouraging of renewables.

Munger summed up that Berkshire is doing more than its share and is charging lower rates.

He noted that the Nebraska Public Power District, a co-operative, was very proud of its record. Today, power is cheaper across the river in Council Bluffs, Iowa, which is becoming a tech haven. Google and the like gobble up electricity with their massive server farms, so they are locating there.

Derivatives and Discontinuities

Buffett warned that derivatives still pose a danger.

The great danger is when there are discontinuities that cause the system to stop such as World War I, September 11, 2001, and October 19, 1987 (Black Monday).

Buffett noted that a major cyber, nuclear, or biological attack is a near certainty that will happen at some point. At times like that, there can be enormous gaps in positions.

Buffett noted that Berkshire would only do derivatives on a collateralized basis. The Gen Re derivative book is still in run-off after a decade of benign market conditions.

Buffett still sees derivatives as a potential time bomb in the system.

Munger summed: "We'd prefer that derivatives were illegal."

Float

Buffett loves the idea of increasing float, which has grown to $88 billion.

With $50 billion in treasuries and another $8 billion coming from the call of its Kraft Heinz preferred, Berkshire will be at around $60 billion in cash.

Low rates are a problem for everyone with fixed-dollar investments. However, Buffett noted again, that Berkshire has so much capital and so many sources of earnings power that it can use its float in ways other insurers cannot consider.

Munger: "I've got nothing to add."

Buffett: "He's now at full strength."

Railroads

With rail stocks down some 35% in the stock market, Buffett was asked if the rails were in secular or cyclical decline.

Buffett admitted that a decline in the usage of coal was likely secular. However, the recent decline in coal orders was overstated due to high inventories by utilities. The high inventories resulted in the utilities temporarily under-ordering.

Overall, Buffett was unabashed, saying, "We love Burlington Northern Santa Fe."

Buffett suggested not to mark the progress of the business by the ups and downs of the stock market. He concluded, "It's a very good business, and we'll hold it forever."

Later on, Buffett shared that railroad depreciation was understated and that Berkshire would have to spend more to keep the railroads in shape. In 2015, Berkshire invested $5.7 billion versus $3.4 billion of depreciation as part of its catch-up effort.

BNSF does more gross revenue ton-miles than any other railway in North America. However, the composition of those revenues is shifting.

With coal, there will be no expansion. With the Bakken, it's a sensible investment but will be less busy going forward. With intermodal, BNSF will be looking to grow.

Basic Advice

Buffett complimented Andy Hayward and his "Secret Millionaires Club" series for helping thousands of kids learn how to handle money, make friends, and become better citizens.

Buffett reminded folks that to buy a stock is to buy part ownership of a business. Don't get hung up on daily price quotes. Instead, think about business performance and what you would pay for the business, just as you would a farm.

Munger added, while it's difficult, to look for people you can trust in dealing with investments.

Buffett assured that American business will be fine over time. Don't be envious. Follow your own course.

Nevada Solar Policy

A controversial decision by the Nevada Public Utility Commission came up for discussion.

The commission decided to stop a rebate experiment that allowed roof-top solar homeowners to sell back to the grid at a subsidized rate. In effect, 99% of the homeowners were subsidizing the 1% who had roof-top solar by paying an inflated price for their power.

Buffett seemed to agree with the decision.

He pointed out that the key question is, "Who pays the subsidy?" In this case, it wasn't right for the 99% to buy at the inflated price to the benefit of the 1%. However, if the entire society benefits, society should pick up the tab.

Greg Abel weighed in, affirming that Berkshire is strongly in favor of renewables, but at a market rate not a subsidized rate. Abel noted that, by 2019, 76% of Berkshire's coal-fired plants would be retired, replaced by solar.

Education in America

Buffett noted that monopoly and bureaucracy were widespread in higher education in America. If you want more financial efficiency in education, you're howling at the wind.

Munger concurred, noting that a rich society has an obligation to the young as well as the old. Endowments have gone up, yet there are no tuition reductions, no increase in students. The only thing up are the professors' salaries. For too many schools, the purpose of the endowment is to make a bigger endowment.

Munger stopped himself: "I've made all the enemies I can afford."

Buffett: "That never slowed him down in the past."

Trump or Clinton?

Buffett claimed that Berkshire will do fine with either candidate.

Despite 50% taxes for many years, price controls, regulations, and more, American business has done extraordinarily well over the last 200 years. America is a remarkably attractive place to do business. GDP per capita is up six-fold in his lifetime.

While aggregate output is very good, the distribution of that output can fall short.

Munger noted that GDP figures understate the real advantages the system has given our citizens—advantages that don't translate easily into monetary figures.

Buffett challenged those who think this is a bad time to be born. They are wrong. Consider the pace of innovation. With phones alone, there are numerous choices that were not available just 20 years ago.

Bank Profitability

Buffett noted you can change the profitability of banking totally with capital requirements. With a 100% capital requirement, you could not make any money. With a 1% capital requirement, you add too much risk to the system.

New, tougher capital requirements for banks are sure to make large banks less profitable, though less risky.

Wells Fargo is Berkshire's largest single marketable security. Buffett likes it extremely well with its huge base of very cheap deposits. Unfortunately, Wells has to lend it out at cheap rates currently, but Buffett expects the spreads will work in their advantage eventually.

Activists

Buffett believes Berkshire's willingness to repurchase shares will keep its stock price at a reasonable approximation of fair value. Breaking up Berkshire is an unlikely event.

Munger noted that worry about activists is good for Berkshire. If a company is being attacked, Berkshire makes a great ally.

Sequoia Fund

After its embarrassing over-concentration in Valeant, the Sequoia Fund came up for discussion.

Buffett reminisced that he was the father of the fund.

When he closed the Buffett Partnership in 1969, the partners wanted to know what to do. Buffett suggested putting some money into municipal bonds and then suggested just two managers: Sandy Gottesman and Bill Ruane—two terrific people with talent and integrity.

Gottesman took on individual clients. Ruane started the Sequoia Fund for clients with more modest means and did a fantastic job up to his passing in 2005.

With Valeant, despite objections by the board, the managers took an unusually large position.* The primary Sequoia manager involved is no longer at the fund. The Valeant business model was enormously flawed and had been touted to Berkshire.

Buffett shared that the Valeant debacle illustrates a principle of Peter Kiewit: "If you need a manager, look for someone with intelligence and energy and integrity. If they don't have the last one, then be sure you don't have the first two. If they have no integrity, I want them dumb and lazy."

Buffett noted that they have seen certain things over and over. Valeant had elements of a chain letter scheme. Many Wall Street things seem to have that element.

Buffett believed that the team at Sequoia going forward were able people. Munger agreed. Sequoia, as it was reconstituted, is reputable. The problem is fixed. As for Valeant, Munger called it a sewer and said those who created it deserved what they got.

---

* At one point, Valeant comprised 30% of the fund.

Bet Update

Buffett gave an update on his bet with Protégé Partners that the S&P 500 would outperform a selection of hedge funds over the decade beginning with 2008.

As of year-end 2015, the score was S&P 500 up 65%, Protégé's hedge funds up 22%.

Buffett is driving home his point about the extreme compensation of hedge fund managers: Getting 2 and 20 for just breathing!* Taken in aggregate, the returns of all managers must be average. With the hedge funds, you get average less the terrific expenses.

In addition, you have consultants charging fees. If the consultants just say, "Buy an S&P 500 Index fund and sit for 50 years," they wouldn't be able to charge much. The hyperactive traders and their "helpers" are, in aggregate, a tax on the system.

In sum, you can skip the fees and get the performance of American industry by owning an S&P 500 Index fund.

This is not new. Buffett mentioned Fred Schwed's classic from 1940, *Where Are the Customers' Yachts?*†

Buffett asserted that far more money is made on Wall Street with selling talent than with investing talent.

Munger shared, again, that finding people you trust is difficult—like finding a needle in a haystack.

Buffett reiterated that he only had two recommendations in 1969: Gottesman and Ruane.

That was it.

Culture

Buffett was pleased to assert that the Berkshire board, managers, and shareholders clearly recognize and embrace the Berkshire culture. It works, and there's not a lot of competition.

Buffett noted that the main problem is Berkshire's size. To a significant degree, size is the enemy of performance.

Munger claimed he was more optimistic, predicting that Berkshire's culture will surprise everyone with how well it works. So much power in

---

* 2% of asset fee plus 20% of the profits.
† Classic line from the book: "They told me to buy this stock for my old age. It worked wonderfully. Within a week I was an old man."

place with so little turnover. Great tenure with people who are not in it for the money.

Buffett noted that Berkshire selects board members with (1) business savvy, (2) shareholder orientation, and (3) special interest in Berkshire.

He asserted that they have the best board they could have. All Berkshire board members have bought stock in the open market. There are no stock options. He lamented that board members too often get options just for breathing.

Buffett suggested we take note of the Christmas picture in the annual report. He hopes it's exactly the same next year. It's a remarkable group. No committees. No makeshift work groups. A cooperative effort by all.

Berkshire Buybacks

When asked about Berkshire's 120% of book value buyback authorization, Buffett allowed that the stock didn't trade to buyback levels, so none was purchased.

Although, he loves the idea as the surest way to make money is to buy dollar bills for less than a dollar.

Over time, the buyback is a backstop for ensuring that a no-dividend policy results in a greater return than paying out a dollar. It's probable, but not certain, to work out.

Buffett noted that Berkshire's intrinsic value has widened from book value. He mused that, if Berkshire gets to $100-120 billion in cash, maybe they'll need to move up the threshold.

Munger noted that buybacks are fashionable, sold by consultants, and often destroy value.

Buffett chimed in that most buybacks are done at any price, which makes no sense. Very rarely do you see metrics to govern the prices paid. Buybacks above intrinsic value destroy value.

Buffett: "A full wallet is like a full bladder. One could get the urge very quickly to pee it away."

Nebraska Furniture Mart

Buffett shared that NFM's new store in Dallas had so much initial volume that they couldn't keep up. It took a while to get deliveries up to standard.

Dallas is already their largest store and will be a $1 billion store before long.

NFM is bringing prices and variety that Dallas hasn't seen before.

Beware CNBC

Cyber, nuclear, biochemical, and chemical attacks, that is.

In a sobering digression, Buffett shared that CNBC is his handle for the world's greatest problems. Buffett warned that something of the sort will happen. It's just a matter of time because a percentage of the population comprises psychotics, megalomaniacs, and religious fanatics.

And the problem is growing. There are more of them when the world population is 7.4 billion versus 3 billion.

Also, we have innovated beyond bows and arrows, and spears, so the potential damage has increased. In 1945, with the dropping of the bomb in Japan, we unleashed a power like the world had never seen. That bomb was a popgun compared to what we can do now.

Buffett recommended visiting the Union of Concerned Scientists website for further study on the issues.

Buffett sees this as overwhelmingly a government problem and a priority for each president.

He suggested you could argue that, if Hitler hadn't been so anti-Semitic, pushing out all the scientists, he would have had the bomb. It was Leo Szilard who got Einstein to co-sign a letter to FDR that convinced the president to move ahead with the Manhattan Project. One side or the other was going to get it.

Referencing 9/11 and the anthrax letter, Buffett noted that the capacity for damage is horrific. And we still don't know just what to do about it. It's a tough problem.

Again, he warned, anything that has a 99.9% chance of not happening eventually will happen.

Get the Details

Asked how he does it, Buffett shared that he and Charlie read a lot.

What matters most to him are micro factors, as opposed to the macro factors that so often get all the attention. He loves to know all the details of a business.

Buffett reminisced that, in 1972, See's Candy had 140 shops. You could look at each shop, see how it did in year one, year two, year three.

It was very interesting. You never know when some fact might pop up as useful.

Buffett compared it to baseball, where every move was interesting, and then, suddenly, you get a double steal.

Free Cash Flow Outlook

A question about free cash flow turned into a lovely ramble about the value of good mentors.

Buffett started with walking through Berkshire's deferred tax item (about $21 billion on some $60 billion of unrealized appreciation), float ($88 billion), and depreciation.

He allowed that Berkshire will outspend depreciation at both Burlington Northern Santa Fe and Berkshire Hathaway Energy for years and year to come.

Buffett noted that annual operating earnings (about $17 billion) and additions to float would equal Berkshire's net new cash available.

That torrent of cash flow to allocate allows for a lot of mistakes.

The goal, again, is to add each year to the normalized per-share earnings power of the company.

Munger quipped that the key is not to be at the mercy of standard stupidities. If so, you'll do well.

He noted that Warren's gift is that he thinks ahead of the crowd. He thinks in such a clear way.

Buffett quoted Yogi Berra: "You can see a lot just by observing."

Buffett said they see very smart people do very dumb things. Rich people leveraging up and other self-destructive behaviors.

Munger chimed in, saying that what is required is the proper temperament of opportunism combined with patience coupled with trying to behave well.

He cited the preacher who, for his grandfather's eulogy, said, "None envied the man's success so fairly won and so wisely used." It's not just about being smart, but also about doing things in a good way.

Then came a reminiscence of mentors gone by.

Munger mentioned that Warren's uncle Fred was one of the finest men he ever met.

Buffett mentioned his four aunts who each reinforced good qualities in him.

Munger joked that he wished Warren would have had more aunts so that he'd have done even better.

Munger remembered Warren's grandfather Earnest working them hard at the Buffett family grocery store and then giving them lectures on self-reliance.

Buffett summed up that they were very lucky to have such people around.

Acquisitions: Quality of the Business + Quality of the People

Buffett said what matters most with an acquisition is whether you have a fix on the basic economics of the business.

He argued that typical due diligence does not get at the real risks. He could think of at least a half-dozen mistakes made, none of which could have been prevented by a checklist. It's all about the future economics.

For example, if you give a manager $1 billion for a business he once owned 100%, will he behave in the future as he has in the past? It's a hugely important question that's not on a checklist.

Munger concurred, noting that the essence of it all is the quality of the business and the human quality of the management. Neither can be assured by "due diligence."

Munger said he didn't know anyone who's done a better job with acquisitions than Berkshire.

Buffett added that he likes to show trust and that trust usually comes right back. That keeps things moving.

In addition, Buffett has found that really able people can handle so much. There's no limit to what talented people can do.

He noted that Berkshire's managers have added billions of dollars of value to Berkshire over the years.

Munger pointed out that the obverse is true: "Not only are the most able easy to trust, the unable you cannot fix. You're forced to use our system if you have your wits about you."

3G Capital Partners and Cost Cutting

3G Capital Partners has come under fire for its cost-cutting approach with Kraft Heinz.

Buffett defended 3G, citing Tom Murphy, CEO of Cap Cities, who said the best approach is to never hire a person you don't need, so you never have to lay anyone off.

Buffett suggested that all kinds of companies have people not doing much. He'd let go of the staff economist and the investor relations department, for example.

His impression is that 3G is extremely intelligent about staffing. In packaged foods, volume trends are not good, so some cutting is needed.

Munger noted that reducing sales volume at times can be quite intelligent. Just as you may need to lose excess staff, there may be times to lose some customers.

He concluded that a lean staff is always better.

Buffett noted that, when sloppy thinking appears in one area, sloppy thinking appears elsewhere. He recommended reading *Barbarians at the Gate* for a lesson on how a great business can get sloppy.

Van Tuyl

On Berkshire's $4.1 billion acquisition of auto deal Van Tuyl, Buffett noted that $1 billion of securities came with the deal, so take $1 billion off the price! In addition, the economics are good, and the CEO, Jeff Rachor, is first class.

NIRP (Negative Interest Rate Policy)

Buffett observed that, while going from 0% to -0.5% interest rates is no different than going from 4.0% to 3.5%, it feels different.

What's most dramatic is that we've had 0% interest rates for so long. That leads folks to pay much more for businesses than when rates are, say, 15%.

Aesop's rule of a bird in the hand is worth two in the bush is being re-written as a bird in the hand is worth 9/10 of a bird in the bush.

Munger noted that we've never had NIRP before. All the Keynesians have been mired in stasis over Japan for 25 years.

Munger noted that his advantage is that he knows he doesn't understand it.

Munger: "If you're not confused, you haven't thought about it correctly."

Buffett: "I've thought about it correctly then."

Compensation

Munger noted the importance of proper incentives. You get what you reward for. Reward for silliness, and you will get silly outcomes.

Buffett shared that GEICO uses just two variables that apply to its 20,000 employees' laddered bonus program: (1) growth in policies in force and (2) profitability of seasoned business.

Buffett noted this approach allows for the expensive nature of first-year policies. It's simple, everyone understands it, and it aligns the goals of the owners with the goals of the staff.

Munger took his annual shot at compensation consultants.

Munger asserted that it is important not to just reward profits. Banks and insurance companies can show huge profits on paper before disaster appears. This was a major cause of the subprime mortgage debacle. Accountants allowed lenders to merely use past loan experience to lend. It was insane—and no one is ashamed. The very greedy CEO enlists others in the industry to make a pyramid, so it doesn't look like he's in it for himself. Stock options get re-priced at low prices.

Munger stopped himself, summing up that intelligent compensation is not as complicated as the world makes it.

Restructuring

A question about restructuring hit a nerve.

Munger retorted, "Would you kill your mother to get the insurance money?"

He noted that Berkshire had never had a restructuring charge and was never going to start.

Buffett said that the key is that their accounting numbers are conservatively stated. The one understatement on the Berkshire balance sheet was the low depreciation at BNSF, which has been openly discussed.

Final Quote

Munger: "I think if you see the world accurately, it's bound to be humorous because it's so ridiculous."

2017

Venue: CenturyLink Center

Attendance: 40,000

Details About This Year:

- Despite the meeting being live-streamed, which reduces the need to travel to Omaha, for the second year in a row, physical attendance was as big as ever.

- One reason for the large turn-out may be that, last year, Warren added an extra shopping day by having The Berkshire Mall open on Friday. This year, shareholders/ shoppers were ready. The place was packed. Past record sales figures for the annual event were probably handily exceeded by this year's eager treasure hunters.

- The festivities began with a one-hour movie. One vignette was a Munger clip from the Daily Journal meeting where he talks about being a nerd and dating. He gets a date with a blond goddess, inadvertently sets her on fire, and douses her with Coke. He encourages fellow nerds to persevere. His version of an inspirational speech, we suppose.

Fortune 500 Ranking: 2nd

- Berkshire now trails only Wal-Mart.

Stock Price: $244,121

One dollar invested in 1964 would now be worth **$19,726**.

Berkshire's per-share book value has grown from $19.46 to **$172,108** (a rate of **19%** compounded annually).

The S&P 500 compounded at **9.7%** annually for the same period.

HIGHLIGHTS FROM 2017'S NOTES

First Quarter Earnings

Buffett opened the meeting with a review of the first quarter earnings.

While the review was relatively short, in a sense, it was a lecture unto itself. It illustrated so many elements of the Berkshire model.

For the quarter, per-share earnings were $4,060 versus $5,589 a year ago.

However, it is not what the numbers are but *what they mean* that matters.

The key question is always, *"Did intrinsic value grow?"* Buffett clearly believed the answer was "yes," making it a good quarter from his perspective.

First, he proudly noted that GEICO had added over 748,000 new policyholders since the beginning of the year.[*]

Competitors increased their rates. Loss costs have increased sharply in the industry,[†] and some competitors decided to slow down taking on new business. Acting more like a cheetah than a lizard, GEICO's response was to accelerate its new-business efforts.

Buffett regards each policyholder as a lifetime stream of premiums. Each policy is worth something like $2,000 to Berkshire. Thus, GEICO added some $1.5 billion of intrinsic value to Berkshire in just the last four months.[‡]

Second, Buffett noted that Berkshire's float had hit a new high of $105 billion, thanks primarily to a deal with AIG where Berkshire received a $10.5 billion premium for taking on 80% of substantially all of AIG's U.S. commercial long-tail exposures for accident years 2015 and prior.

It's good for AIG, allowing them to unload a troublesome book of business that was depressing earnings.[§] It's also good for Berkshire, who gets lots of money up front (float) to work with in exchange for paying out claims over many years.

By highlighting these two events, Buffett was teaching the shareholders several essential lessons:

For one, focus on intrinsic value growth, not reported earnings. Again, it's not what the numbers are but what they mean that matters.

---

[*] For comparison, GEICO added 707,000 policies in 2015 and 974,000 in 2016.
[†] Largely due to "distracted driving." Texting is dangerous.
[‡] 748,000 x $2,000 per policy.
[§] AIG is currently in the sights of activist Carl Icahn.

Each business will have a couple of unique factors that are essential in evaluating its progress. Often, *those unique factors are not immediately reflected in the reported earnings.* In our short-attention-span world, analysts and the media so often focus on reported earnings and look no deeper.

With GEICO, one of those essential factors is the policyholder count. Buffett is telling us that. Another is the combined ratio, which reflects the profitability (or lack thereof) of those policies over time. There's also the generation of float.

With GEICO, these are the things that matter—and they are all growing in a good way. In particular, growth in policyholders has accelerated.

For the Berkshire insurance operation, the growth of no- or low-cost float is primary. Adding $10.5 billion of float (an 11% increase in one fell swoop) is a major addition to intrinsic value. If the float comes with little or no cost, it acts much like equity.

No wonder Buffett is delighted with the AIG deal.

Another lesson is how Berkshire's laser focus on long-term intrinsic value growth and comfort with lumpy earnings puts it at a major advantage compared to its publicly traded peers.

In the case of GEICO, competitors are ceding market share to shelter profit margins.

Under pressure from analysts, shareholders, and other constituencies, public companies are often driven to forgo the long-term, rational decision in favor of short-term gratification.

In the case of AIG, with Carl Icahn breathing down its neck, the company is ceding 80% of its pre-2016 U.S. commercial book to improve the optics of its quarterly earnings.

This dynamic has created tons of value for Berkshire over the years.

Third, it highlights the value of momentum and share of mind for GEICO.

GEICO has long been the low-cost operator in auto insurance. In addition, GEICO management has invested heavily to make the company ever more efficient.

To top it off, after years of massive marketing, GEICO has also created a large share of mind. *Who doesn't know where they might save 15% on their auto insurance?*

When companies raise prices, consumers shop. GEICO immediately and successfully responded to this ripple in the market by putting the pedal to the metal on its new-business efforts.

Fourth, it highlights the value of Berkshire's Fort Knox balance sheet and reputation for fiscal soundness.

When an insurance company cedes a book of business to a reinsurer, it is still on the hook if the reinsurer fails to pay.

AIG had 10.5 billion reasons to only do that deal with Berkshire. No other company could have done that AIG deal.

So again, quarterly earnings were down. Digging deeper, Buffett let us know that it was a good quarter for growing intrinsic value. And that's what counts at Berkshire Hathaway.

Driverless Cars

Buffett noted that driverless cars were a threat to both GEICO and the railroads.

Safer roads would bring down economic loss costs, which would mean fewer premium dollars for GEICO. Safer trucks would provide stiffer competition for the railroads.

However, Buffett added that he thinks it's all a long way off.

Munger: "I think that's perfectly clear."

Buffett: "Finally, approval after all these years."

Technology

A question about technology turned into a fascinating revelation on Buffett's investments and non-investments in this arena.

For one, Berkshire sold some IBM. Buffett admitted that he has been wrong on IBM. He thought it would do better over the last six years.

For another, Berkshire has recently accumulated an $18 billion stake in Apple. Buffett explained that, while Apple obviously has products with lots of technology built into them, the big question is, *"What will its customers do over the years ahead?"*

Munger noted that Buffett's purchase of Apple suggests that either he is crazy or he is learning, most likely the latter.

The Technology Age

Buffett rocked the meeting by declaring that people don't appreciate how much the world has changed.

He noted that the five largest companies in the U.S. by market cap (excluding Berkshire)—some $2.5 trillion of market value—now represent 10% of the whole market.

These five companies (Alphabet, Amazon, Apple, Facebook, Microsoft) require no equity capital to run them. None.

It's a very different world. It used to be that growing and earning larger and larger amounts of money required large reinvestments of capital. Not so with these top five, which generate *almost infinite returns on capital*.

Buffett mused that Andrew Mellon would be baffled. In his world, growth could only come with more capital. More trucks. More factories. More plant and equipment. Our capital system was built on real tangible assets with innovation.

Munger cautioned that venture capital has been chasing this trend hard and has lost lots of money doing it. Only a few will win big.*

Google

Munger asserted that they have no advantages in technology. That they weren't smart enough to figure out Google when it was right in their laps.

Buffett agreed that they were very close-up on Google. They knew GEICO was paying $10 a click, and they were happy to do it. Furthermore, Google had no incremental cost. The owners even came to see Buffett before the IPO.

Buffett confessed: "I blew it."

Munger added that they saw Wal-Mart as a total cinch and blew that one too.†

Amazon

While Berkshire also does not own Amazon, Buffett saw this as less of a miss.

He noted that it is difficult to predict winners in new areas. Even more amazing is when a person builds two major businesses from a standing start, as Jeff Bezos of Amazon has done with retail and the cloud.

Buffett noted that Bezos laid out his vision in the 1997 annual report.‡ Even knowing what his plans were, the successful execution of them would have been a long shot.

Munger observed that what Amazon has done was very difficult and not at all obvious. Missing Google was worse.

Munger concluded that Jeff Bezos is a different species.

---

* What we hear Buffett saying, in a sense, is that as huge as the "FANG" type stocks have been, *they are still underappreciated*. From this, we infer that these stocks may still not be fully valued as people do not understand just how radically different their capital models are from past models.
† Munger is a long-time board member of Costco, so he knows big-box retailing. Why has Berkshire never taken a meaningful stake in Costco?
‡ He also recommended checking out the Charlie Rose interview of Bezos.

Indexing

Buffett had John Bogle, who was turning 88 years old, stand up for recognition.

Buffett joked that, in two years, Bogle would be eligible for an executive position at Berkshire.

He praised Bogle for his lifelong championing of the idea of index funds.

Later in the meeting, Buffett discussed his big bet with a fund of funds back in 2007.

He reviewed his reasoning that a fund of hedge funds, which charge 2 and 20,* in aggregate, simply could not beat the index. By definition, a large group of aggregated returns will be average. Subtract large fees and the result must be worse than average.

Buffett asserted that it's the sales culture of Wall Street that's perpetuated the scheme.

Munger joked that a hedge fund manager was asked, "Why do you charge 2 and 20?" The manager replied, "Because I couldn't get 3 and 30."

The Wells Fargo Error

In a response to misdeeds at Wells Fargo, Buffett noted that Berkshire benefits from decentralization. However, with hundreds of thousands of employees, there is no question that, somewhere, a few are behaving inappropriately.

Berkshire leans heavily on principles of behavior rather than loads of rules. He claimed that a culture that self-selects is better than a 1,000-page manual.

Buffett sends a letter every other year to all the managers with the "Salomon pledge": *"Lose money for the firm and I will be understanding. Lose one shred of reputation for the firm and I will be ruthless."*

With Wells Fargo, Buffett observed that there were three errors, but one of them, in particular, dwarfed the others.

One error was to inadvertently incentivize bad behavior. In addition, as with any strong sales culture, there is a risk of pushing too hard. But the giant error here was that, when the program runs off the rails, *the CEO must act.*

---

* 2% of the assets plus 20% of the profits.

Buffett recalled the Salomon scandal. Paul Moser of Salomon was flim-flamming the Treasury auctions with phony bids. The then-CEO, John Gutfreund, got the news and said he'd take care of it. He didn't. In fact, Gutfreund compared the infraction to a "traffic ticket." Then Moser did it again. The pyro-maniac had lit another fire. That's when things imploded for Salomon. This "traffic ticket" nearly brought down the enterprise.

There are times when the CEO must act.

With Wells Fargo, the top brass underestimated the impact of fraudulent account openings. The fines totaled $185 million, not an amount that seemed all that offensive. It was a huge miss. The CEO did not act.

Buffett revised Ben Franklin: *"An ounce of prevention is worth a ton of cure."*

Ideal Buy

Buffett said he knows a great deal when he sees it.

Although every situation is unique, in general, he loves a competitive advantage that can last for decades, talented and eager managers who fit the Berkshire culture, and of course, a good price.

Buffett reviewed how buying See's Candy in 1972 was a watershed moment.

They paid $25 million net for an entity earning $4 million pre-tax that has since generated $2 billion of pre-tax earnings.

See's Candy was special then, and it's special now. However, for a slightly higher price, they would not have bought it.

Munger: "We were young and ignorant."

Buffett: "Now we're old and ignorant."

Continuous Learning—Early Stupidity Helped Us

One of Buffett's annual themes is the value of learning. He noted that life properly lived is learning, learning, learning all the time.

He observed that being wrong is when he learns the most.

Munger chimed in that there's nothing like personal painful experiences to help you learn.

He added that they had a lot of early experiences fixing horrible businesses and that it helps to have your nose rubbed in it.

Buffett agreed that their early stupidity really helped them.

Munger put it more graphically, *"Painful experience is a lot like eating cockleburs. It really gets your attention."*

Buffett added that if you want to be a good evaluator of a business, run a lousy business for a while. You can see how awful it can be and that having a high IQ doesn't help.*

Durable Competitive Advantage

Asked about some of his more challenged investees (such as American Express, Coca-Cola, Wells Fargo, and the airlines), Buffett reminded us that these companies were not purchased because they would never have problems or competition, but because they had *durable competitive advantages.*

In the case of American Express, he noted that the Platinum Card is doing very well.

Berkshire is now the largest holder of four of the largest airlines—while the industry has its problems, it also has some strengths.

There is also a judgment on the ability of management to ward off competitors.

Buffett noted National Indemnity, purchased in 1968 for $8 million, has become a huge asset for Berkshire after years of warding off marauders.

He summed up that what you want is an economic castle with a very wide moat and an honest, talented knight to handle marauders.

Munger: "I have nothing to add."

Buffett: "We'll cut his salary if he doesn't participate."

Airlines

Remarkably, Buffett very clearly laid out his rationale for Berkshire's airline investments. Seldom does he lay out his cards so directly.

Operating at 80% of capacity in seats/miles, Buffett sees it as very likely that revenues per passenger mile will rise for the next 5–10 years.

Surprisingly, the airlines are earning higher returns on capital than UPS or FedEx.

---

* We can't help but feel a little vindication.

In 1986, one of my questions was whether owning the Berkshire textile mills, while an economic mess, did add value to Berkshire by lessons learned and showing Buffett's patience and loyalty with owned businesses. Buffett made a joke about my question, I blushed, and I don't remember what he said after that.

In any case, at this year's meeting, they clearly made the case that those early mistakes were formative in building the Berkshire compounding machine.

In addition, the airlines are buying in lots of stocks at very low multiples. Even if business proves to be flat, the stocks will be worth more on a per-share basis in years to come.

Buffett cautioned that it's no cinch. Will pricing be rational or suicidal? What will happen with oil prices? While labor relations seem more stable, there is a shortage of pilots.

Munger noted that the railroads were terrible for decades and decades. Then things changed, and they got good.

Buffett summed up that the keys will be operating margins, fewer shares, and the intensity of pricing competition.[*]

Intrinsic Business Value

Buffett noted that intrinsic business value can only be calculated in retrospect: cash generated between now and judgment day discounted back to the present at an appropriate interest rate.

While book value is a starting point, even 120% of book[†] understates Berkshire's intrinsic business value.

Going back to 2007, Buffett estimated that Berkshire has compounded at about 10% a year. Going forward, Buffett mused that it will be tough to achieve that rate of growth with interest rates so low.

The one statistic Buffett would want to know for the future would be, *"What will the interest rates be over the next 20 years?"*

Buffett's guess is that rates will be somewhat higher in the next 20 years. If so, maybe 10% a year for Berkshire will be achievable. If rates stay low, Berkshire will likely do less than that.

However, Buffett affirmed that Berkshire is built to last.

He asserted that the chances of Berkshire having a terrible return are as low as you can find. And the chances of Berkshire having a sensational return are also as low as you can find.

Munger noted that size is the anchor of performance, and they are proving it.[‡]

Munger also asserted that Berkshire's collection of businesses is superior to those of the S&P 500, on average.

Buffett agreed, noting that Berkshire's culture is significantly more shareholder-oriented than that of the companies in the S&P 500.

---

[*] Again, Buffett teaches us that every industry has a few essential variables. These are the ones for his airline bet.
[†] Berkshire's stock buyback hurdle.
[‡] Although, size also has its advantages: Only Berkshire was big enough to do the AIG deal.

Berkshire's owner-oriented culture and mindset are distinctly different from most public companies, which are subject to all sorts of pressures.

Buffett went even further: "There's nothing I can think of that would break Berkshire."

Berkshire has such a wide variety of earnings streams. In every way, Berkshire is structured to handle stresses.*

Munger insightfully concluded: "A lot of people are trying to be brilliant. We're just trying to stay rational. That's a big advantage. Trying to be brilliant is dangerous."

Tax Cuts

Regarding the proposed tax cuts, Buffett observed that effects can vary widely.

For Berkshire's regulated businesses, returns are regulated, so all benefits would flow through to the customers. For other businesses, the gains may be competed away. For monopolies, all the benefits would flow to the corporate bottom line.

History shows that overall benefits would be split between businesses and consumers.

Risk Averse

Munger noted that, if things went to hell in a handbasket, Berkshire would do much better. While he doesn't wish adversity on anyone, Berkshire benefits from times of chaos.

Buffett noted that, when the world is fearful, people have a hard time believing things will get better. Berkshire has no such trouble.

Buffett's trust that things will recover, time and again, has allowed him to put lots of money to work in troubled times. And when fear hits, things can happen faster than you can believe.

As an example, Buffett noted that, in 2008, with $2.5 trillion in money market funds, $750 billion flowed out in a week.

As a cute aside, Buffett recalled that his Aunt Katie, who lived to age 97, lived simply and owned $200 million worth of Berkshire stock. Yet she would write to Warren every 3–4 months: "Sorry to bother you, but am I going to run out of money?" He would write back: "Dear Katie, It's

---

* Buffett often brings up this diversification of earnings streams. It's what allowed the Berkshire Insurance Group to show a profit after Hurricane Andrew. He's also been building this diversification into the utility subsidiaries and operating businesses.

a good question. Because if you live 986 years, you're going to run out of money."

He concluded: "There's no way in the world, if you've got plenty of money, that it should become a minus in your life."

Capital Allocation

For his successor, Buffett emphasized that proven capital allocation abilities would be the key.

Buffett estimated that Berkshire will need to allocate some $400 billion over the next decade. That far exceeds all the money put into Berkshire to date. Clearly capital allocation will need to be the foremost talent.

Buffett noted that such a person would need a "money mind." Even someone with an IQ of 140 can have a very different mind where they do poorly at investing. It takes a money mind to think well about money and investing.

Precision Castparts

Buffett has been pleased with this acquisition, noting that the company has a strong position in the aerospace industry and extraordinary management.

Buffett noted that Precision Castparts (PCP) earnings are understated to the extent that there is $400 million of annual amortization from the purchase.

Buffett loves the long-term prospects for aircraft parts and that they are unlikely to be digitally replaced. He noted, "There will be no 3-D printing of aerospace parts."

Overall, Buffett believes PCP has a great future.[*]

---

[*] We anticipated that part of the appeal of PCP was its ability to make acquisitions, and PCP has done two deals already.

PCP CEO Mark Donegan told Corey that he loves working for Warren. Presumably, when Donegan sees a deal worth doing, all he has to do is pick up the phone and call Omaha.

In addition, Berkshire gives Donegan the freedom to invest in developing long-term aerospace contracts. While such aerospace parts cycles are expensive upfront, they can create very long-term, lucrative earnings streams.

Back when PCP was a public company, the lumpy earnings process caused Donegan plenty of headaches working with shareholders, bankers, and analysts. Now, working at Berkshire, he is free to build long-term intrinsic value without undue concern for short-term turbulence in profit cycles.

Productivity

Buffett fielded several questions about 3G Partners and its aggressive cost-cutting ways. The discussion quickly expanded to an overview of productivity.

As he did in the 2016 Berkshire annual report, Buffett reflected on the history of productivity improvement.

He noted that, without it, we'd still be living as we did in 1776. Eighty percent of the American working population was on farms 200 years ago.

Farming, steel, retail—all these areas have always been getting more productive. America is a story of constantly finding better ways to do things.

With Kraft Heinz, 3G found it could run things with fewer people.

Buffett asserted that 3G was fair in severance.

Munger chimed in that he would not care to be a subsistence farmer, nor does he miss the elevator operator. While it's unpleasant for those involved, productivity and change are part of life.

He noted that textiles, Berkshire's original business, were headed for oblivion. While it wasn't fun, it was pro-social for textile production to move where it could be more efficiently done. Berkshire's mills were closed, and 2,000 people were let go.

Munger agreed that there is nothing wrong with improving productivity. However, he did allow that, just because you're right, doesn't mean you should always do it.

With artificial intelligence, Buffett observed that more change will be coming. Almost certainly it will cause less employment in certain areas while being good for society overall.

Buffett offered a thought problem: Let's say one person could push a button and the entire U.S. GDP would be produced 150 million workers would be without jobs. It would be an enormously disruptive transformation and pro-social eventually.

Munger discerned that it is a matter of how fast people adapt. When air conditioning came along, acceptance was immediate. No one wanted to go back to being stinky and sweaty in the South.

He wrapped up the topic by opining that change will continue, but it won't happen that quickly—so people don't need to worry so much.

Berkshire Hathaway Energy: Wind and Solar

Buffett is proud of Berkshire's large investments in wind and solar and has a large appetite for more. He said that, if there were a $5 billion solar project, they would look at it.

Iowa has proved to be a bonanza for wind projects. In 2016, wind generated 55% of all megawatt-hours sold to Iowa retail customers. New projects are underway that will take that figure to 89% by 2020.

Buffett concluded that Iowa is terrific for wind and California is terrific for solar.

One of the keys is that Berkshire pays lots of taxes, so the tax subsidies for wind and solar have real value to Berkshire.

In contrast, most public utilities (1) don't have much cash after dividends to invest and (2) don't pay much real tax, so the tax subsidies are of little or no value.

Buffett said that Greg Abel has done a sensational job.

Berkshire Hathaway Energy's prices are 21%–33% lower across the states they serve.

While utilities in the Midwest region produce power on average for 9.7 cents per kilowatt, MidAmerican Energy is getting it done for just 7.1 cents.

Buffett predicted that in the next 10 years, Berkshire will have significantly more money invested in utility systems and that Berkshire is the buyer of choice with utility commissions.

Opportunities

Munger suggested that you must fish where the fish are. China has lots of fish. In the U.S. market, there are too damn many boats.

Healthcare

Corporate tax rates are down over the past 50 years. Meanwhile, healthcare costs have soared. Buffett reported that, in 1960, corporate taxes were 4% of GDP and healthcare costs were 5% of GDP. Today, corporate taxes are 2% and healthcare is 17% of GDP.

Buffett labeled medical costs *the tapeworm of American economic competitiveness*. The rest of the world spends 5%–10% of GDP on healthcare, mostly with socialized medicine.

Munger piped in that there is much in medical care that he doesn't like. Too much chemo for the almost dead, doctors doing too many unnecessary surgeries.

He asserted that it is not moral. However, vested interests are hard to change. We are in love with our lifesaving technologies. The system is crazy, and the costs are wild.

Munger predicted present trends will only get worse.

Looking Back and Looking Ahead

A local audience member, born in 1965, said that Buffett had run Berkshire Hathaway his entire life. Looking back all those years, the 52 year old was interested in hearing a memory from Berkshire's first annual meeting.

Continuing on, the local man said he'd asked Buffett in 2011 what he would like to be known for 100 years from now. Now, in 2017, he'd like to know the same for Munger.

Munger responded with one answer to this man's two-part question.

Munger recalled that his earliest memory of the meetings was Buffett's answer to this age-old question of legacy, "They asked him what he wanted said at his funeral, and he said, 'I want them to all be saying that's the oldest looking corpse I ever saw.'"

Buffett quipped, with a laugh at his often-told joke, "That may be the smartest thing I ever said."

Then, becoming earnest, Buffett shared that his ideal legacy is very simple. What he really likes is teaching. He's been teaching both formally and informally all his life. He's also had some of the greatest teachers one could imagine. So he figures that, if somebody thought he did a decent job of teaching, he'd feel very good about that.

Munger concluded: "And to make the teaching endurable, it has to have a bit of wise-assery in it. And that we've both been able to supply."

APPENDICES

APPENDIX I:
IN THE BEGINNING . . .
THERE WAS CAPITAL
ALLOCATION

The story of Buffett's takeover of Berkshire Hathaway begins with capital allocation.

It was the company's massive buyback proposal at the 1962 shareholders' meeting that caught Buffett's attention. This at a time when buybacks were virtually nonexistent.

We thought the whole thing was fascinating, so here's Buffett's telling of the story in the 2014 Berkshire annual report:

> "On May 6, 1964, Berkshire Hathaway, then run by a man named Seabury Stanton, sent a letter to its shareholders offering to buy 225,000 shares of its stock for $11.375 per share. I had expected the letter; I was surprised by the price.
>
> Berkshire then had 1,583,680 shares outstanding. About 7% of these were owned by Buffett Partnership Ltd. ("BPL"), an investing entity that I managed and in which I had virtually all of my net worth. Shortly before the tender offer was mailed, Stanton had asked me at what price BPL would sell its holdings. I answered $11.50, and he said, "Fine, we have a deal." Then came Berkshire's letter, offering an eighth of a point less. I bristled at Stanton's behavior and didn't tender.
>
> That was a monumentally stupid decision.
>
> Berkshire was then a northern textile manufacturer, mired in a terrible business. The industry in which it operated

was heading south, both metaphorically and physically. And Berkshire, for a variety of reasons, was unable to change course."*

"That was true even though the industry's problems had long been widely understood. Berkshires' own Board minutes of July 29, 1954, laid out the grim facts: 'The textile industry in New England started going out of business forty years ago. During the war years this trend was stopped. The trend must continue until supply and demand have been balanced.'

About a year after that board meeting, Berkshire Fine Spinning Associates and Hathaway Manufacturing—both with roots in the 19th Century—joined forces, taking the name we bear today. With its fourteen plants and 10,000 employees, the merged company became the giant of New England textiles. What the two managements viewed as a merger agreement, however, soon morphed into a suicide pact. During the seven years following the consolidation, Berkshire operated at an overall loss, and its net worth shrank by 37%.

Meanwhile, the company closed nine plants, sometimes using the liquidation process to repurchase shares. And that pattern caught my attention.

I purchase BPL's first shares of Berkshire in December 1962, anticipating more closings and more repurchases. The stock was then selling for $7.50, a wide discount from per-share working capital of $10.25 and book value of $20.20. Buying the stock at that price was like picking up a discarded cigar butt that had one puff remaining in it. Though the stub might be ugly and soggy, the puff would be free. Once that momentary pleasure was enjoyed, however, no more could be expected.

Berkshire thereafter stuck to the script: It soon closed another two plants, and in that May 1964 move, set out to repurchase shares with the shutdown proceeds. The price that Stanton offered was 50% above the cost of our original purchases. There it was—my free puff, just waiting for me, after which I could look elsewhere for other discarded butts.

---

* Charlie Munger once referred to textiles as "congealed electricity," so the move of production to the TVA southern states was inevitable. In his classically understated way, he concluded that the New England textile business was a "totally doomed, certain-to-fail business."

Instead, irritated by Stanton's chiseling, I ignored his offer and began to aggressively buy more Berkshire shares.

By April 1965, BPL owned 392,633 shares (out of 1,017,547 then outstanding), and at an early-May board meeting, we formally took control of the company. Through Seabury's and my childish behavior—after all, what was an eighth of a point to either of us?—he lost his job, and I found myself with more than 25% of BPL's capital invested in a terrible business about which I knew very little. I became the dog who caught the car.

Because of Berkshire's operating losses and share repurchases, its net worth at the end of fiscal 1964 had fallen to $22 million from $55 million at the time of the 1955 merger. The full $22 million was required by the textile operation: The company had no excess cash and owed its bank $2.5 million. (Berkshire's 1964 annual report is reproduced on pages 130-142.) For a time I got lucky: Berkshire immediately enjoyed two years of good operating conditions. Better yet, its earnings in those years were free of income tax because it possessed a large loss carry-forward that had arisen from the disastrous results in earlier years.

Then the honeymoon ended. During the 18 years following 1966, we struggled unremittingly with the textile business, all to no avail. But stubbornness—stupidity?—has its limits. In 1985, I finally threw in the towel and closed the operation."

A Tutorial on Capital Allocation

While Buffett grills himself for buying a dying textile business out of pique for Stanton Seabury's chiseling, we think he doth protest too much.

In truth, Buffett's maneuvers in the years to follow constituted an amazing exercise in aggressive capital reallocation.

Here are the numbers: In 1964, the year before Buffett took control, Berkshire's per-share book value stood at $19.46 with per share earnings of $0.15. *At year-end 1969, Berkshire's per-share book value was $43.18, up 120%, with per share earnings of $8.07.*

How the heck did Buffett do that with a dying textile business? Let's take a look.

Buybacks

At the time of purchase, Berkshire was undergoing a dramatic buyback program.

In 1964, Berkshire bought in 469,602 shares, leaving 1,137,778 shares outstanding, a 29% cap shrink!

Furthermore, this was done at an average price paid of $11.32 share, far below book value.

Massive per share value was being created by shrinking the capitalization at very low prices.

Under Buffett's command, Berkshire bought in an additional 120,231 shares to further shrink the cap. In all, Berkshire's share count went from 1,607,380 in 1964 to 1,017,547 in 1969, a 37% reduction.*

Hidden Value

As of 1964, Berkshire had $5 million of "tax loss carry-overs."

With the accounting rules of the day, this asset was not included in the calculation of book value. In addition, this asset could be especially valuable at the time since the top corporate tax was 48%.

We estimate this asset added over $2 per share of value as Berkshire used up the tax loss carry-overs within a few years, sheltering a significant portion of earnings from taxes.

Investments

Buffett created cash for investment through additional asset sales and reductions in inventory and overhead.

He invested in securities that appreciated significantly, liquidating the portfolio during 1968 and 1969.

He reported net per share earnings from the gains on those sales of $2.20 ($1.49 from the parent and $0.71 from insurance subsidiaries) in 1968 and $4.16 ($3.87 from the parent and $0.29 from insurance subsidiaries) in 1969, adding a total of $6.36 of after-tax value.

---

* Compare this to just over 1.6 million shares outstanding today. Berkshire has had little share expansion over the past 50 years.

Acquisitions

In 1967, Berkshire bought National Indemnity for $8.4 million, which became the base for building Berkshire's insurance empire.

As of the 1969 report, Berkshire was moving into surety, workmen's compensation and reinsurance.

In 1969, Berkshire purchased The Illinois National Bank and Trust Co. of Rockford, Illinois.

Earnings and Earnings Power

With these two new lines of business, Buffett transformed Berkshire's earnings power.

Of those $8.07 of per share earnings in 1969, $4.66 came from operations: $0.79 from the textile operation, $2.31 from the insurance subsidiaries and $1.56 from the banking operation.*

The key to note here is that the bulk of *Berkshire's future earning power was no longer in the textile operation but in the insurance, banking and investment operations.*

Note that the $43.18 book value in 1969 represented a far better company, more diversified, with more earning power and better growth prospects than the $19.46 book value of 1964, so the increase in *intrinsic per share value* was even greater than the 120% increase in per-share book value.

Despite its beginnings in the ill-fated textile industry, Buffett's ability to re-allocate resources transformed Berkshire Hathaway into a dynamically growing juggernaut within just five years.

---

* Again, $4.16 of those earnings represented non-recurring gains from the liquidation of the investment portfolio.

APPENDIX II:
THE
SPECTACULAR GROWTH
IN POPULARITY

As Buffett's fame and wealth have grown, so has the frenzy around his once humble meetings:

- In the 1970s, Berkshire's annual meetings consisted of a half dozen shareholders in a local coffee shop.

- In 1980, there were only 13 people at the meeting.

- In 1984, Corey, my now partner, was newly employed in the audit department at Berkshire and joined a few dozen of the faithful at the Red Lion Inn.

- My first meeting was in 1985. The meeting was moved to the Joslyn Art Museum to handle the "crowd." There were about 300 in attendance.

- In 1989, the year's meeting was delayed 15 minutes as over 1,000 people squeezed in. Buffett noted, "A lot more people turn out to talk about their money than to look at old paintings."

- In 1994, attendance continued to grow with 3,000 shareholders squeezing into the Orpheum Theater. Buffett mused that the only place large enough to hold next year's meeting might be the local race track, AK-SAR-BEN. He remarked that in moving from a temple of culture (the Joslyn Art Museum) to an old vaudeville theater, then on to a den of gambling, Berkshire was sliding down the cultural scale.

- In 1997, a throng of 7,700 stakeholders filled AK-SAR-BEN's auditorium.

- In August 2001, 10,000 plus fans were in attendance at the currently titled CenturyLink Center.

- By 2003, attendance nearly doubled with a packed-to-the-rafters event with 19,000 in attendance.

- In May 2008, with 31,000 of Warren's closest friends in town, Buffett had now taken over Omaha.

- May 2013 was the largest attendance by far: 45,000 of Warren Buffett's friends joined him at the CenturyLink Center.

- In 2016, Professors Buffett and Munger presided over the first-ever live-streaming of the Berkshire meeting via Yahoo Finance, creating a global audience. The live streaming decreased attendance by about 10%.

APPENDIX III:
LESSONS FROM THE
BERKSHIRE MALL

One of the secrets to the explosion in meeting attendance has been the festive shopping event that Buffett shrewdly added in the mid-1990s.

Ever the entrepreneur, Buffett realized the spending power of his shareholder base. The weekend began morphing into a target-marketing retail bonanza for Berkshire subsidiaries. They have since capitalized on the huge attendance numbers by rolling out "The Berkshire Mall."

Today, Berkshire's shareholders head en masse to the ground floor of the CenturyLink Center. And there awaits a mini-mall comprising booths of subsidiaries selling their goods.

The mall shamelessly plugs as many Berkshire enterprises as can be fit into the showroom. These have included the following:

- Benjamin Moore Paints
- Borsheim's Jewelry
- Clayton Homes
- Cort Business Furniture
- Dairy Queen
- Fruit of the Loom
- GEICO insurance
- Ginsu Knives
- H.H. Brown shoes
- Justin Boots
- Kirby vacuum cleaners
- Larson-Juhl custom framing
- M&T Bank
- Nebraska Furniture Mart
- Pampered Chef
- Quikut knives
- See's Candy
- Shaw Carpets
- World Book

If that weren't enough branding, purchases and free handouts are taken home in shopping bags featuring the Coca-Cola logo. Cartoon caricatures of Buffett festoon as many of the products as possible—including boxers, T-shirts and even competing ketchup bottles.

This is not gimmickry, though. Far from it.

In 2008, Nebraska Furniture Mart did a record of $7.5 million in sales during the event. An amount considered a great year for most retail outlets. In 2012, Buffett proudly announced that Berkshire shareholders spent $35 million on everything from See's Candy to Borsheim's jewelry, an average of $1,000 per attendee. And in 2014, Nebraska Furniture Mart did over $40 million of business the week of the meeting—equivalent to 10% of its annual sales.

Not only is Buffett enabling Berkshire shareholders to do their part to augment the company's sales, but the mall also functions as a great teaching aid. The mall educates shareholders on how Berkshire has become a powerhouse collection of operating businesses.

In a not-so-subtle way, it's as if Buffett is tacitly shouting to the public that Berkshire outgrew being primarily an investment holding company years ago.

APPENDIX IV:
CASH/BOND/STOCK
RATIOS

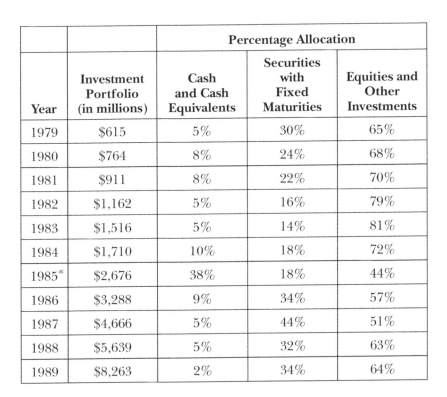

Year	Investment Portfolio (in millions)	Percentage Allocation		
		Cash and Cash Equivalents	Securities with Fixed Maturities	Equities and Other Investments
1979	$615	5%	30%	65%
1980	$764	8%	24%	68%
1981	$911	8%	22%	70%
1982	$1,162	5%	16%	79%
1983	$1,516	5%	14%	81%
1984	$1,710	10%	18%	72%
1985*	$2,676	38%	18%	44%
1986	$3,288	9%	34%	57%
1987	$4,666	5%	44%	51%
1988	$5,639	5%	32%	63%
1989	$8,263	2%	34%	64%

*In 1985, cash swelled due largely to the buy-out of General Foods by Philip Morris, and the 1998 General Re Corporation merger shifted the percentage in equities from 76% to roughly 55%.

Year	Investment Portfolio (in millions)	Percentage Allocation		
		Cash and Cash Equivalents	Securities with Fixed Maturities	Equities and Other Investments
1990	$8,994	3%	34%	63%
1991	$12,283	6%	19%	75%
1992	$14,948	8%	14%	78%
1993	$16,487	11%	13%	76%
1994	$18,355	2%	15%	83%
1995	$26,362	10%	6%	84%
1996	$35,537	4%	18%	78%
1997	$47,548	2%	22%	76%
1998	$74,589	18%	29%	53%
1999	$73,565	5%	41%	54%
2000	$77,086	6%	43%	51%
2001	$72,471	7%	51%	42%
2002	$80,494	13%	50%	37%
2003	$95,589	33%	27%	40%
2004	$102,929	39%	22%	39%
2005	$115,615	34%	23%	41%
2006	$125,715	30%	20%	49%
2007	$141,217	27%	20%	53%
2008	$122,025	20%	22%	58%
2009	$145,982	19%	22%	59%
2010	$147,772	24%	23%	53%
2011	$153,909	22%	20%	58%
2012	$176,331	24%	18%	58%
2013	$211,308	20%	13%	67%
2014	$228,906	25%	12%	63%
2015	$236,803	26%	11%	63%
2016	$244,531	29%	9%	62%

APPENDIX V:
ON CURATING
THIS BOOK

Whereas this is a historical document, the original newsletters are not reprinted here exactly as they were sent out to clients. Instead, these are the curated highlights of the original text.

This was done because these newsletters were never conceived to be reprinted in one volume. Therefore, many redundancies exist from one year to the next. Understandably, such repetition would be tiresome to the reader. So, wherever possible, redundancies have been removed.

Those original newsletters have also been edited. As this is a historical document, I have preserved many typos. However, as Corey and I assembled this collection, some errors were so glaring that we could not help ourselves. So light editing was done. Stylistic changes were made.

Nothing of note was omitted. All the information is the same.

ACKNOWLEDGMENTS

Daniel Pecaut

Huge thanks to my partner and best friend, Corey Wrenn, who has been so instrumental in my understanding of Berkshire. Thanks, Corey, for the copious notes you took which, along with my notes, were the raw material for this book. Attending these meetings with you at my side has been an absolute blast. Thank you for believing in me, especially when I didn't believe in myself. Your support has been invaluable.

Thanks also to our clients at Pecaut & Company. Without you, these newsletters would never have been written. Many of you have been with us through so many ups and downs of the markets—and of life itself. We deeply appreciate our relationship with you.

I want to acknowledge my gratitude to Austin Pierce for having the vision to see the possibility of this book. You inspired me to take it from an idea and turn it into a reality. I wouldn't have done it without you, Austin.

An even bigger thank you to my assistant, Shelby Pierce, who actually started this whole thing by introducing me to her husband, Austin. Shelby supports me each and every workday with an indefatigable work ethic and sunny disposition. Everyone should have a Shelby in their life.

Thanks to Gayle Rupp, our long-time administrator at Pecaut & Company, who keeps things running smoothly so I can do crazy projects like this book. We have a great team at work, and I appreciate their support day in and day out.

Thanks to our beta readers: David Aycock, Dan Boyle, Helen Burstyn, Frank Franciscovich, Andrew Henshon, Phil McLaughlin, Mary Pecaut, and Robert Roy. Your feedback has made this a far better book. I'm deeply grateful to all of you.

Deep gratitude to my parents, Dick and Dottie, who taught me so many of life's lessons and created an environment of love and curiosity for our family to grow in. While they're no longer alive, their voices of teaching and encouragement still resonate.

Thanks go to my children, John, Charlie, and Danielle, who've helped me grow in a thousand ways. Until recently, I always thought what I wanted for them most was to be happy. Now I see what I've really wanted for them is to take 100% responsibility of their own lives. And they have. I couldn't be happier for them.

Most of all, great love and thanks to my wife, Kay, my high school sweetheart and greatest teacher. She has loved me and supported me throughout. She doesn't care that much about money. She does care that I show up with integrity, generosity, and love.

Big thanks to Warren Buffett and Charlie Munger. We couldn't have done this book without you. Thanks for the last three decades. See you next year.

Corey Wrenn

I would like to thank my partner and dear friend Daniel Pecaut for believing in and welcoming me into the Pecaut and Company family 24 years ago. I believe he is one of the finest individuals I have ever known. He is an excellent writer, teacher and investor. I have learned and continue to learn much from him.

I would also like to thank our clients who are like family to me. It has been a privilege and honor to have worked with and for them over all these years.

I feel incredibly lucky to have worked with the many faces at Pecaut and Company, including Dick Pecaut. Dick was smart, had an encyclopedic memory, was quick-witted, and passionate about investing.

I am very grateful to Gayle Rupp, who my family refers to as my right hand. She shows an amazing attention to detail, is a tireless worker, and someone I have counted on for over 25 years.

I would like to also acknowledge Shelby Pierce. She brings youthful energy and a joyful spirit to Pecaut and Company. She is outstanding and, remarkably, manages Daniel and me effortlessly.

Thank you for your hard work on this book, Austin Pierce. You have a unique skill set and an ability to herd an unruly crew to a final destination.

I am very grateful for all the paths I crossed at Berkshire. It is an incredible organization filled with brilliant, talented and focused individuals. Those who worry about succession there clearly don't understand how deep the bench is. It was an honor to work there.

I am exceedingly grateful for my mother, who single-handedly raised a gaggle of children. She built a successful business that served her customers—with $0 of beginning equity with elbow grease and sheer determination. She was loved by anyone who crossed her path, by her employees and her customers. I learned the art of dealing with people, integrity and making the most of every situation from her.

I am extremely grateful for my three daughters and son-in-law. Each has unique strengths, talents, and gifts that helped me to become, in many ways, the man I am today. I love them all dearly and am very proud of the paths they have chosen.

Finally, I am humbled by and over-the-top grateful for my beloved wife Lisa who has always believed in me. Supporting me through the highs and the lows, she is the glue that holds our family together. Je t'aime ma chérie.

INDEX

Blankfein, Lloyd, 203
Bluhdorn, Charles, 225
Blumkin, Rose, 214
BNSF. *See* Burlington Northern
  Santa Fe
Board of directors, xxv
  CEOs and, 146, 159
  executive compensation and, 31,
    159
  of Salomon Brothers, 105
Bogle, John, 308
Bolt-on acquisitions, 271
Bonds, 102, 160
  cash/bond/stock ratios, 329–330
  derivatives for, 192
  government, 36
  junk, 16–17, 124, 127, 156
  municipal, 170–171, 203, 211
  zero-coupon, 16, 75
Bond-stock ratio, 71–73
Bonuses, 123
Book value, 33
Borsheim's, 58, 80
BPL. *See* Buffett Partnership Ltd.
Brady, Nick, 150
Brandon, Joe, 102, 197, 237
Brands, xviii, 17, 80, 177, 282
  vs. generics, 37–38
  market share of, 37
  vs. retail, 96
Branson, Richard, 244
Buffalo News, 99, 161, 242
Buffett, Howard, 221, 263
Buffett, Warren, xi–xvi. *See also Specific
    topics*
  advice from, 260–261, 292
  energy of, 259
  happiness of, 268, 288
  legacy of, 225
  misquotations of, 214
  philanthropy of, 165
  popularity of, 325
  predictions by, 282–283
  prostate cancer of, 245
  track record of, 2–3
Buffett Partnership Ltd. (BPL), 154,
  319–321
Burger King, 278

Burlington Northern Santa Fe
  (BNSF), xix–xx, 169, 206–207,
  229, 241, 252–253, 270
  coal and, 291
  dangerous substance safety by, 283
  market share of, 276
  return on equity of, 210
Business acquisitions, 48, 112–113,
  170, 271, 323. *See also* Good busi-
    nesses; *Specific companies*
  competitive advantage for, 258–259
  dollar decline and, 157–158
  filters for, 65–66, 279–280
  of good businesses plus manage-
    ment quality, 299
  ideal buys for, 309
  100% ownership in, 44–45, 168
  value calculations for, 161–162
  waiting for fat pitch in, 109, 118
Business cycle, predictions of, 11
Business moat, 37, 50–51, 55, 80–81,
  209, 220, 282, 310
Business risk, 63–64
Buybacks, 56, 296, 322
BYD, 195–196, 209, 228
Byrne, Jack, xix, 248

C

Cadbury's, 213
California, 93–94, 135, 187, 229, 315
Capital allocation, 32, 43, 268–270,
  313, 319–323
Capital Cities/ABC, 4, 24, 58
Capital gains, taxes on, 65, 71, 73
Carmax, 169
Carry trade, 132, 138, 157
Cash, 75–76, 143, 206–207
  for business acquisitions, 271
  vs. dividends, 179, 243, 272
  in Treasury bills, 230
Cash flow, 33, 36, 80, 106, 206
  free, 298–299
  IBV and, 17
Cash/bond/stocks ratios, 329–330
Catastrophe coverage, 42, 66–67, 197,
  210, 218, 236
CDOs. *See* Collateralized debt obliga-
  tions

PECAUT & COMPANY

Pecaut & Company is a federally registered investment advisor. If you would like more information about our services, you may contact us at:

Pecaut & Company
401 Douglas Street, Suite 415
Sioux City, IA 51101

712-252-3268
800-779-7326

www.pecautandcompany.com

Made in United States
North Haven, CT
04 May 2023